THE PARTITIONING OF EUROPE

WOLFGANG WAGNER

THE PARTITIONING OF EUROPE

A History of the Soviet Expansion
up to the Cleavage of Germany
1918-1945

DEUTSCHE VERLAGS-ANSTALT

STUTTGART

INTRODUCTION

Fifteen years after the end of the second World War, mankind's consciousness has grown accustomed to the new picture of the world that has emerged out of the chaos. The irresistible upheaval brought about by the war has raised two Powers up to a lonely height above all others. It has let half a dozen States decline into mediocrity, thereby giving whole continents, which, seemingly without a history of their own, had passed their days in colonial dependency, the chance to take their fate into their own hands. Today, mankind's destiny is largely determined by the fact that the two World Powers are measuring their strength one against the other.

For a long time the Western World has been reflecting on the historical beginnings of these transformations, in which process German historians and political writers have been participating, their special attention being understandably focused on the pernicious partitioning of Germany. The historical facts are for the most part exposed, even if broad spheres of Eastern politics are still shrouded in darkness. But views diverge widely in the interpretation of the events. The purpose of this book is to provide some contribution to the rational discussion of the problem.

As a result of lengthy studies the conviction has become firm that the best-known contemporary analyses suffer from three weaknesses: a false appreciation of the nature and origins of the East-West conflict; an overrating of the historical importance of the great war conferences; and the taking of too narrow a view when forming an opinion about the carving-up of Germany. None of these three weaknesses has come about fortuitously. Their roots lie deep in history.

In general, the conflict between East and West is looked upon as a feature of the post-war times or at best of the last phase of the war, whereas it is actually a product of much earlier times. It dates from at least as far back as the Russian revolution of 1917, when the Communists declared their intention to wage war on the entire world. This curtailment of the historical perspective continues the deception in regard to Soviet aims and intentions, so fraught with fateful consequences, that was suffered by the Western World during the war from 1941 to 1945. The dream of the "one indivisible world" is no longer a political dream, though still effective in the writing of history. Through the usual differentiation between two phases of the East-West relations, the period of cooperation and the period of conflict, the fact that, over and above all tactical manœuvring, Soviet policy has continued to pursue the same aim of expansion threatens to become obscured. Clearly this differentiation has been accepted without criticism from the reminiscences of Western politicians and military personalities, although it is obvious that a strong element of self-justification lies at the bottom of the blunder of these memoirs to credit the Soviets during the war with an internal transformation, which, when the war came to an end, was followed by a return to sentiments of a revolutionary nature. The writers therefore allege that political and military decisions which, in the light of the Soviet expansion, have later shown themselves to be faulty ought for this reason to be excused.

The overrating of the historical influence of the great war conferences, particularly the "summit meetings" at Teheran, Yalta and Potsdam, goes hand in hand with an underrating of the political significance of the military events of the second World War. Here, too, one-sided points of view originating in the war period are transmitted to the historical record. At the time, the action of the Allied armies seemed to pursue the sole aim of defeating the Axis Powers. Today, however, we see that the Soviet Union was simultaneously aspiring to the extension of its sphere of influence over large parts of Europe. The meetings of the Allied Heads of Government and their Departmental Chiefs played but a trifling part in the monstrous consequences of this expansion. In regard to the war conferences, George Kennan, one of the clearest-sighted observers of contemporary history, has rightly affirmed: "If it cannot be said that the Western de-

6

mocracies gained very much from these talks with the Russians, it would also be incorrect to say that they gave very much away. The establishment of Soviet military power in Eastern Europe... was not the result of these talks; it was the result of the military operations during the concluding phases of the war."

When giving a description of how the partitioning of Germany has arisen, writers, particularly the German, tend to regard the event as being solely, or predominantly, a *national* misfortune. However, if one suffers Germany's partitioning to be a development of the various discussions of the Allies in regard to the carving-up of the Reich, the most important connection relative to this process is concealed. In reality, the partitioning of Germany is part of an enormous historical catastrophe, the Soviet inundation of half Europe, which is not to be understood under the usual aspects of national historiography.

In the pages which follow, an attempt will be made to tell the story, on this foundation, of how the new Europe, split into two parts, has arisen. Since only facts speak a language that is convincing, it is unavoidable that the informed reader should stumble on much that is well-known, though frequently in a new environment and freshly illuminated.

The author is convinced that the history of our times is no longer conceivable as the history of individual States. All the events of the last decades are overshadowed by the growth of totalitarian ruling societies, with their contempt for humanity and their monstrous pressure to expand. The Europe of old can be regretfully conscious of how very much its own precipitous development contributed to the rise of the mass society through rapid industrialisation, to the social distress in town and country, to the unrestrained increase in competition with its devastating consequences, to the world-wide imperialism, to the unemployment and embittering of certain sections of the middle-classes, and, finally, to the growth of an unbridled fanaticism. But today there is no consolation in perceiving that the sources of totalitarianism lie in our own world. The extreme newness of these frightful régimes has become the challenge of our age.

If one lays the blame for the outbreak of the second World War on National Socialist Germany one need summon no further witnesses or king's evidence. Seldom have the historians found so little opportunity for well-informed controversy. However, not everywhere is it apprehended that it was not something specifically German that exhausted its fury in National Socialism, but that the German people had only fallen a victim to the typical illness of the 20th century. After having brought about fearful calamities, the German people have been cured by the shock therapy of the military defeat. But now we are witnessing how the same malady, in a form only slightly changed, is spreading over the earth with frightful rapidity. The course taken by the second World War provided the totalitarian régime of the Soviet Union with the chance to extend its domination over East and South-East Europe as far as the Elbe. It was used with the same unscrupulousness as was formerly one of Hitler's characteristics. In the meantime, Communism has laid hold of the largest nation of the earth, the Chinese. The pressure on the remainder of the world will increase from year to year.

All other political problems pale before this tremendous challenge. It may disturb the æsthetic sense of the European that the "appallingly simple" antithesis between West and East cloaks all other problems and drowns the customary, well-attuned orchestra of the Powers with rude beats of the drum. But he who wishes to comprehend the happenings of our times in their just proportions must appreciate the commanding significance of the Soviet expansion. Advanced by Hitler's mad and blinkered policy, it has transformed the face of Europe, leaving to freedom only a niggardly asylum in the fringes of the continent to the north, west and south. Europe, once the fervently-beating heart of the world, is divided into two parts.

Chapter One

THE FIRST PHASE OF THE SOVIET EXPANSION
(1918–1921)

> Russia, which has just carried out its execrable attack
> on Georgia, is no longer a proletarian community but
> a Bonapartistic one.
>
> *Karl Kautsky in "Georgia" (1921)*

The peculiarity of the October Revolution in Russia lies in the
fact that, from the very beginning, it was not regarded as a
purely national upheaval but at the same time as the starting-
point of a convulsion embracing the whole world. Perhaps the
revolutionaries who stormed the Winter Palace in St. Petersburg
on October 25 (November 7), 1917, wished in the first place to
bring about the collapse of the decadent feudalism of the Czarist
Empire and the bourgeois régime of the democrats. But out of the
fog of the future their leaders saw a new world-embracing Utopia
taking shape, the origination of which could have started equally
well from Berlin or Paris.

It would have seemed narrow-minded to the leaders of the Bolshevist revolution in Russia to give a thought to the happiness
of their people. In their year-long preoccupation with the theories
of Karl Marx and Friedrich Engels, they had learned to think
internationally. Indeed, during the endless ideological discussions
that were so characteristic of the early period of the development
of Lenin's party, the dominant conviction was that, even with a
successful revolution in Russia, it would not be possible to realise
a socialistic * order so long as the spark did not flash over to
other, more highly industrialised, countries. For this reason, the

---

* In the following pages, the concept of "socialism" is always employed
in the way usual in the Soviet sphere and therefore not in accordance
with what is customary in the language used by the Social Democratic
parties.

outbreak of the first World War seemed to them to offer promise. The weapons of international revolution had to be forged in the fire of this global conflict. Even as early as the end of 1915 Lenin was occupying himself with the question of what a Bolshevist Government would do in this war. His answer betrays the revolutionaries' far-flung aims. "To all those waging war we would offer peace on condition the colonies and all dependent, oppressed and dispossessed nationalities were freed. Neither Germany nor England nor France would accept this condition under their present Governments. We would therefore have to prepare for, and wage, the war of revolution. That is, we... would... stir up all colonies and dependent countries of Asia (India, China, Persia, etc.) and, above all, incite the socialistic proletariat of Europe... to rise up against their Governments. There is no doubt that a victory of the proletariat in Russia would result in unusually favourable conditions for the development of the revolution in both Asia and Europe." [1]

Bolshevism was born with the mole of the revolutionary pressure to expand. From the very beginning, the foundation of the Soviet Union was not intended to be the final aim but an interim stage. A few years later Stalin publicly stated: "The significance of the October Revolution in world history consists not only in the fact that... it is the first harbour of socialism in the ocean of the imperialist countries but also in the fact that it is the first stage of world revolution and a mighty base from which to launch its further development." [2] What we call the "Russian Revolution" is in Russia itself rightly designated the "Great Socialist Revolution". The leaders of the Revolution regarded the country in which they came to power only as "a sort of headquarters for the international movement on the road to world conquest". [3]

1. WAITING IN VAIN FOR WORLD REVOLUTION

Since power was seized in October, 1917, the Bolshevist Party and the Russian State have amalgamated to become one inseparable unit. While in democratic States one party which succeeds in gaining governmental power customarily subordinates its particular aims to reasons of State, in Russia at first the opposite happened. The Bolshevist Party did not place itself at the service of its country but, instead, the means of the State were placed at the service of the Revolution. Only after some time had elapsed was there any endeavour, at least outwardly, to make a formal differentiation between the revolutionary aims of the Party and the country's foreign policy.

In the beginning, when Lenin and his associates still believed in the imminent outbreak of World Revolution, they considered any foreign policy of the usual kind to be superfluous. The only task of the Soviet State was to promote the revolutionary development in the remaining parts of the world. Shortly after his appointment as Commissar for Foreign Affairs, Trotsky said: "What kind of diplomatic work are we likely to have? I shall issue a few revolutionary proclamations to the peoples and then shut up shop." [4] Certainly there were also other means of State that could serve the Revolution. The "Council of People's Commissars" resolved, "in view of the fact that... the struggle against war and imperialism can lead to full victory only on an international scale", to place two million roubles at the disposal of the parties of the Extreme Left all over the world and, without bothering about the rules normally prevailing between States, made public the direction to place this money at the disposal of the diplomatic missions.[5]

The Soviet negotiators even tried to exploit for their own ends the proceedings in respect of the armistice and the Brest-Litovsk treaty. Trotsky made fiery revolutionary speeches but, in spite of his famed eloquence, the German generals replied only with an astonished shaking of the head. It went beyond their powers of imagination that such strange ideas should find any sympathy outside uncultivated Russia. It might be good to conclude a peace with this mixed society of professional revolutionaries who, for years on end, had allowed the struggle against their Government to be paid for with German money. Since their Revolution had smashed the front, one could dictate a hard peace to them. Russia had to relinquish all claim to the Baltic Provinces and evacuate Finland as well as the Ukraine – which is what the loss of those territories signified.

11

The new masters of Russia were thereby faced with a decision that struck at the very foundations. They had awaited the outbreak in Europe of the revolution which was to extend their sphere of domination. Instead, they were now to relinquish large parts of the country that were already in their hands. In the Central Committee of the Bolshevist Party, national scruples asserted themselves. Ought the Revolutionary Government make so ignominious a peace? But Lenin took a decision which showed with exciting impressiveness that he looked on his country only as an instrument of the Revolution. "If the Germans should demand the overturn of the Bolshevik Government, then, of course, we would have to fight", he said. "All other demands can and should be granted. Even if we give up Finland, Livonia and Esthonia, we still retain the Revolution." [6]

Lenin and his comrades in the struggle would not have concluded the treaty of Brest-Litovsk had they not been convinced, in a sort of religious fanaticism, that the victory of the Revolution was not to be retarded. They awaited the outbreak of the revolution in Europe with the same imperturbable confidence "as the first Christians the coming again of the Lord." [7] In January, 1918, Lenin declared at a mass assembly of soldiery: "The peoples are already awakening. Already they hear the fiery call of our Revolution and soon we will not be alone. In our army will stream the strength of proletarian masses of the other nations." [8]

Nevertheless, 1918 brought at first only set-backs and dangers. In the spring civil war broke out, extensive regions seceded from the revolutionary movement, and considerable armies took up a stand against the Soviets and their troops. At the same time, British troops landed in the north and north-east of the country, the Japanese followed suit, and finally there also came French, American, and, indeed, Italian units. In Moscow an uprising flamed up. Only by means of ruthless terror could the Bolshevists remain masters of the situation. Human life was of no consequence. With terrifying pride, Zinoviev, the leader of the Petersburg Soviet, proclaimed: "The bourgeoisie kills separate individuals; but we kill whole classes." [9]

The outbreak of the November Revolution in Germany was the passionately-awaited signal for the Bolshevists. Trotsky was already prophesying the origination of a "mighty block" formed of Russia and Germany, with 200 million inhabitants, "on which all the waves of imperialism will break".[10] Lenin, who for more than a year had had the Spartacist League headed by Karl Liebknecht and Rosa Luxemburg financially supported, appointed the crafty Galician Karl Radek director of Bolshevist propaganda in Germany.[11] On December 30, 1918, the Communist Party of Germany was constituted, and a few days later the Spartacist uprising broke out. In Moscow it was anticipated that the Reich would be Bolshevist by March. The door to the world would thereby be open.

At first the uprising made rapid progress. The national over-enthusiasm of the first years of the war had left behind at the collapse a mood of dejection that made some of the workers and the soldiers amenable to the words of international socialism. In many towns "Soviet Republics" were founded; in the Ruhr a "Workers' and Soldiers' Republic" was proclaimed. Meanwhile the Soviet Government tore up the treaty of Brest-Litovsk, invaded the Baltic Provinces, and at the beginning of February pushed forward with their troops into East Prussia. Sure of victory, the Soviet Government that had been set up in Lithuania declared in a manifesto: "Behind us stands the coming revolution that in the shortest space of time will lead not only in Germany but also in the other parts of Europe to the general Federation of Soviet Socialist Republics." [12]

In March, Europe was staggered by the news that a second Communist uprising had broken out. In Hungary the wild bands of Béla Kun inaugurated a rule of terror. At once the Soviet Government promised the Hungarian dictator economic aid. Had the Red troops not been chained down in the Ukraine by the struggle with the "Whites", they would have joined forces with Béla Kun's army. Appropriate instructions to this effect had been issued by Moscow.[13] Apparently a military thrust over Poland towards Germany was also planned. In the middle of April, the Communists in Munich, led by the Russian delegate Eugen Leviné, succeeded in establishing a Communist Soviet Republic, which announced in telegrams to Moscow and Budapest that it would "do all in its power to assist the great historical task which

In his reply, Zinoviev, the President of the Communist International that had been set up shortly before, expressed the "un-
shakable conviction that the time is no longer distant when the
entire German Reich will be a Soviet Republic", and Lenin tele-
graphed thirteen pieces of advice as to how the Soviet system
could be strengthened.[15]

But the flood, rising menacingly, was halted. In Germany it was
chiefly due to the Ebert Government and the Social Democrats
that the Spartacist uprisings were defeated. The East Prussian
boundary was defended by volunteers and the von der Goltz
division. In Hungary, the Communists, to whose aid this time no
Soviet divisions were able to hurry, were put to flight by the invading Roumanian troops, so that towards the end of the year a
new bourgeois régime could be established. Smaller uprisings in
Czechoslovakia and Vienna were suppressed. The Soviets' first
attempt to carry the Revolution into the heart of Europe had
miscarried.

2. AN ABORTIVE THRUST TOWARDS THE WEST

In the spring of 1919 Zinoviev had declared: "The Movement
advances at such a dizzy speed that it may be said with confidence: within a year we will already begin to forget that there
was a struggle for Communism in Europe, because within a year
all Europe will be Communist." [16] 1919 was not, however, the
year of Bolshevist triumph in Europe but the year of extreme
jeopardy for Communism. Up to the middle of 1920 the Soviet
régime experienced a series of defeats which in another country
would have put an end to any thoughts of expansion. In revolutionary Russia, however, the purpose of the expansion survived
even these set-backs.

Communist Russia was near to exhaustion. To put an end to the
war with Poland, the Soviet Government made an offer of an
armistice and peace. On February 4, 1920, the all-Russian Soviet
Executive Committee gave the assurance that the Russian Communists were not trying to assist the spread of Communism in

14

other countries by force. "The reorganization of Poland in the interest of the working masses must be the work of those masses themselves." [17]

In view of the situation prevailing in Russia there can be no doubt that the Soviets were at that time seeking peace. However, in a dramatic series of events, the atmosphere was reversed within the space of a few months. Marshal Pilsudski, the virtual master of Poland, has seen with mounting care how the hoped-for ruin of Russia in the civil war held off. Now he desired to create a wide belt of independent States between the Baltic Sea and the Black Sea, in order to keep in check the dangerous power in the East. [18] But he had overestimated the strength of his young country. The surprising success at the outset which had brought Kiev into the Polish hands in May was soon followed by the set-back. The Ukrainian support remained behind expectations, and the Soviet counter-offensive quickly gained back the lost ground. In July, the Russian troops were standing along the Bug: the ethnological boundary between Poland and Russia had been reached. Now it must be seen whether or not the Soviet régime really wanted to assist the spread of Communism without the use of force.

The question was posed the Soviet Government in the most urgent form imaginable, since it was precisely at this moment that Lord Curzon, the British Foreign Secretary, addressed a Note to the Soviet Government in which he proposed an immediate armistice and a provisional drawing of the frontier along the Bug – a proposal that took into consideration the prevailing balance of power in favour of Russia. To a Russian State concerned solely with the safeguarding of its own territory, this boundary, which was known as the Curzon Line [19], would have offered advantages enough.

In the Soviet command there were heated discussions. [20] Trotsky advocated breaking off the advance and concluding peace. Radek and the sinister Cheka head, Dzerzhinsky, agreed with him. But it was no moral scruples that prompted them to give this advice. They, too, longed passionately for nothing more than the spread of the Revolution, only they feared the Polish people's power of resistance in the struggle for Warsaw. Lenin, supported by

15

Zinoviev, and after some hesitation by Stalin also, called for the march into Poland. He hoped the Red Army would incite the Polish workers to revolt. Once again he saw the chance turn up to carry the Revolution across Poland and, beyond, to Germany. Europe was to be "put to the test with the bayonets of the Red Army".

Lenin prevailed. Now that the Soviet Government felt itself strong enough, the principle that the Revolution should not be advanced by force was thrust to one side. Whether the interests of Russia demanded a continuation of the struggle played no part. Just like a foreign conqueror, the totalitarian dictator regards the treasures and forces of his own country only as a "source of loot and a means of preparing the next step of aggressive expansion." [21] After rejecting a peace offer, the Soviet troops started up their advance again, inflamed by the cry of their Commander-in-Chief, Tukachevsky: "Soldiers of the Workers' Revolution! Turn your eyes towards the West! There will be decided the final outcome of World Revolution. The road of the world-wide conflagration leads over the corpse of White Poland!" [22]

The Red Army stood the test as the Army of the Revolution. As soon as it had occupied the first Polish city, Bialystok, a "Revolutionary Committee", headed by the old Polish Communist Julian Marchlewski, was set up.[23] The Committee, clearly looked upon as the nucleus of a future Soviet Government of Poland, issued a proclamation "to the Polish working population in town and country", in which the Poles were enjoined to dispossess the factory-owners and landed proprietors. "In the towns the powers will be handed over to the workers' deputies; in the villages, community-soviets will be formed." Everywhere where the Soviet Army arrived, action was taken on the lines of this proclamation. Every step towards the west signified an extension of Bolshevism.

Since that time, one has come to speak of a "miracle on the Vistula", to which Poland owes its survival, in August, 1920, as an independent State. The miracle consisted of a variety of elements. Apart from war material, the West had sent the French General Weygand to assist. The Poles struck out desperately and the rivalry of the Soviet Army commanders exposed the weak spots in their deployment, which Marshal Pilsudski cleverly exploited. But whatever the measures, even individually, may have been, it was a miracle that in the summer of 1920 the Soviets were prevented from giving the impulse to the revolution in Central Europe by force of arms. In the hour of decision it was not that they themselves abstained from doing so but that in attempting to do so they failed.

The Peace of Riga, which was concluded the following year, fixed a boundary-line between Poland and the Soviet Union that had nothing more to do with the Curzon Line and the ethnological conditions. The Soviet Government accepted this frontier because it had not the strength to continue the war to a successful conclusion. After hopes of a swift World Revolution had foundered, Russia fell into a condition of exhaustion. A "cordon sanitaire" came into being in front of its western frontier. Europe isolated itself from the alien world that had developed there in the East. For two decades the Soviet pressure to expand westwards was halted.

3. THE FIRST CONQUESTS BY VIOLENCE

While Europe withdrew its intervention troops and reconciled itself to the existence of Bolshevist Russia, for the first time some smaller peoples fell victim to the Soviet pressure to expand. Georgia, Azerbaidjan and Armenia were forced within the Soviet empire by trickery and violence. The peoples of Transcaucasia were unable to maintain their freedom because Europe left them in the lurch.

It was not until during the 19th century that, through aggression which from time immemorial had been stigmatised by the Bolshevists as "Czarist imperialism", the regions in the southern foothills of the Caucasus between the Black and Caspian Seas became constituent parts of the Russian empire. Repeated attempts at revolt, especially on the part of the valiant Georgians, had not borne fruit, but the desire for independence had remained alive. Side by side with the social questions, the nationality problem continually formed a source of unrest in the Czarist empire.

For this reason, the Socialist Party had early on concerned itself exhaustively with this problem. Even as emigrés, Lenin and his associates used to discuss this complicated question of the self-determination of the non-Russian nationals. In his basic statement shortly before the outbreak of the World War, Lenin, who advocated self-determination with particular emphasis and defined it expressly as the "right to separate", maintained that it was "the misfortune of the nation that, while it subjugates other nations, it strengthens the reaction in the whole of Russia." [24] These words already contained the hint that, for the Bolshevists, the struggle for self-determination was less a political principle than a tactical manœuvre.

When in the spring of 1917 the Revolution broke out, the then weak Bolshevists endeavoured with all the means at their disposal to gain new adherents. Thus they also made use of the efforts towards self-determination of the non-Russian nationals since at their party conference in April they announced in a "resolution concerning the problem of nationality" [25]: "The right to voluntary separation and the formation of an independent State must be recognised to all peoples who belong to Russia. The denial of this right and the neglect of measures guaranteeing its practical feasibility are synonymous with supporting the policy of conquest or annexation. Only the recognition on the part of the proletariat of the right of nations to separate safeguards the complete solidarity of the workers of the various nations and promotes the real democratic understanding between the nations." Here, too, was once more indicated, at least in the last words, the hope that the Bolshevists had finally made support of efforts at self-determination one of their accepted principles.

Even after the October Revolution Lenin adhered to this policy. As early as November 2 (15), he, together with Stalin, who had become People's Commissar for Nationality Questions, promised in a decree: 1. Equality and sovereignty for all the Russian peoples; 2. Self-determination up to separation and complete independence from Russia; 3. Abolition of all national and religious privileges and restrictions; and 4. Unfettered evolution of the national minorities and ethnological groups in Russian State territory. [26] The Transcaucasian peoples, who, making use of the confusion, had extricated themselves from Russian domination, could, therefore, hope that their self-determination, which they reinforced in May, 1918, by establishing national Governments, was respected by the Soviet Government. However, Stalin soon gave the decree a suspicious twist when he wrote: "It is necessary to limit the principle of free self-determination of nations by granting it to the toilers and refusing it to the bourgeoisie. The principle of self-determination should be a means of fighting for socialism." [27]

A few months after the Revolution, the non-Russian peoples struggling for independence received a grim warning. Under the impact of the nationalities decree and of an appeal to the Mohammedans of the empire and of the East which followed shortly afterwards, about the turn of the year 1917–8 autonomous Mohammedan Governments had set themselves up in Turkestan and Kirghizia side by side with the Soviet organs.[28] They expressed their loyalty towards Soviet Russia but demanded that the Russian supreme power should not interfere in the internal affairs of their countries. At first the Soviet Government seemed to respect these wishes, but in February, 1918, a sudden onslaught on Kokand, the seat of the Turkestan Government, was set in motion from Tashkent, supported by a Bolshevist group in the country. The town was captured, laid waste, and most of it burned down. The people of Kirghizia did not fare much better. With the aid of the Soviet troops, their bourgeois Government, too, was overthrown and replaced by a sort of Popular Front régime.

It would be possible to regard these proceedings as episodes of the civil war if special circumstances did not point to the development of a manner of overthrow which has significance beyond the individual case. Immediately after its instalment, the Kirghizian Government had started up negotiations with Moscow in order to establish friendly relations with Soviet Russia. Alikhan Bucheikan, the Government chairman, acted as the spokesman with Stalin, who, as the People's Commissar for Nationality Questions, declared that the Soviet Government unreservedly recognised the autonomy of the people of Kirghizia and that it would not interfere in their internal affairs. However, immediately after the discussions were concluded, Stalin, in his capacity of member of the

Central Committee of the Party, got in touch with the Bolshevist chairman of the district soviet in question and ordered him to overthrow the bourgeois Government. The Red Army was then summoned from inside the country to help, and completed the work of sovietisation. Without the literal breaking of his word, Stalin, by combining revolutionary with State means, had secured the removal of the bourgeois régime.

These proceedings were carefully noted south of the Caucasus. For a time, the independent Governments felt themselves secure, to some extent, in the protection of, respectively, German and British expeditionary corps. But the traditional enmity between Armenians and Tartars, heightened by the proximity of the grasping Turks, obstructed the establishment of a solid front of defence against Bolshevism. As early as May, 1918, the "Transcaucasian Federative Republic", which had been established after the October Revolution and on April 22, 1918, had proclaimed its autonomy, broke up and three independent States set themselves up, side by side with which there still existed for some time a Communist régime in the port of Baku. After a chequered career[29], on January 11, 1920, Georgia and Azerbaidjan experienced the satisfaction of being recognised by the Allied Governments as independent States. But they were soon to know that no one was prepared to defend their independence against the encroaching Bolshevism.

In February, 1920, the Central Committee of the Russian Communist Party established a special "Caucasian Bureau" (Kavbiuro), under the direction of the Georgian Ordzhonikidze. The members of the Bureau went off forthwith to the Eleventh Red Army, which was stationed in the northern Caucasus. This circumstance alone shows that the Soviets had given up hope of being able to seize power in the Transcaucasian States by an internal revolution and were considering conquest from outside.[30] At the same time, the Soviet Government camouflaged its intentions by addressing to the Governments of Azerbaidjan and Georgia Notes which called for cooperation in the struggles against the "Whites" but at the same time contained an expression of the recognition of independence.

Azerbaidjan was the first victim of the Soviet expansion towards the south.[31] The oil of Baku exercised a strong power of attraction. In addition, relatively favourable conditions for the Communists prevailed here. In Baku, the seat of Government, there was a strong Communist party, which had at its disposal 4,000 armed men. While the Government plunged into the adventure of a war against Armenia and denuded the northern boundary of the country of troops, the Kavbiuro issued an order on April 24 to the effect that the Communists in Baku should present an ultimatum to the Government, at the same time calling for help from the Soviet Union. And so it happened. The twelve hours given by the ultimatum had not yet expired when the news reached Baku of the invasion by the Red Army. The next day Ordzhonikidze was in the capital, arranging for the assumption of governmental power.

The Eleventh Army did not remain stationary on the frontiers of Azerbaidjan but continued the march forward in the direction of Tiflis and Erevan, the capitals of the other two Transcaucasian republics. But Georgia and Armenia were once again saved. Precisely at this moment war with Poland broke out. Moscow ordered the retreat. Once again the intentions, already made public, had to be camouflaged. The Commissariat for Foreign Affairs opened negotiations, and on May 7 concluded a treaty with Georgia in which the Soviet Union recognised "without reservation" the independence and sovereignty of the Georgian Republic and expressly bound itself to abstain from interfering in the internal affairs of the country.[32] In a secret clause it undertook to allow the Communist Party a free rein. Moscow had another jumping-off place for later developments. Shortly afterwards a Soviet envoy was despatched to Tiflis. It was Kirov, the deputy chairman of the Kavbiuro.

In Armenia there was no strong Communist Party such as there was in Azerbaidjan. But there, too, circumstances came to the Soviet aid. For years the Armenians both inside and outside the country had been exposed to persecution by the Turks. Shortly after the signing of the treaty of Sèvres, which provided for a free and independent Armenia, in the late summer of 1920 the Turks once more invaded the country. In a short time they had advanced so far that they were in a position to dictate peace

21

conditions. While the Armenians were still negotiating with the Turks, the Kavbiuro received instructions to attack Armenia.[33] In an ultimatum, Legran, the Soviet Union's diplomatic representative in Erevan, called upon the Armenian Government to hand governmental power over to a "Revolutionary Committee of the Socialist Soviet Republic of Armenia", which had in the meantime been set up on Azerbaidjan soil. In the belief that the Soviet Union wished to assist Armenia against the Turks, the Government concurred in the establishment of a sort of Popular Front Government and, while Eleventh Army units were marching on Erevan, concluded a regular treaty[34] with Legran, in which Armenia was called an "independent Socialist Republic". Notwithstanding this, the "Revolutionary Committee", which entered the capital some days later, tore up this treaty on the spot, and on December 21 placed all Soviet laws in force for Soviet Armenia also.

After Armenia had been occupied Georgia was almost encircled. Nevertheless, the Soviet Government hesitated. The country had a Menshevist Government, which was regarded favourably by the Social Democrats in the Western countries. Only when Lloyd George expressed the opinion that, in the British view, the whole of the Caucasus belonged to the Soviet sphere of interest was Georgia's fate sealed.[35] On February 12, 1921, the Kavbiuro staged a Communist uprising on the border between Georgia and Armenia. In accordance with the prototype that had stood the test, a "Georgian Revolution Committee" was set up and at the same time the Eleventh Army crossed the border. Although the Armenians thereupon rose up against the Bolshevist domination and outside Tiflis the Georgians resisted valiantly, the superiority of the Red Army gained the victory. On February 25 the capital was occupied. In triumph, Ordzhonikidze sent telegrams to Lenin and Stalin: "The proletarian flag waves over Tiflis!"

This first phase of Bolshevist expansion was quickly forgotten when, for a long time afterwards, the Soviet Union busied itself solely with its own problems. Paying no heed to the raped peoples in Transcaucasia, the conscience of Europe soothed itself with the comfortable interpretation that one could not gainsay the Soviets the right to territories which had belonged to even the

Czarist empire. However, in a historical description of the revolutionary policy of the Soviets, this first phase of the expansion must not be omitted, since in it there stood out some peculiarities of this policy containing significance for the future too.

The first point that stands out is that the Soviets did not make a start with the conquest of the Transcaucasian countries until a moment when Europe had clearly shown that it was disinterested. In this, the Soviets exhibited an astounding foresight. However, when they believed that the right moment had come for the attack, it did not in the least disturb them that they were annexing a country whose independence they had beforehand contractually recognised. Finally, the method of attack is worthy of note. The Soviets were not satisfied with the employment of military means alone but simultaneously set up a revolutionary façade. The false appearance of a civil war was given to the struggle through an artifice.

Lenin sharply criticised the brutal methods that Stalin, Ordzhonikidze and Dzerzhinski, the Cheka head, applied in Georgia for the "political coordination" after the annexion.[36] He spoke of a "quagmire" in which one lands if one gives the Great Russians, whom he abruptly equated with chauvinists, the opportunity to oppress other peoples. But this criticism did not prevent Stalin from using the same methods when he entertained hopes of their success.

Chapter Two

EBB AND FURTHER FLOW OF THE REVOLUTION
(1921-1940)

> The greatest crime of Hitler was that his actions had
> resulted in opening the doors of Eastern Europe to
> Asia.
>
> *Averell Harriman, Potsdam, July 29, 1945*

The revolutionary tactics that had been developed in the years
of the civil war and the first violent conquests were scarcely used
for nearly another two decades. Only in the years 1920 and 1921,
after Transcaucasia had been conquered, did they play a role,
with the subjugation of the Emirate of Bukhara and the Khanate
of Chiwa [1] as well as in the Far East. The Soviet Union appeared
to become a State too occupied with its internal problems to
bother about enterprises in foreign parts. It would, however, be
wrong to suspect behind it all a slackening of the revolutionary
urge to expand. Soviet Russia was far from feeling itself satiated.

In these days Stalin advanced the theory of revolutionary ebb
and flow. Revolution does not, he averred, progress steadily.
After a period of success it requires rest in order to collect strength
for further strokes.[2] In 1921 the Soviet Union was exhausted. The
defeat in the war with Poland had shown the Soviet leaders that
the World War, the Revolution, the civil war and the frantic
attempt to transform agrarian Russia into a "socialist society"
had brought the gigantic empire to the brink of the abyss. Russia
needed rest. It was, indeed, because of this that Lenin had originally been opposed to the attack on Georgia.[3] He had just
despatched a trade mission to London and hoped to achieve the
assumption of diplomatic relations. The "storm and stress" period
of the Revolution was over.

In these years Europe protected itself against Bolshevist Russia
by a "cordon sanitaire" of independent States which, for a time,

aroused the impression of being strong enough to hold their own. The Soviet Union lay shut away beyond them, apparently inactive and paralysed by the experiment of socialism, though actually full of gathering energy. The Soviet command, which after Lenin's death in 1924 devolved on Stalin, never let the aims of the Revolution out of its sight. Only the methods changed, and the new methods produced their effect on the aims. While all over the world the Communist International attempted to improve the conditions for revolution, in the Soviet Union there were built up a heavy industry and a military apparatus which were meant to provide the bastion of socialism with the weight of one of the first Powers in the world. The Communist urge to expand took on imperialistic characteristics.

1. SOCIALISM IN ONE COUNTRY

At the beginning of the 1920s, the Soviets, despite their successes in the Soviet Union, had to despair of their own theory. In year-long deliberations prior to 1917, the principle was, in general, recognised that if the Revolution were to be launched from an agrarian country such as Russia and not, as Marx had expected, from one of the industrial countries in the West, it could not thrive without the full development of socialism extending to the other countries. Indeed, it had mostly been accepted that an individual socialist State could hold its own only for a short while in "capitalistic" surroundings. But these prognostications showed themselves to be false. The Revolution did not spread to other countries, nor did it unite the "capitalistic" world in order to take on the challenge of the Communists.

While the incorrigibles still awaited the outbreak of World Revolution, a new mood gradually came to prevail among the Soviet leaders. The Revolution began to establish itself in the conquered territories and to await the further course of history. This entailed in the first place a re-framing of economic policy. In order to put an end to the privation from lack of food and to get the economy viable again, in 1921 Lenin broke off the socialistic experiment at a moment's notice, and in the "new economic policy" once more left room for private initiative. At the same time, the Soviet Government concerned itself with the resumption of trade relations with foreign countries. After the Western States had reconciled themselves to the existence of the Soviet Union, they made no more difficulties in principle. In spite of this, for a time the Soviet Union remained diplomatically in the role of the outlaw, until on April 16, 1922, with the Russo-German Treaty of Rapallo, it succeeded in penetrating the wall of disdain.

Little by little the Bolshevist revolutionaries grew into the part of leaders of State. Industry was driven forward vehemently; diplomats were despatched to other countries. Between the ideology that forbade the origination of an isolated socialist State and the Soviet reality, there developed an inconsistency that could in the long run be bridged only by an amendment of the theory. This step was completed by Stalin in the autumn of 1924 when he propounded the theory of "socialism in *one* country".[4] The success of the new idea that socialism need not await the successful outcome of the Revolution in other countries but could be realised in Russia alone was mainly due to the mood of optimism that spread among the Bolshevists of conviction. After waiting in vain for World Revolution, there they were set once more a realisable goal on the attainment of which all their strength could be concentrated. The doctrine of "socialism in *one* country" became the "national creed".[5]

In the Western countries the new dogma evoked bewilderment. The reasoning of the Soviets that, without waiting for a further gaining of ground, socialism could be realised in Russia was confounded with a deliberate resignation to the spread of Communism. This was not, however, the design of Lenin's theory. It kept in view the aim of World Revolution. In the first place the methods changed. Trotsky, Stalin's protagonist in the contention over the new thesis, never wavered from the belief that in Western Europe Communism would gain the victory in class warfare by virtue of its own power. Secondly, as the years went by, Stalin grew more sceptical[6], and it was only a matter of consistency when he, in contrast to Trotsky, kept his eyes more and more on the necessity to support Communists abroad with the

Soviet power of State. This was reason enough for the application of all energies to the industrial development of the Soviet Union.

Nevertheless, with the adoption of newer methods the aims also changed. After the Soviet Union had become the stronghold of socialism, the Soviets' ideological consciousness of mission assimilated elements of the old Russian conception of the "Third Rome". Now it no longer seemed material whether in the course of the Revolution the centre switched from Moscow to Berlin or Paris or whether new centres developed side by side with Moscow. Rather, under the leadership of Stalin the Georgian there developed a Soviet state-consciousness, an odd mixture of Marxist and nationalist elements. Inside the revolutionary world movement, the Soviet Union, as "Fatherland of the Workers", put forward, in matters to do both with tactics and with theory, a claim to leadership, which was granted it without substantial resistance. At the same time, the revolutionary urge to expand of the early days was overshadowed by a leaning to extend the Soviet State power. The conception of a number of socialist States with equal entitlement was replaced, almost unnoticed, by the goal of the domination of as great a part of the world as possible by the Moscow leaders. There was a mingling of the urge for World Revolution and Soviet imperialism.

This change is to be seen particularly significantly in the development of the Communist International. The Comintern's inaugural congress took place in March, 1917, in the Kremlin – characteristically at the invitation of the Soviet People's Commissar for Foreign Affairs[7], who at the time regarded the propagation of World Revolution as his most important task. It was still a threadbare assembly, consisting of a few Communists, some prisoners-of-war, and foreign Extremists who chanced to be in Russia. However, even to the second congress, in June, 1920, there streamed delegations of Communist groups from 37 countries. Through the acceptance of Lenin's "21 points"[8], the Comintern became a centrally-directed instrument of revolution, with organs covering the whole world. Among other things, the political parties associated in it bound themselves to lay their programmes before the Comintern for approval and, side by side with their official organisations, to establish secret machinery which would be "of great use in the revolutionary periods of the Party". All over the world, rigidly-controlled Communist parties were built up after the prototype of the Bolshevist Party, ready at all times to carry out the directions of the Moscow headquarters.

The Comintern did not lose its importance when the Soviet leaders went over to the policy of socialism in *one* country, though it had to suffer a change of structure. While in the beginning it was superior to the Russian party, now it was subordinated to it.[9] Stalin made it an instrument of command, whereby his directions could reach to the furthermost corners of the earth.[10] Inured to strict obedience, everywhere the Communist parties became the Soviet Union's "fifth column", long before this concept made its mark in the Spanish Civil War. Just as, after the October Revolution in Russia, the Soviet leaders disposed over, at one and the same time, the means of power of both Party and State, and used it alternately at will, so now could they pursue their aims abroad, now via "their" parties, then via "their" diplomatic representatives.

The Comintern also helped to school and train Communists all over the world for the revolution to come. Communists from abroad were summoned to Moscow, there to be instructed in the tried and proved technique of revolution. The tactical rules were laid down in secret manuals, and in the committee headquarters in Moscow and the Frunze Academy, material on the military aspects of communist expansion was assembled.[11] The secret handbooks placed the greatest emphasis on incessant acts of aggression by means of which the Communists in the various countries had to snatch the power from the existing governments. They also took into account, however, as we know from one example, of the "possibility of military support from a foreign country in which the revolutionary class has already seized power." [12]

In spite of the existence of the Comintern, the activity of the Communists abroad was, in the first years, disappointing for the Soviet leaders. To mention only a few instances, neither in 1923 in Germany nor in England during the world economic crisis did they manage to stage a successful coup d'état. In China, after years of cooperation with the Kuomintang they were thrown out by Chiang Kai-shek, and in the Spanish Civil War they were unable to hold their own against Franco. From Moscow's point of view, through such failures the Communist parties abroad ceased, in the course of the years, to be the "vanguards of World Revolution". They were more or less demoted to being "frontier-guards of Soviet Russia".[13] To Stalin, every factory that was built in Russia seemed more important than all expectations of a revolution abroad.[14] He concentrated all energies on realising the great Five Year Plans that were intended in mighty strokes to transform Russia from being an agrarian country that had lagged behind the times to being a modern industrial State.

There was a time when Stalin himself had set his face against the idea that behind this transformation there lay concealed a renunciation of the revolutionary aims and a restriction to the old national ambitions of Russia. When the writer Emil Ludwig wished to compare Stalin with Peter the Great, Stalin retorted that his task was "not the strengthening of any national State but the strengthening of a Socialist, and that means international, State".[15] In these words Stalin's policy is restricted in two ways. On the one hand, he always considered it his task to build up a Soviet State with all the means at the disposal of those in power; on the other hand, he regarded this State as not being for ever and aye the territory lying within the boundaries of the Czarist empire. Stalin's most conspicuous quality was his more temperate instinct for power. To ensure the progress of World Revolution he backed the greatest Power that stood at Communism's disposal. This was the Soviet Union, with its population of millions, with its far-flung lands and the rich mineral wealth that allowed a great deal of elbow-room for modern industrial development. But the consolidation of the State received its meaning only with the prospect of being able to advance the historical process of supplanting capitalism by socialism. Indeed, from Stalin's point of view it was not illogical to assert that the Soviet Five Year Plans mobilised "the revolutionary substance of the working-classes *of all countries* against capitalism." [16]

Every epoch learns from its own experiences. The Bolshevist revolutionaries never forgot that their success in Russia was primarily due to the chaos and confusion of war. From this empiricism it was but a short step to the concept that fresh wars are suited to preparing the soil for the further spreading of Communism. The Soviet leaders had therefore from the beginning had a penchant for the idea that fresh global conflicts are unavoidable.

For the Soviets, belief in another world war was facilitated by Lenin's dogmatic theory of "imperialism as the highest stage of capitalism", since in this system peace is signalised as being the "breathing-space" between two wars. Among the Soviet leaders, war was so certain that the establishment of the League of Nations was looked upon from the very beginning as being merely an episode. There was, however, early recognition that not every war is good for Communism. Above all, the preference was for wars between the "capitalist" States. The Soviet Union must, so far as possible, remain aloof from any conflict – in the first place because at first it had not enough strength and, secondly, because it must save its strength for the final coming-to-grips between "capitalism" and socialism.

Early signs of subscription to this war theory are to be found even with Lenin, who at the end of 1920 declared before the Moscow Communists: "If war does not materialise by itself, it must be instigated. If we are compelled to tolerate such scamps as the capitalist thieves, each of whom is whetting his knife against us, it is our immediate obligation to direct these knives against each other." [17] Stalin elaborated this theory, while to a certain extent categorising the various conceivable conflicts, placing them in a definite relationship to each other. Thus at the 15th Party Congress of the Communist Party he said that, though war with the capitalist countries was unavoidable, it must, in the interest of the socialist development, be postponed "until the proletarian war breaks out in Europe or the colonial revolutions have fully developed or the capitalists are embroiled in a war concerning the distribution of the colonies among them." [18]

Such pronouncements clearly betray that the Soviet leaders in no way despised the means of war. In 1930, Stalin, in a letter to Gorki, expressly turned his back on a pacifistic frame of mind. "We are certainly not against *every* war", he wrote. "We are *against* the imperialistic war as a means of counter-revolution. But we are *for* the liberating, anti-imperialistic war, notwithstanding the fact that, as is well-known, such a war is not only not free of the 'terror of blood-shedding' but is liberally endowed with it." [19] Nor did it disturb the Soviet leaders that an intervention with violence was theoretically contradictory to the certain expectation that the victory of socialism was historically a matter of compulsion. Even Lenin had scoffed at the Communists who, placing their confidence in the correctness of the Marxist theory, believed that they could allow themselves any mistake.[20] Stalin, with his highly-developed instinct for power, advocated more than ever promoting the Revolution with all disposable means. At a given point of time the proletariat dictatorship was to serve in *one* country "as a base . . . from which to overthrow imperialism in all countries." [21]

It was one of Stalin's most peculiar accomplishments that he recognised early on how incorrect it would be were the Soviet Union to rush with revolutionary fervour into every conflict that flared up. He saw clearly that the most favourable time for the Soviet Union lay in the final phase of a new World War, if it were possible to save the Soviet troops till then. First let the "capitalist thieves" quarrel among themselves, then exploit their condition of weakness in order to give them the finishing stroke – such was the cold-blooded theory that, as early as 1925, Stalin elaborated before the Party's Central Committee. "Our banner remains, as before, the banner of freedom. But when war begins we shall not have to place our hands in our lap. We shall have to come forward, but be the last to come forward. And we shall come forward in order to throw the decisive weight into the scales, the weight that can turn the scales." [22] From the 1920s to 1941, this new theory of the "third man with the laugh on his side" was the determining factor in Soviet foreign policy above all tactical twistings. The Soviet leaders attempted to avoid every war in which the Soviet Union would have to fight from the first day.

It is true that it certainly now looked at first as if the Communist expectations would be disappointed. There neither developed a "proletarian war" in Europe nor did the revolutionary developments in the colonies proceed with the hoped-for speed. Much less did there break out any conflict concerned with the apportionment of colonies. The vacuum that threatened to arise because of this in Soviet policy was, however, filled up by another political current. With their inflated national ambitions, the authoritarian States brought into the world the unrest and keen antagonisms that had been vainly awaited in Moscow from an increase in economic competition among the "capitalist" States. While Japan with its attack on the land-mass of the Far East and Italy with its Abyssinian adventure could, after a fashion, be classified as falling within the pattern of Leninistic theories, Nazi Germany was already giving cause for anticipating difficulties of a seriously substantial nature.

The rise of National Socialism in Germany set the Soviet leaders a riddle. It must have surprised them that it was not the idea of class-warfare that succeeded in mobilising the masses but a "movement" which, from the Communist point of view, was composed of an indigestible mixture of socialist and capitalist elements and which inscribed the National Socialist password on its flags, for which there was absolutely no place in Leninism's schematic concepts. But even if the inevitable unintelligibility of this phenomenon long continued, the Soviet leaders soon comprehended that the authoritarian States were introducing to the world a new constellation that brought with it not only special dangers but also opportunities.

In the first years, Moscow apparently rated the hazards higher than the opportunities. Since the Soviet Union did not yet consider itself by far strong enough for a big war, it now pursued a peaceful policy the sincerity of which was not to be doubted. Through entrance into the League of Nations and the conclusion of a whole wad of treaties of non-aggression, it attempted to ensure for itself a lengthy period of peace in which there was to be built up not so much "socialism" as an efficient armaments industry. For the first time, the concept of "peaceful co-existence", which had put in its appearance as early as 1927, played in this period

32

a bigger part. It was of moment for the Soviet Union to free itself of the suspicion that because of an internal lawfulness it was the enemy of the whole world.

It was soon recognised, however, that in the increasing power of the authoritarian States there also lay an opportunity for Communism. Looking back, one sees that in the 1930s Communism had no better allies than National Socialism and Fascism, even if these were attuned to anti-Communism and subsequently concluded the "anti-Comintern pact." Indeed, the rabid determination with which especially the German National Socialists drove forward the development in the direction of a new European civil war was possibly more welcome to the Soviets than a successful Communist uprising in Germany, which could precipitate the danger of a premature duel between the "capitalist" and socialist parts of the world.[23] It is possible to explain the striking holding-back of the Soviet Union in the Spanish Civil War as being due to similar considerations.[24]

Soviet foreign policy of the 1930s, with its curious pacifism, is to be explained only as being due to the anticipation that a new global conflict was unavoidable. In this connection, the analysis of the world position that Stalin gave before the 17th Party Congress in January, 1934[25], is very well worth noting. It began with the stony statement: "Another war is clearly approaching." Stalin then differentiated among four possibilities: a war against one of the great Powers; a war against a large, but weak, country such as China; a war waged by an allegedly "superior" race against an allegedly "inferior" race; and, finally, a war against the Soviet Union. In each of the four cases he came to the conclusion that such a war could not help but be useful to the spread of Communism, but the most disagreeable possibility, the war against the Soviet Union, was, he said, the "most dangerous war for the bourgeoisie", since his belief was that in such a conflict "the numerous friends of the working-class of the Soviet Union in Europe and Asia" would stab their "oppressors" in the back. Stalin followed this false prognostication with a sentence that, in the light of later events, seems to be a genuine prophecy: "And may the bourgeois gentlemen not cast reproaches upon us if the day after such a war they miss some of the Governments intimately connected with them which, safe and sound, are now ruling 'by the grace of God'."

When, five years later, on March 10, 1939, Stalin appeared at the 18th Party Congress, for him the new war had already begun[26], and he had succeeded in keeping the Soviet Union out of the conflict. "The new war of the imperialists has become a fact", he asserted in regard to the aggressive actions of Japan, Italy and Germany. But this war had not yet developed into another World War because the "non-aggressive, democratic States" had taken up a position of neutrality. With a clarity the Western Powers then lacked, Stalin predicted: "In reality, however, the policy of non-intervention signifies a coming down in favour on the side of aggression, the unleashing of war, and, as a consequence, its transformation into a World War."

This speech of Stalin's on the eve of the second World War is only to be understood if one brings to mind the situation in Europe at the time. In the Soviet Union, which as a non-participant had to look on, Chamberlain and Daladier's surprising unanimity with Hitler at Munich had increased the suspicion that the Western Powers wished to divert in the direction of the Soviet Union Nazi Germany's urge to expand. Stalin gave clear expression to this suspicion without, however, going more deeply into the matter. The speech has justly been called a "rare masterpiece of double entendre".[27] Both sides, the Western democracies and the Axis Powers, could each feel that it was to them that the words were addressed.

A few days later there started that episode the diplomatic documents of which constitute for the reader of today perhaps the pre-war era's most dramatic recording.[28] The European democracies, led by the United Kingdom, sought to safeguard themselves against Germany and Italy's further appetite to expand by guaranteeing the integrity of the countries that came into question – Poland, Roumania and Greece. But because of the unfavourability of the geographical conditions, it was plain to all the world that they could afford no protection to Poland or Roumania. They therefore fell back on the desperate idea of offering the Soviet Union an alliance for the protection of these countries, not without the weird feeling of, under certain circumstances,

34

setting a thief to catch a thief. Faithful to the tactics of the third man with the laugh on his side, the Soviet Government showed little enthusiasm for this proposal, which could involve them all too soon in a war with the powerfully-armed Reich. Instead of this, Stalin let it be known that his mind was not unable to conjure up the picture of a Russo-German rapprochement.

It is difficult to penetrate the purport of the diplomatic game that developed and from which in August the Western Powers emerged beaten and Hitler the apparent, Stalin the real, victor. And yet a profound logic resides therein. The Western democracies' mistrust of the Soviet Union was even surpassed by the anxieties of the countries immediately bordering the Soviet empire. Poland, Roumania and the Baltic States had no appetite for entering into any alliance with the Soviet Union. Poland's Marshal Rydz-Śmigly spoke for them all when he said: "With the Germans we would lose our freedom; with the Russians – our soul." On the other hand, Nazi Germany knew no plague of scruples. With all their militant aversion to Communism, Germany's rulers, themselves bent entirely on acts of violence, had practically kindred feelings when in the course of the negotiations they found it confirmed that the Soviet Union, too, was on the prowl for plunder. For the Soviet Union, it was a question, in the most prosaic sense, of business – not only on account of the territorial gains agreed in the secret supplementary protocol to the Hitler-Stalin pact of August 23, 1939 [29], but, above all, on account of the fact that the new World War would flare up without at first Soviet participation. Thus Stalin hoped out of the global conflagration, to the kindling of which he emboldened Hitler by the conclusion of the pact, "to draw the greatest benefit at the smallest cost." [30]

It would be a mistake to imagine that the Soviet Government believed it had placed itself at the side of the strongest battalions. Stalin knew that the democracies, weak though they had shown themselves in the last years, were stronger than the Axis Powers. He had unmistakably expressed himself thus in his March speech.[31] He had, it is true, overestimated the French powers of resistance [32] and counted on a protracted Franco-German war on the Continent. In this, he did not at all wish to be sure of standing

on the side of the victors. The Soviet attitude is difficult to understand without taking into consideration the historic *Leit-motive*
that the Bolshevist leaders kept constantly before their eyes. In
this case it was perhaps the example that Stalin often advanced
yet again in later times – the Peace of Tilsit, which gave the
Czar Alexander I a breathing-space of four years before the war
with Napoleon. Perhaps it was also the hope that the situation in
1918 would repeat itself – a Europe shattered by the strains and
the dishevelment of war; masses aflame with a revolutionary
temper; and a whole society of States, this time delivered up,
defenceless, to the unbroken might of the Soviet Union.[33]

3. THE SECOND PHASE OF THE SOVIET EXPANSION

Hitler's unscrupulous attack on Poland not only unleashed the
second World War. At the same time it thrust open the gateway
to Europe to the Soviet Union.[34] What at first in September and
October seemed only a fourth partitioning of Poland was the
beginning of a second phase of Soviet expansion. Stalin's declaration at the 16th Party Congress that the Soviet Union did
not desire "a single square metre of foreign land" was forgotten
now that, for the first time since the beginning of the 1920s, they
once again had the chance of territorial gains in Europe.
Seldom, however, has expansion by force been made so easy for
a country as it was for the Soviet Union in 1939–40. In their
negotiations, the German leaders offered the Soviets everything
the latters' appetite could desire. The assurance that from the
Baltic to the Black Sea there was no clash of interests between
Germany and the Soviet Union had to be looked upon in Moscow
as a formal invitation. Since at that time the Western Powers
had no possibility whatever of affording effective assistance to
the countries in Eastern and South-Eastern Europe, it is not to be
wondered at that the Soviets accepted the irresponsible German
offer. Rather is it surprising that they were satisfied with the
eastern portion of Poland, the Baltic States, Finland and Bessarabia. In August, 1939, Hitler, wildly anxious to conclude the
treaty, would have presented them with large parts of the Balkans

also [35], but in this they were not interested. Here, too, their motives are not at first sight transparent, though their further actions provide pointers for the forming of convictions.

In this phase of the expansion, the Soviet Government's first conspicuous step was the re-defining, in September, 1939, of the spheres of interest. In the secret supplementary protocol of August 23, 1939, the Soviets were promised the regions east of the rivers Narev, Vistula and San as well as the Baltic territories minus Lithuania. The possibility of a Polish State arising out of what was left over remained open. The rapid defeat of Poland was so surprising to the Soviets that they had difficulty in occupying their sphere of interest promptly. At the same time, the dissolution of all State authority rendered the preservation of a rump-State difficult. The Soviet Government was, therefore, suddenly faced with the question as to whether at this early stage of the great global conflagration they ought to draw upon themselves the odium of annexing a foreign country. The decision taken by Stalin apparently eight days after the Red Army's march into Poland [36] does honour to his statesmanship. He proposed to the German Government a reduction of the Soviet sphere of interest in Poland to approximately the territory east of the Curzon Line, thereby creating the preliminary conditions for the annexation of the whole of the Polish territory gained. The Western Powers could neither reproach the Soviet Union with appropriation of territory that had never belonged to Russia nor with carrying the Revolution beyond the borders of its own State. The Soviet restraint did not, in fact, remain unnoticed in the West.[37] In any case, in the new secret protocol of September 28, Stalin traded for his partial renunciation in Poland the incorporation of Lithuania within his sphere of influence.[38]

Even the form in which the Soviet Union completed the annexation of Eastern Poland was unusual. The Soviet Government placed value on not invading Poland as a wager of war, and for that reason planned to call for the dissolution of the Polish State even before Poland was finally defeated in order to engineer the necessity of placing the "life and property of the population" under the protection of the Red Army.[39] In a broadcast speech, Molotov circulated the version that the Soviet Government deemed it its "sacred duty to extend a helping hand to our Brother Ukrainians and Brother White Russians who live in Poland." [40] Thus, in order to avoid the impression of a Communist expansion, arguments having a national ring about them were chosen, the phraseology being more appropriate to the vocabularies of the nationalists. Indeed, some weeks later the Soviet leaders put themselves to the trouble of holding "elections" in the newly-gained territories so that it could be given out later that a "popular referendum" for attachment to the Soviet Ukraine and Soviet White Ruthenia had been held. [41] Legality was preserved so far as mere form was concerned.

As the Soviet Government busied itself with engineering accomplished facts in the remaining lands of their "sphere of interest", they also placed value at first on external rectitude. The procedure adopted stands in striking contrast to the methods used at the end of 1924 with the first attempt at the annexation of Esthonia. Then, at short notice, Zinoviev despatched a few dozen officers to Tallin, where a bloody, though unsuccessful, coup d'état was staged.[42] Now, the Soviet Government first secured, on September 28, that the Esthonian Government concluded a "pact of mutual assistance", under which naval bases and airports were ceded to the Red Army.[43] President Päts, the Esthonian Head of State, had feared that non-compliance with the Soviet demands would lead to war and the extermination of his people. On October 5, Latvia was forced to follow the Esthonian example, and on October 10 a similar "pact of mutual assistance" was signed with Lithuania.[44] The Baltic States had to surrender their independence since they saw that Germany was not willing, and the United Kingdom not in a position, to afford them protection. It was soon to be seen that the loss of independence precluded the maintenance of neutrality and was the first step on the road to annexation by the Soviets.

In the middle of October, the Soviet Government addressed to Finland demands going further than those made on the Baltic States. The Finnish frontier was to be withdrawn on the Karelian peninsula, not far from Leningrad, and the south-west tip of Finland with the port of Hangö was to be leased to the Soviet Union for 30 years. It was wished to establish military bases

38

there, as in the Esthonian harbour of Baltic Port opposite, in order to be able to block access to the Gulf of Finland.[45] But here for the first time the Kremlin met with a resistance that unveiled its aggressive intent. While M. Paasikivi, the Finnish Prime Minister, was willing to yield in all points, he felt he could not acquiesce in the transfer of Hangö because the strategic security of the country depended on possession of this peninsula. In mid-November the negotiations were broken off. Thereupon the Soviet Government showed that the fears of the Baltic States were not unjustified. On November 28, the Soviet Government cancelled the Finno-Soviet pact of non-aggression, and two days later Soviet divisions attacked at eight points the long frontier between Finland and Russia.

The circumstances attending the attack deserve close study.[46] In the first place, it is striking that the Soviet Government did not regard the Finnish refusal unreservedly to accept the demands contained in the Soviet ultimatum as a sufficient reason for going to war but sought a pretext in an alleged surprise attack by Finnish artillery. However, in the days prior to the attack, the Soviet Press accused the governing circles of Finland not only of adopting an aggressive attitude towards the Soviet Government but at the same time accused it of oppressing the Finnish "workers". In Finland, this accusation must have aroused the gravest fears, but on November 29 Molotov, in a broadcast speech, gave the express assurance that the Soviet Union would not interfere in Finland's internal affairs but would only attend to the security of Leningrad. The following day, when the Soviet attack began, the Central Committee issued a proclamation to the Communist Party of Finland calling for civil war. One day later, in the town of Terijoki, which had been occupied by Soviet troops, the Finnish Communist Kuusinen formed a "People's Government" after the pattern of the Armenian and Georgian Communists. The very same day this "Government" was recognised by the Supreme Soviet as the legitimate Government of Finland. The next day Molotov and Kuusinen signed a Finno-Russian treaty, which fulfilled every one of the Russian demands. When a few days later, in Helsinki, the legal Finnish Government proposed to the Soviet Union via Sweden the resumption of negotiations, the Soviet Government replied to the effect that it was not able to negotiate with the "so-called Finnish Government" since it no longer recognised it.

Since the Soviet Union was now in league with a Finnish Government and did not recognise the Government it was fighting, Molotov was able in a despatch to the Secretary-General of the League of Nations flatly to contest that there was any Finno-Soviet war at all. Molotov peremptorily asserted that the Government of the "Finnish Democratic Republic" with which the Soviet Union had been allied since December 2 through a pact of mutual assistance had asked the Soviet Government for military aid.[47] The Foreign Commissar passed over the fact that the Soviet "aid" had already started before there was any Finnish "People's Government" at all and that this "People's Government" in turn had to thank the Soviet "assistance" for its existence. He could therefore act, as previously in the case of the Transcaucasian countries, as if it were a matter of a civil war. But the League of Nations did not permit itself to be misled. On December 14 it adopted a resolution expelling the Soviet Union because of its aggression.

Seemingly the Soviets had reckoned that their military attack would lead at once to a popular uprising and the overthrow of the Government. In such an event the Kuusinen "Government" would have assumed power and been able to lay the ground for the same development as in the Baltic States. But it was precisely the establishment of this Communist counter-Government that proved to be a mistake. In view of the clear Soviet intention to sovietise the whole of Finland, the Finns sprang to their defence in a mood of desperation. Favoured by the wintry weather, for several months they were able to keep the numerically greater Soviet troops at bay and seriously damage the prestige of the Red Army. With mounting sympathy the whole world watched the Finns' struggle for freedom. Exclusion of the Soviet Union from the League of Nations was not the end of the matter. On February 5, 1940, the Supreme War Council of the Western Powers resolved to despatch an expeditionary corps to Finland.[48] The execution of the resolution foundered only because, in the first place, Sweden and Norway refused to allow the British and

French troops to cross their countries and, secondly, because as a result of the Soviet break-through in the spring, Finland was compelled to conclude a precipitate peace.[49]

Still, it was now no longer possible for the Soviet Union to keep to the intention of sovietising the whole of Finland, since all the world had seen that the affirmation of a Finnish "civil war" was untrue. In the peace treaty which the Soviet Government concluded on March 12, 1940, with a Government with which they had not allegedly been carrying on a war, the Soviet Union annexed only parts of Finland, although considerably larger areas than they had demanded in the autumn of 1939. Finland had, above all, to relinquish the whole of the Karelian peninsula with the city of Vyborg, as well as the Gulf of Vyborg with the islands, the western and northern shores of Lake Ladoga, and part of the Ribachi peninsula.[50] However, in the scuttling of the marionette stage, the Kuusinen "Government" vanished.

The indignation of the West at the Soviets' violent procedure did not prevent the Soviet leaders from a fresh attack on the Baltic States following the victory over Finland. It seems that the impulse was given by a further act of aggression on the part of Nazi Germany – the occupation of Holland, Belgium and Luxemburg. Even on May 16, 1940, the Soviet Government organ "Isvestia" came to the conclusion: "The latest war events have shown once more that the neutrality of small States which have not sufficient strength to maintain themselves is pure imagination. For the continuance of the neutrality and independence of small countries there remains, therefore, little prospect." In the Baltic area, there was comprehension of the threat. The very next day, the Latvian Cabinet gave full powers to its envoy in London should their country be occupied by the enemy.[51] Lithuania followed suit.

In the "pacts of mutual assistance" the Soviet Union had undertaken the express obligation "not to influence in any way the sovereign rights" of the Baltic States, "in particular their economic and State systems", and on October 31, 1939, Molotov, while addressing the Supreme Soviet, had asserted that "the principle of non-interference in the internal affairs of the young States" had thereby been brought into prominence.[52] However,

41

shortly after the fall of Paris, the Soviet Government, under the threadbare pretext that the maintenance of the "pacts of mutual assistance" had not been adhered to, addressed ultimata to the Governments of the three Baltic States calling for their agreement to the reorganisation of the Government and acquiescence in the occupation of the whole of their countries. Within a few days, Esthonia, Latvia and Lithuania were occupied. In order to achieve the formation of more compliant Governments, the Kremlin sent three of its highest functionaries, Zhdanov, the Secretary of the Central Committee, and Vishinsky and Dekanosov, the Deputy Foreign Commissars, to Tallin, Riga and Kaunas. As in Eastern Poland, the attempt to simulate a formal legality was only partially successful.[53]

In Lithuania, Dekanosov was confronted with the difficult problem of who could possibly instal a new Government, since in view of the Soviet menace, President Smetona had gone abroad, without renouncing his office. But the Soviet Government's plenipotentiary knew what to do. He got M. Merkys, the officiating Prime Minister, to make a declaration in which, clearly contradictory to the country's Constitution, the sojourn abroad of the President was signalised as flight and the laying-down of his office. On the basis of this declaration, Merkys assumed the right to appoint as his successor the writer Paleckis, who was nominated by Dekanosov. Paleckis formed the desired "People's Government" out of Communists and members of the Extreme Left.

Vishinsky had an easier task in Riga, where the Communists had demonstrated in the streets even as the Red Army marched in. President Ulmanis had not left the country. There was fighting in the streets when he refused to sign the Cabinet list placed before him by Vishinsky. It is unknown whether or not Ulmanis gave way under the impression caused by this. At any rate, on June 20 the formation of a "People's Government" under Professor Kirchensteins was announced by the secretariat of the President, without it being seen from the announcement whether or not the President had given his sanction for it as laid down in the Constitution.

In Esthonia, Zhdanov met with the greatest resistance. But is was precisely these difficulties that gave the spur to his revolutionary imagination and enabled him to discover a new method of overthrow providing a guide for the future. After discussions with the country's Communist Party leaders, he first proposed to President Päts a new Government headed by the poet Dr. Vares-Barbarus. Päts, who had commissioned Professor Uluots's resigned Government with the execution of affairs for the time being, refused, however, to confirm the new Government composed of Communists and members of the Extreme Left. Thereupon the official residence of the recalcitrant President, Castle Katharinental, was cut off from the surrounding world by Soviet troops. For four days Päts remained resolute, and on the fifth day Zhdanov staged a Communist "popular uprising". A Communist "organisation for the protection of special interests", equipped for the most part with Soviet weapons and strengthened by Bolshevist shock troops from Leningrad, stormed the Government and Parliament buildings and hoisted the Red Flag on "Long Hermann", the symbol of Tallin. Officials and police were arrested and officer-candidates beleaguered in their barracks. In order to prevent further bloodshed, the President gave way.

The establishment of "popular democratic" Governments in the Baltic States soon showed itself to be a connecting link on the road to Soviet annexation.[54] Only a few weeks later, on July 14 and 15, 1940, "elections" took place throughout the Baltic countries under particularly grotesque circumstances. The Communists and the Extreme Left came forward with single lists of candidates, and at short notice the other candidates were almost without exception refused a licence. Thus in general the "elections" took place according to the Soviet pattern. The results corresponded to those habitual with their Soviet prototype. In Lithuania it was officially announced that there was a 99.2% poll, in Latvia 97.6%, and even in Esthonia, where the Communist Party had always had few adherents, 92.9%. Since such results would have been conclusive of very little with a smaller number of people casting their vote, participation in the "elections" was noted on the identity card. Non-voters were defamed as "enemies of the people". Nevertheless, the number of votes cast seems to have been less than was officially given out, and even some forging of the election results was necessary.

In July 17, after talks in Moscow, Zhdanov returned to Tallin, where Dekanosov and Vishinsky awaited him. After he had proclaimed the attachment of Esthonia to the Soviet Union, the following day there were Communist demonstrations during which this demand was seized upon "spontaneously". On July 21, in the first session of the new Chamber of Deputies, it was resolved to declare Esthonia a "Socialist Soviet Republic". The following day the Esthonian Soviet Republic announced its accession to the Soviet Union. Events in Lithuania and Latvia were synchronised, so that in the final days of August the Supreme Soviet could deal, one after the other, with the three new Soviet Republics "petitions of acceptance" and pass appropriate laws.[55] The sovietisation of the Baltic States followed in the shortest possible time. Molotov's statement on October 31, 1939, that "the babbling over the sovietisation of the Baltic countries is of use only to our common enemies and all possible anti-Soviet provocateurs"[56] had not remained applicable for even one year. The sovietisation was carried out with the most brutal means of terror, with deportations and arrests.[57]

When on August 7 the Supreme Soviet decided to incorporate the Baltic region constitutionally into the Soviet Union by a law amending the Constitution, it was also able at the same time to take into consideration the annexation of another region. At the end of June, under the pressure of a Soviet threat of war, Roumania had to relinquish Bessarabia, the northern part of Bukovina, and the northern tip of Old Roumania.[58]

The annexation of the Roumanian border regions followed the classic pattern of the well-prepared use of political threats and measures of violence. This time there was a desisting from revolutionary plotting. After Molotov had, as early as March, 1940, given an intimation in a threatening manner, on June 26 he suddenly summoned the Roumanian Ambassador Davidescu to him and handed him an ultimatum demanding the surrender of the territories within 24 hours.[59] A request for postponement was rejected. In Bucharest the first reaction was extreme perturbation. It is true that they had anticipated that the Soviet Union would at some time or another demand the return of Bessarabia, which apart from a few interruptions had belonged to the Czarist empire since 1812 and in 1918 had been occupied and annexed by Roumania in the turmoil of the Russian civil war, but it caught the Roumanian Government entirely unprepared that other territories which had never been in Russian possession should also be demanded and that the demands should be presented in so caustic a form. It was not at the time known in Roumania that originally the Soviet Union wished to annex the whole of the Bukovina and had desisted from claiming part of the province only out of regard for Germany, because of the *Volksdeutsche* – the ethnic Germans – living there.[60]

The period of consultation was short. Since for some months Roumania had been seeking an association with Germany, the Government first turned to Berlin. It was promptly advised to accede to the Soviet demands. The Reich Government had already been informed of the Soviet intentions and had intimated approval. Nevertheless, opposition made itself felt in the Privy Council convened by King Carol. In view, however, of the threatening concentrations of Soviet troops along the Dniester and on Roumania's northern frontier, military resistance seemed to be hopeless. In order at least to gain time, on June 27 the Roumanian Government declared itself ready to send plenipotentiaries to Moscow to discuss Soviet conditions. The Soviet Government did not, however, go into the matter but peremptorily announced how the handing over of the territories should be accomplished. Within four days the Roumanian troops were to be withdrawn and make way for the advancing Red Army. Berlin once again interposed, and managed to achieve a short postponement. In point of fact, the Soviets did not, however, keep to their promise but outflanked the Roumanian troops in order to seize greater quantities of war material.[61]

The Soviet policy of annexation in regard to Roumania had a little sequel in the autumn of 1940. Supported by small ships-of-war, Soviet border units occupied by force the river narrows of Stari-Stamboul and certain islands in the estuary of the Danube. With the maximum of amiability, Vishinsky told the Roumanian Ambassador that these islands were of no use to Roumania but that for the Soviet Union they were of great value.[62]

4. THE MOTIVES OF SOVIET POLICY
FROM 1939 TO 1940

The motives which led the Soviet leaders to seize the Transcaucasian territories in the years 1920 and 1921 are not generally contested. The method of procedure alone shows that, apart from economic interests and the aim of forging ahead as far as the frontiers of the Czarist empire, a strong revolutionary impulse played a part. On the other hand, the opinions expressed in pertinent writings as to the motives of the Soviet annexations in the years 1939 and 1940 vary.

The view extensively held is that the Soviet Government was endeavouring to advance its strategic frontiers for genuine security needs. This point of view seems plausible with, for example, the annexation of Eastern Poland. The Russo-German pact of August 23, 1939, had in no way removed the Soviet leaders' mistrust of Germany, and, in view of the unavoidable extension eastwards of the German sphere of power, it was obvious to them that they should ensure a corresponding expansion of the approaches to their country westwards.[63] If this way of looking at matters is correct, a further equalisation of the increase of German power must be seen in the establishment of Russian military bases in the Baltic countries and Finland, the refusal of which had led to the winter war in Finland. The annexation of the Baltic States and the Roumanian provinces would have to be interpreted as a reaction to the German troops' victory in France. On the Soviet side there has been strong emphasis on the security point of view. Even in 1939 Molotov made use of this argument, without, however, saying against whom the Soviet Union wished to protect itself. Only after the war did an anonymous publisher from the east, writing about the Soviet annexations in 1939 and 1940, make this assertion: "In this manner was completed the establishment of the Eastern front from the Baltic to the Black Sea which was set up against Hitlerian aggression."[64]

Others are of the opinion that the measures taken at this time by the Soviets reflect a transformation of the Soviet Union from a revolutionary State to an imperialistic Great Power which had become possessed of the territory of the Czarist empire.[65] This observation is certainly correct if the direction and extent of expansion in the first years of the war are kept in mind and the predominance of the traditional means of State in effecting the expansion is taken into consideration. Even before the war, Russian Communism, probably impressed by the success of National Socialism in Europe, had taken on patriotic characteristics.[66] Under the influence of Zhdanov, a "Soviet patriotism" permeated with pan-Slavistic notions had replaced the former cosmopolitan conception in the educational affairs of the Soviet Union, whereby nationalistic inclinations began to compete with socialistic impulses. It is no accident that Zhdanov was at the same time the most determined champion of expansion to the Baltic.[67] When, in addition, one takes into consideration that, based on racial and national arguments, a new "assembling of the Russian world" was also given out as the reason for the annexation of the eastern parts of Poland, one cannot fail to detect a national component in Soviet policies in these years.

Nevertheless, neither of the two explanations embodies the whole of the truth. They presuppose a change of attitude on the part of the Soviet leaders – a renunciation of revolutionary ardour contradicting their own utterances. What was it that caused Stalin, who as late as 1936 was still promising great progress for the Revolution from another war, to let this point of view slip his memory three or four years later? It would be an all-too-ingenious interpretation of events were one to impute to Russia, the Great Power, that, the more easily to achieve its national ends, it had turned to account in 1939 in Finland, and in 1940 in the Baltic States, the idealism of Communist revolutionaries. If one sticks to facts one must infer that the annexations of this period represent a new phase of Communist expansion in which henceforth the struggle for World Revolution and an original Soviet imperialism are inseparably merged.

In any case this interpretation only tallies with the pronouncements of high Soviet functionaries in the years before the war. As early as the end of 1936, Zhdanov, at a Soviet congress in Moscow, had uttered violent threats against the small border-States, and to the Baltic States he had called particularly to mind: "If they do not mind their own business we shall be compelled to open our borders, and it will be too bad if we are compelled

47

to use the Red Army on them." [68] Still more clearly did the principal political commissar of the Red Army, T. Mechlis, express himself on the eve of the war when, to the applause of the 18th Party Congress, he gave the assurance that, in the event of an attack on the Soviet Union, the Soviet Armed Forces would carry their operations forward on to enemy territory "to fulfil our international obligations and increase the number of Soviet republics".[69]

In these years the Soviet leaders can scarcely have had any ideological doubts about their policy. For them, the value of the Soviet Union lay first and foremost in the fact that it formed a strong bastion of Communism. After the war had broken out, this bastion must be safeguarded in every possible way. There must be no recoiling either from menaces or from the use of violence. If thereby the Soviet Union's sphere of power was extended, there could at the same time be a spread of Communism. There seemed all the more purpose in this since the securing and strengthening of the Russian bastion was not, indeed, merely an end in itself but a prerequisite for further extending the domination of "socialism". Thus there is a fusing of Soviet patriotism, security needs and the Communist urge to expand. Every "capitalistic" State is an immediate or a presumptive opponent; every neutral State is a potential assembly area for the opponent. At all times, therefore, the "patriotic" defence of the country and the safeguarding of the Communist bastion demand the occupation of further countries until the "capitalistic encirclement" is redressed by the attainment of World Revolution.[70]

Even if it was clear to all the world that the Soviet annexations of 1939 and 1940 depended solely on the employment of military force, the Soviet leaders themselves did not desist from an infusion of revolutionary motives. After the inhabitants of Eastern Poland had been congratulated on their "deliverance from the enforced domination of capitalism", Molotov said of the inhabitants of Bessarabia and Northern Bukovina that they were now starting "a new life, the life of a people freed from the domination of Roumanian boyars, great landowners and capitalists." The counterfeit elections in the Baltic States had, according to his bold statement, "shown that the ruling bourgeois cliques of Lithuania, Latvia and Esthonia did not correspond with the will of their peoples but represented only a small group of exploiters."[71]

In the Soviet periodicals the revolutionary motif reappeared in a coarser form. There was a particular predeliction for citing Stalin's description of the October Revolution as a "first stage of the World Revolution and a mighty base for its further extension." In 1940, *"The Bolshevik"*, whose articles Stalin said had to pass for "directives" for Party functionaries, characterised the Red Army as an "army of the deliverance of the workers from national and social oppression", and, adopting the words of its principal political commissar, added that they were called upon "to fulfil their international obligation to assist the workers of the capitalist countries to free themselves from the yoke of exploitation."[72] In the spring of 1941, another Soviet periodical triumphantly asserted that "the fraternal family of the peoples of the land of socialism is growing and multiplying. Its illimitable boundaries are expanding, forcing the capitalist world to contract."[73]

In view of the German and the Soviet bent for expansion, it is practically a matter of indifference whether it was with Stalin or with Hitler that suspicion first arose. With both of them the revolutionary urge for expansion was coupled with an ultra-sensitive mistrust, not only in its character but in its political nature. He who seeks to reshape the world by force sees opponents everywhere and booty everywhere. Therefore, two totalitarian systems with their seeking for expansion can exist side by side with even more discomfort than can a totalitarian and a democratic system which, at least for lengthy period, can indulge in "co-existence". The honeymoon of the Russo-German understanding was soon to be followed by disenchantment. Exchanging amicable words, both sides suspiciously watched how quickly the other pocketed an advantage. The Soviet action in Finland and the Baltic was noted in Berlin with the maximum of discomfort. On the other hand, when after peace had been concluded, Germany delivered arms to Finland, and, indeed, as a temporary measure, landed troops there, the tocsin was sounded in Moscow. Similarly with Roumania. The Soviet annexations involved the Reich

Government in a crisis of confidence, but the German doubts flashed over to the Soviet Government when, in accordance with the Vienna arbitrament, the Reich guaranteed the Roumanian frontiers and despatched to Roumania a German military mission together with training personnel.[74]

After the Soviet Union and Germany had become immediate neighbours from the Baltic to the Carpathians, their rivalry had to be concentrated on the Balkans. Perhaps it was only through weakness, though also with premeditation, that in the middle of 1940 the United Kingdom officially gave the Soviet Government a free hand in South-East Europe.[75] If from without it was wished to separate Hitler and Stalin, this was the step that had to be taken. It is not known whether or not the Soviet Union succumbed immediately to the temptation. In the autumn of 1939, it had without further ado tolerated Bulgaria's refusal of an offer of non-aggression.[76] Perhaps Moscow took the decision only in the autumn of 1940, when Nazi Germany, intoxicated with its victories, wished to proceed with dividing up the world among the anti-democratic States and proposed to the Soviet Union a "limitation of their interests in accordance with secular standards." [77]

At no other point of the barely two-year cooperation between Russia and Germany is the inevitability of the straining of relationships between the two revolutionary Powers to be perceived so clearly as with Molotov's visit to Berlin on November 12 and 13, 1940.[78] At the same time, Hitler and Ribbentrop let their apprehensions and their pipe-dreams be glimpsed as they tried to direct the Soviet Union's interest away from Europe, southwards towards the Persian Gulf. This offer could have been attractive to Russia the Great Power had the latter shared Hitler's imaginative assessment of the situation that Great Britain had lost the war and was holding its "estate in bankruptcy" in readiness for the victors. Since, however, the Soviet Union sized up the position in a soberer fashion and felt no desire to plunge into the war prematurely, it seemed to the Soviets more appropriate for the moment to harvest all the advantages that could still be drawn from the Russo-German alliance. In silence Molotov gave ear to Hitler and Ribbentrop's ideas of dividing up the world so that whenever there was a pause he could, with his well-known stubbornness, come back again and again to concrete interests the Soviets had in Europe. The Finnish problem had to be cleared up and, what was more, after the fashion of the Baltic States and Bessarabia. The southern portion of the Bukovina had to follow the northern. The problem of the straits had to be settled, not only on paper but "in fact". What was the position of the Reich Government in regard to a Soviet-Bulgarian non-aggression pact? What did Berlin think of the future fortunes of Roumania, Hungary, Greece and Yugoslavia? And, finally, there still remained the question of the outlets to the Baltic.

On the Communist side, these questions, in which Molotov persisted with undiplomatic obstinacy, were later given out as "sounding".[79] But this discourse breathed a wholly different spirit. Perhaps M. Gafencu, the former Roumanian Foreign Minister and at the time the Roumanian envoy in Moscow, sized up Soviet policy correctly when he wrote: "The Soviet Union had drawn so much advantage from the destruction of the equilibrium in the world caused by the German victories that it would have no interest whatever in a restoration of this equilibrium ... Under the cloak of certain neutrality and peace formulæ that served its propaganda without damaging its policy, Soviet Russia desired to draw its advantages from the general confusion ... Its (the Soviet Union's) constant anxiety was that not Germany alone should profit from its efforts at extension in the south-east ... The idea of having to share everything pleased the Russians whereas to the Germans it seemed to be merely a burden."[80]

After the talks with Molotov, Hitler was profoundly disturbed. They seem to have contributed directly to the fact that on December 18, 1940, he gave the instruction for preparations to be made for the destruction of the Soviet Union.[81] From the 1940–41 winter on, Nazi Germany pursued a policy towards the Soviet Union in which there was no compromise. Indifferent as to the Soviet claim to Bulgaria, troops were massed on the Bulgarian frontier for marching into the country which a short while previously had rejected the Soviet offer of a pact of mutual assistance.[82] The Soviet Government thereupon clung to its last friend in the Balkans. Relations with Yugoslavia were fostered in an ostentatious manner. On May 5, 1941, a treaty of friendship was concluded between the Soviet Union and Yugoslavia. Two days later, the German campaign in the Balkans was launched. In a surprisingly short space of time the Soviet Union lost its only allies in South-East Europe.

Nevertheless, the Soviet leaders had from the very beginning counted on attaining their most important successes in the final phase of the war. The war was not over yet by a long way. It had not even reached its climax. The German attack on the Soviet Union on June 22, 1941, ushered in another phase at the end of which the Soviet flood returned and, with the exception of Greece, submerged all those countries in which Molotov had interested himself in the autumn of 1940 as well as what was left of Poland, Czechoslovakia, and parts of Austria and Germany.[83]

Chapter Three

THE UNNATURAL ALLIANCE BETWEEN
EAST AND WEST
(1940–1944)

> As long as we have not conquered the whole world ...
> we have to adhere to the rule of understanding how to
> profit by the contradictions and antagonisms among
> the imperialists. *Lenin, November 26, 1920*

The German attack on the Soviet Union completely changed the
world situation. From that day on, the Soviet Union harboured
a hatred of Germany the seeds of which were to shoot forth dis-
astrously in later years. When Molotov took his leave of the
German ambassador with the bitter words "We have not deserved this"[1] he was sincere. The Soviet Union had tried to keep
to the 1939 alliance, and the annexations it took in hand from
1939 to 1941 seemed merely an appropriate compensation for the
military successes that, during this period, Nazi Germany, with
no better right, had been able to secure, thanks to the Soviet
cover in the rear. Now Hitler was breaking the agreement that
had brought so much profit to both sides. His fear that during the
course of the war the Soviet Union wished to invade Central
Europe was a legitimate one. At this point of time, however, it
is probable that the Soviet Government did not want to go warring yet awhile.[2] The war had not yet progressed sufficiently to
suit its policy of the third man with the laugh on his side. The
tremendous sacrifice demanded of the Soviet Union by the German attack allowed the Soviet leaders to strive for profit all the
more implacably when the war was over.

Another outcome of the German attack was to show itself as still
more fraught with momentous consequences. Hitler drove the
warring Western Powers, who were joined a few months later by
the United States, to an unnatural alliance with the Soviet Union.
In retrospect, there can be no doubt as to what was the more
decisive historically: the enforced agglomeration of such a tre-

mendous abundance of power, to which sooner or later the Axis Powers would have to yield, or the unhappy perplexity that this "strange alliance" brought about in the West. It was through the combination of these two elements that there subsequently resulted the historical circumstance that determines the political picture of Europe today: the antagonistically-inclined allies came face to face with each other on the soil of their common enemy, and at the point where they collided with one another the Continent was rent in twain.

The Soviet leaders were particularly successful in turning to full account the unexpected combination of "capitalist" and Soviet might. Without relinquishing their aims of expansion, they took advantage of the West's war potential. This policy presupposed deceiving the rest of the world, but within a few months the West allowed its anxieties to be allayed. It vigorously supported the Soviet struggle against Nazi Germany and decisively contributed to the fact that the Soviet Union was able to come forward as the dominating land Power when the war was over.

In these circumstances, Stalin's prediction that Communism would emerge from a new war with new successes proved to be correct. But there was equal confirmation of that result of the first two phases of the Soviet expansion which must sadden a revolutionary. This was that, outside Russia, nowhere in Europe was Communism able to come to power by its own strength but, everywhere, only with the help of the Red Army. After the war had been thrust upon it, the fateful question was, how far the Red Army could advance in the course of the fighting. In the decisive months, leading Western statesmen failed to appreciate the historical importance of this question. Even when the Soviet Union, with the surging forward of its troops, began to crush freedom in every country it occupied, the deception and the "brothers-in-arms" feeling still lingered long enough to facilitate the Soviet success.

1. THE SOVIET TACTIC OF CONCEALMENT

The ease with which after the German attack the Soviet leaders were able to convince the Western public that they had abandoned their revolutionary aims still seems astonishing, even if one takes into consideration the firmness of the West's deception and credulity. For years the Soviets had been prating of revolution and the spreading of Communism by force, and in the Western world there had been no inclination to disbelieve the earnestness of Soviet intentions. Now, suddenly, the Soviet Union was posing as a peaceful State having no ugly intentions, and almost overnight world opinion swung round to this new impression.

The rapid change of mind on the part of the Western public can be explained only as arising out of an underrating of the revolutionary theories of Lenin and Stalin, of the significance of which non-Communists have from times long since not been really clear. Yet the Soviet philosophy of life is not correctly comprehended if the exposition of the principles is neglected. Even if Stalin did not approach Lenin as a theoretician, he himself put express emphasis[3] on the importance of a clear foundation of theory and placed value on writing comprehensive screeds dealing with it. Only a short while before the war, he supplemented his compositions of the 1920s, which laid down the doctrinal rudiments, by the "short course" on the history of the Communist Party of the Soviet Union, which was expressly to be regarded not as a historical dissertation but as a directive concerning traffic in revolution. Had the significance of the theory not been misinterpreted in the West, the fact that millions of copies of these and other screeds were, even during the war, assiduously printed and circulated must have been disconcerting.[4]

Just as E. Varga, the economic theoretician, had expounded as early as the spring of 1941, a true Communist revolutionary could have no doubt that the antagonism between the "capitalist" and the "socialist" systems is an "eternal antagonism" which has "not ceased even today" and continues to exist "up to the complete destruction of the capitalist system".[5] Nor could he conceive that the war had effaced the truth of the dogmas that had held good till then, since for a doctrine that likes to make use in politics of military concepts such as "cadre", "reserves", "attack" "retreat", "encirclement" and "manœuvre", war forms in very truth the real element of life.[6] Basically, the Soviet State must always regard its relations with other countries as more or less a condition of open conflict. Even in times of cooperation with "capitalist" countries, scarcely anything could change so far as that was concerned.[7] A temporary alliance with the West was always, of course, only a tactical manœuvre.[8]

However, the new situation did not even require of the Soviet leaders a fundamental change of their political tactics. Ever since 1936, Stalin had, as occasion offered, contested with foreign visitors all intentions to expand and had designated an "exportation of revolution" as nonsense. Just as in 1939 he had to deceive Hitler, so had he now to delude Churchill and Roosevelt. In doing so, scruples of conscience will hardly have disturbed the man who, as early as 1913, had said of diplomacy: "Words are one thing, actions another. Good words are a mask for concealment of bad deeds. Sincere diplomacy is no more possible than dry water or wooden iron."[9] Even if this characterisation was intended to hold good for "bourgeois" diplomacy only, Stalin did not shrink from employing the same methods if the interests of the Soviet Union required it. He thus denied in the most decisive manner all revolutionary intentions. Particularly notorious is his declaration at the 24th anniversary of the October Revolution, on November 6, 1941: "We have no war aims and can have no war aims such as the conquest of foreign territories or the subjugation of foreign peoples ... We have no war aims and can have no war aims such as the goal of imposing our will and our régime on the Slavs and other subjugated peoples of Europe who expect help from us ... No interference whatsoever in the internal affairs of other nations!"[10] To be sure, the Soviet Union had also given this promise, which it itself broke, in the "pacts of mutual assistance" with the Baltic States, but once again it had propagandistic success. The fact, too, that by signing the Atlantic Charter the Soviet Union undertook not to seek territorial or other aggrandizement and to observe the right of all nations freely to choose their form of Government had a soothing effect on the West.

The Soviet Union was successful in concealing its revolutionary aims because it put on a mask that appeared authentic to the world – the mask of patriotic sentiments. Nevertheless, it would not be right to attribute the switching over of Soviet propaganda from revolutionary socialism to "Soviet patriotism" solely to an intention to deceive foreigners. Of at least equal importance for the Kremlin was the fact that new powers of resistance against the German armies that were surging forward were aroused thereby in the Russian people. As early as the Polish invasion in 1920, the Soviet leaders had found that patriotic sentiments could spur on even the rural population – little accessible to revolutionary slogans – to the courageous defence of the country and thereby of the Communist régime also. Nor had twenty years of socialist upbringing changed this situation. The guerilla fighters were held together less by political commissars than by the primitive feeling of having to protect "Little Mother Russia". Since, this apart, Russian patriotism always contained not a little consciousness of a mission, the bridge to Soviet Communism was not difficult to build.[11]

Outside the country, however, the stressing of the "attachment of our country", combined with the avoidance of any idea of revolutionary internationalism, had an effect similar to the sudden conversion of a heathen tribe clasped, in rapturous astonishment, in the arms of the Christian missionaries. Entirely aware of this, the Soviet leaders did their utmost to strengthen this impression and to demonstrate themselves worthy of the new society known as the anti-Fascist front. Indeed, the "Internationale" fell victim to the purge, though only as a national anthem. In the Communist Party there was still a bleating of "Arise, ye prisoners of starvation!"[12] The most important propaganda success, and at the same time the most penetrating encroachment on the institutions of Revolution, was, however, the dissolution of the Comintern in May, 1943.

For two decades the existence of the Comintern had been the best evidence for the world public of the revolutionary plans of the Communists and their direction from Russia. When in war the Soviet Union was transformed from the "Fatherland of the Workers" to an ordinary State defending its territories against attack, the Communist International no longer fitted into the picture. Since it had already become in the 1920s an "authority of the Soviet State"[13], the Soviet leaders were now able to sacrifice it without difficulty in the course of their new foreign policy. Moscow had already shown a notable elasticity in this respect when the Communist Party in the United States had been permitted to secede from the Comintern in order to dispel the mistrust of leading American circles. In spite of this, the disbandment of the Comintern came as a complete surprise even to the members themselves.[14]

In one respect, the official reason, that the Communist parties had become sufficiently mature to be able to continue their operations without central guidance, was not really inexact. Clearly, the Communist leaders in the other countries understood at once that basically nothing would be altered.[15] Nor did they let themselves be misled by repeated assurances that it was more than a tactical manœuvre. And they were right. It is true that the Comintern headquarters was disbanded in name, that the secret Comintern school in Ufa, in which Communists from many countries had been prepared ideologically and practically for "work in their homeland", was shut down[16], and that the periodical "*Communist International*" was replaced by a new organ entitled "*The War and the Working-class*", but we know from the testimony of Castro Delgado[17], a member of the Spanish Comintern, that the International continued its operations in secret. Dimitroff took possession of the Russian Party's Central Committee building, but from there he continued to direct the operations of the individual Communist parties. These sent their delegations to him and obeyed the instructions of the Comintern's foreign representatives.

In retrospect, the dissolution of the Comintern seems to have been, and not only in regard to propaganda, a highly sensible precaution. The timing of the decision, a few months after the turning-point of the war outside Stalingrad, had a particular significance. At this moment the Soviet leaders saw, for the first time, a real chance of being able, by pursuing the Germans, to thrust deep into Europe with the Red Army and to sweep away some of the bourgeois Governments ruling "by the grace of God". This gave rise to the new task of making prompt provision for a strict control by the Soviet Union over the régimes newly originating. In the Comintern, other countries' victorious Communist parties would have been able, under certain circumstances, to form a counterbalance to the Bolshevist Party, particularly if they united to form a non-Russian parliamentary group. It was better to get the foreign parties accustomed in good time to the fact that every single one of them was directly subordinate to the Kremlin. Not by accident did Zhdanov, the most determined champion of "Soviet patriotism" in the Politburo, then take over the reins of superintendence in the Comintern. His leadership brought with it a change of course not only in the direction of more camouflage and increased aggressiveness but also of still more rigid subjugation of the other Communist parties to Moscow's will.[18] What remained of the Comintern was unfitted for acts of resistance to the Russian party.

At the same time, the dissolution of the Comintern allowed the non-Russian Communists more freely to mark time with the other political forces in their respective countries. As early as the end of 1941, Stalin had prophesied that the Soviet Union's "nationalist" war would "merge with the struggle of the peoples of Europe and America for their independence, for the democratic freedoms".[19] Now it was a matter of investing the impending Soviet extension of power with a semblance permitting the interpretation of a "national struggle for freedom". To this end preparations had to be made not only for coalitions generally but, in certain circumstances, for entirely different tactics in invidual countries. It would have been cramping had the Comintern issued from time to time public, universally-binding instructions. Through the dissolution of the International more political elbow-room was secured.

As a foremost historical illustration, Stalin probably made use of the Communists' China policy, which had so fervently moved the Soviet leaders' minds in the 1920s. Just as at that time Stalin, in contrast to Trotsky, had recommended for China an alliance with the national forces, so did he now give out the catchword of the "union of the progressive forces . . . to a unified national camp of freedom". This occurred quite publicly at an interview with Reuters, the British Press agency[20], though not without a fresh use of the tactics of camouflage in that he added that the lies that Moscow desired to "bolshevise" other countries would thereby be unmasked. At that time the actual tendency of Soviet foreign policy was characterised by the fact that in 1943 the Soviet Union already regarded eight European *émigré* Governments in London as "traitors".[21] Thus the first step towards interference in their internal affairs was taken.

In the spring of 1943, the "union of progressive forces" was fully active in Russia, where for years the cadres for future revolutions in other countries had been trained and assembled. Seemingly the start was made by the Poles, who as early as March had founded the "League of Polish Patriots". Although the Association of Polish Communists in exile, which was established at the end of 1941 under the leadership of Wanda Wasilewska, was absorbed by the "Union of Patriots", it was, of course, under Communist command. The same thing happened with the "National Committee of Free Germany", founded on July 12, 1943.[22] Here, too, tried and trusted Communists such as Wilhelm Pieck, Walter Ulbricht and Erich Weinert constituted the hard core which, through its direct connection with the highest Soviet quarters, held all power in its hands while the officers admitted were employed as an effective cloak. With the members of other nations the association was perhaps looser, though similar exertions were observed among the Roumanians, Hungarians and Austrians.[23]

There has since been much guesswork as to what really were the Soviet intentions at that time by this assembling of "progressive forces". Was their essential purpose to undermine the war morale of the peoples concerned by radio broadcasts and printed matter? Or were they regarded from the outset as future Governments, something after the pattern of the Kuusinen "Government" of Finland during the 1939–1940 winter? The answer is simple. For the Soviet leaders these "Committees" were something akin to pawns at chess, about which at the beginning of the game it is not known whether when they reach the winning end of the board they will be transformed into a queen or a castle or a bishop or a knight. They formed an instrument which could be employed in one manner or another, each according to its need. For example, the original intention of the "Union of Polish Patriots" was assuredly to constitute a counterbalance to the Polish *émigré* Government in London, which was hostile to Moscow. Later, when the Red Army succeeded in occupying Poland, it became the "Provisional Government". So far as the German National Committee is concerned, there is reason to suspect that the Soviets feared the proclamation in England of an anti-Fascist German group and wished to anticipate this.[24] Possibly they also believed in a successful uprising in Germany and wanted in such an event to dispose over a substantial group of men, permeated with Communists, which with their support could put forward a claim to participation in a future German Government.[25] In certain circumstances the National Committee could certainly, as it once looked like in 1943[26], have also served as the nucleus for a pro-Soviet German Government.

At the back of all these precautions was a circumstance of great significance. At this period the Soviets clearly imagined that, in all European countries, the Communists would not be strong enough after the war to be able to carry through the Revolution immediately. On the other hand, however, professional revolutionaries, such as Walter Ulbricht, Georgi Dimitroff (Bulgaria), Ana Pauker (Roumania), Mátyás Rákosi (Hungary), Jakob Berman (Poland) and Ernst Fischer (Austria), who had been quartered in Moscow for years, were naturally all aflame with the desire to dispose of the hated "capitalism" in their respective countries and have a hand in the victory of "socialism". Now, therefore, there was a resumption of the old Comintern campaigns: "People's Front" and "National Front" were to give the Communists the opportunity gradually to build with their superior tactical skill a firm basis from which as time went on they could prepare the Revolution.

The tactics demanded that for the time being there was no talk of revolution and socialism. But the trained Communist knew exactly what was meant when a high Soviet functionary wrote: "One of the most serious, one of the most important aims of the present war must be the establishment of such a social order upon earth under which adventurists, provocateurs and imperialistic parties would be deprived of the opportunity periodically to drag the majority of peoples and States into bloody wars."[27] In accordance with Communist doctrines there is only *one* "social system" which has this capacity.

It was no contradiction of the Soviet inclination to expand that only a short time after the German attack started Stalin demanded of the West the setting up of a "second front" in Europe. Rather did it reflect the old aspiration to let the West bleed unwillingly for Communism and the Soviet Union. The more the German troops were chained down in the west, the greater and swifter the progress that the Soviet Armed Forces could make in the east. It was, moreover, important to keep the West on a chain to a certain extent, for, as seen from Moscow, the West must indeed have a natural inclination to conspire with the Fascists against the Soviet Union in a reversal of the alliances. On the other hand, there was no ideological barrier to prevent the Soviets, when the chance was presented, of entering into an armistice, or indeed a separate peace[28], with Germany, thus allowing the Soviet troops, in certain circumstances, to achieve their aims in Central and South-East Europe without a fight.

2. THE BLIND CONFIDENCE OF THE WEST

At the end of the 1930s, the Western democracies found themselves in a position which did not in any event hold out good prospects for the future. From two flanks had they been given notice of battle: from the authoritarian States in Europe and the Far East, and from the Soviet Union. George Kennan has rightly pointed out[29] that only with the help of the other opponent could the West gain the victory over each of these two adversaries and must therefore from the point of view of humanity put up with seeing this allied adversary among the victors. In that Hitler first unleashed the civil war in Europe and then attacked the Soviet Union, he grouped the victorious Powers together. From then on, only with difficulty could the Western democracies prevent the Soviet Union from coming out of the war on the winning side. However, the successes of the latter could have been kept within a smaller framework if during the war the West had remained alive to the fact that, even as an ally, the Soviet Union was an adversary. It is universally recognised in contemporary recordings that the West's unjustified confidence in Soviet policy during the war facilitated the Soviet leaders' military and political successes. Nevertheless, opinions differ as to the extent to which Western credulity influenced the course of events. At this point, therefore, an examination of the Western attitude must be made.

During the first years of the war, relations between the Western Powers and the Soviet Union were tense. Up to the middle of 1940, Soviet propaganda, in clear contrast to the facts and to former speeches of Stalin, blamed the "capitalist" West for the outbreak of war and made it solely responsible for its continuation and extension. The Soviet action against Finland aroused the anger of the Western public more than did this propaganda. At the climax of the tension, in the spring of 1940, the French and British General Staffs drew up plans for an intervention not only in Finland [30] but also in the Caucasus. This second undertaking was mainly directed towards cutting Germany off from oil supplies in the Caucasus but, as a subsidiary effect, it was hoped to unsettle the Mohammedan population in this region. [31] Only the course taken by military events prevented the carrying out of these plans, the realisation of which would have involved the Western Powers in hostilities with the Soviet Union. The Finnish enterprise miscarried through the armistice and the conclusion of peace, and the attack on Baku through the lightning war in France.

In 1940–1941, the relations between Moscow and the West improved in something like the same space of time as those between Berlin and the Kremlin became cooler. Prior to the German attack, the Soviet leaders were repeatedly warned by the Western Powers via diplomatic channels. Nonetheless, on June 22, 1941, the allies for the future were far from enjoying a genuine friendship. Even at the beginning of 1942, Cordell Hull, the American Secretary of State, warned his President of the "tremendous ambitions" of the Soviet Union in regard to Europe. [32]

Had those in charge of affairs of State in the West, just as those in the Soviet Union, been dominated by the idea that the course of the history of mankind depended on the outcome of the great controversy between "capitalism" and "socialism", for them there could have been only one logical concept in this situation: to let the two totalitarian disturbers of the peace fight it out together and shed each other's blood until both no longer represented a danger to the bourgeois-capitalist world of the West. At the outset there was no lack of advice to this effect. Senator Harry S. Truman, the subsequent President of the United States, recommended that the Germans and the Russians should be allowed to fight it out to the death between themselves[33], and Lord Brabazon, a British Minister, gave expression to the same idea.[34]

The Governments in London and Washington permitted themselves, however, to be guided by other considerations. Particularly in Great Britain, where after the German attack on the Soviet Union there was feeling of being freed from the nightmare of invasion, the dominating conviction was that the German Armed Forces, after their lightning victories in Poland, Norway, France and Yugoslavia, would have no difficulty in Russia also. The tremendous successes of the first weeks and months strengthened the impression that the Soviet collapse was only a matter of time and circumstance. Proceeding on these lines, it seemed to the Governments imperative to assist the Soviet Union in order, in the interests of the West, to strengthen its capacity to resist. It was a matter of complete honesty when, in the summer of 1941, Sumner Welles, the United States Secretary of State, said that the offer of aid to the Soviet Union was based on the assumption that the Soviet resistance was "in the interest of the national defense of the United States." [35] This mood is incomparably expressed in the words with which Prime Minister Churchill greeted the new allies: "If Hitler invaded Hell I would make at least a favourable reference to the Devil in the House of Commons." [36]

In another connection, too, the Soviet reverses in 1941 made it easier for the Western Powers to decide to assist them. In retreating, the Soviets had to give up all the territories they had gained under the aura of their alliance with Hitler. They were freed unwillingly from the odium of annexation by force. Moreover, moral weight shifted as Finland and Roumania replied to the Soviet aggression by participating on the side of Germany in the campaign against the Soviet Union.

It was soon seen, however, that in the struggle the democracies suffered from a curious incapacity to keep a tight rein calmly on their feelings towards enemies and ally.[37] As hatred of Germany and Japan immeasurably increased, after a few months an excessive sympathy for the new allies outgrew all former repugnance. The enormous losses sustained by the Soviet armies excited pity all the more since Great Britain and (since its entry into the war) the United States were not standing directly in the fighting-line. In London it soon became the fashion to wear the hammer and sickle on clothing. In the cinemas Stalin's portrait was greeted with applause, and in the streets banners appeared with the words "Quiet nights – Thanks to Russia!"[38] A mood developed in which "criticism of Russia became tantamount to treason".[39]

The Western State leaders could not permanently withstand this surge of sentiment. From the doubtful query as to whether it might possibly be that Stalin had not after all experienced a transfiguration from the state of being a Russian revolutionary to take on the stature of a Russian statesman was a long trail to the blind expectation that the Soviet Union would not comport itself differently from all other States. The trail was covered with astonishing rapidity. Shortly before his first meeting with Stalin, Mr. Roosevelt, the United States President, is said to have decided to invest his negotiation tactics in regard to Stalin with the principle of "noblesse oblige", as if he had to do with an old aristocrat. At the Teheran Conference he even greeted the Soviet Union's representative as "a new member of the family circle".

The Western attitude during these years is not correctly understood if there is not perceived therein an element of faith-healing. The Western spokesmen treated the Soviet revolutionaries as American senators or British lords in the firm hope of convincing them of the advantages of living like gentlemen. At the same time they tried to persuade themselves that Stalin was nothing more than an amiable "Uncle Joe". An American scientist has characterised the West's attitude towards the Soviet Union with a biting, if pertinent, parallel: "It was as though Queen Victoria had locked her debutante daughter in a room with Jack the Ripper to prove the strength of her belief in mankind."[40]

It is difficult to estimate to what extent the military aid rendered by the Western Powers to the Soviet Union helped to overcome the German assault and, later, in the Soviet pursuit of the beaten enemy, to succeed in thrusting forward with their armies into Central Europe. Certainly in 1941 the West underestimated the Soviet powers of resistance, but the Western aid must not be shrugged off as insignificant, as is done in Soviet literature. "Without the American tinned goods . . ., without the delivery of immense quantities of uniform material, army boots, weapons, railway material and motor vehicles, the Soviet Union would probably have lost its breath prematurely." [41] The total value of the deliveries, some $ 11,000 million [42], gives only an inadequate idea of the significance of the Western aid. Even if the Soviet Union itself produced by far the greater part of its weapons, it was largely dependent on the Western Powers for means of transport. Moreover, the Western aid had an effect the great consequence of which was not seen until after the war. The technical information which, in part legally, in part illegally, the Soviet Union understood how to get hold of under the Lease-Lend Agreement [43] advanced the country's progress enormously in the field of armament techniques. It is scarcely to be contested, therefore, that later on the aid proved to be a boomerang for the Western democracies. [44]

Not even when in the last months of the war it became increasingly clear that the Soviet Union was misusing its military superiority in Europe for political purposes was a cessation of Lease-Lend deliveries seriously considered. [45] It is one of the ironies of history that the Ulbricht clique which in the spring of 1945 was despatched from Moscow to Berlin to realise Soviet policy in Germany was able to make use of a Douglas transport plane delivered by America. [46]

More important than the large-scale deliveries was an indirect aid which the West allowed to accrue to the Soviet Union: the foregoing of a purely Western strategy directed not only against Germany and Japan but also pursuing the aim of preventing a new Communist dictatorship in Europe after Hitler's downfall. Since, for comprehensible reasons, the voice of Germany was not heeded, it fell largely to the task of the Poles continually to remind the Western Powers that a Soviet overrunning of large parts of Europe was not to be thwarted by diplomatic snake-charmers but only by a strategic planning that allowed the Western troops to steal a march on the Soviet armies.[47]

As early as June 22, 1942, the officer commanding the military groups of the Polish underground movement put forward the proposal that Poland should be "occupied for a time by Anglo-American Armed Forces". After Stalingrad, the Polish underground movement planned an uprising for the moment when Soviet troops set foot on Polish soil but, again, declared that the success of the project depended on the dropping, "predominantly in the eastern part of the country", of Anglo-American parachute troops "as a visible sign of the link between us and the Anglo-American nations." At the end of 1943, the Poles were once more hoping that, thanks to the German resistance, the eastern front could be stabilised somewhere east of the Polish frontier, so that, in an audacious thrust straight across Europe, the British and the Americans could preserve the freedom of Poland from suppression by their own allies. Nevertheless, ideas of this kind quickly showed themselves to be pipe-dreams.

Whether at any point of time whatever during the war the Western Powers would have been in a position to plan their strategy so as to reach Poland and the Balkans before the Soviets is primarily a matter for military experts. At least one must be on one's guard against accepting as inevitable the course of the fighting as it was actually experienced. Had the West's political and military commanders set themselves the goal of keeping the Soviets out of Central and South-East Europe and had all their enterprises – the invasions of Europe just as their aid to the Soviet Union – been planned accordingly, the war would probably not have followed the course it did. For our consideration of the matter, it is decisive that this attempt was never made, since the Western statesmen, not to speak of the military men, did not recognise the task soon enough. In this case the main reproach also affects Hitler and Nazi Germany, who had brought upon them the hatred of all the world and had thereby clouded the West's eye for political realities.

Churchill's suggestion of making a landing in the Balkans has been made too much of in post-war literature.[48] In accordance with his own deposition[49], he had never thought of using a Balkan landing as a point of departure for a thrust towards the north to drive a wedge between the Soviet troops and Central Europe. Nevertheless, he certainly emphatically advocated that the main invasion in Northern France should not mean neglecting the advance in Italy that would bring the Western troops speedily to the critical sector Trieste–Vienna–Budapest. Particularly in the last year of the war was the British Prime Minister increasingly alive to the fact that, according to possibilities, the Western Powers must obstruct a deep penetration of Europe by Soviet troops. In this, neither with President Roosevelt nor with General Eisenhower, the Supreme Allied Commander, did he find agreement and, moreover, he also transgressed his own principles when, during the German offensive in the Ardennes in the 1944–1945 winter, he approached Stalin and begged for a swift attack on the Eastern front.

By and large, up to 1945 the Western leaders of State did little to prevent the Soviet armies doing, in extensive areas, what in 1939 the Soviet principal political commissar had designated the fulfilment of their "international obligations". In America, as early as the summer of 1943 people had become reconciled to the view that the Soviet Union "would occupy a dominant position in Europe after the war", and shortsightedly came to the conclusion that friendly relations with the Soviet State were "even more essential".[50] British policy was more sceptical, but even Churchill still for a long time hoped that it would be possible to arrest the Soviet expansion at the Curzon Line.[51] Thus did the two Great Powers of the West knowingly fall victim to the delusion that the Soviet Union had become a State similar to all others. So far as Moscow's expansive tendencies were not to be overlooked, they were interpreted as a security claim – exaggerated, it is true, but nevertheless a claim in the nature of realist politics – which Roosevelt hoped to satisfy by the establishment of the great United Nations security organisation.

3. POLITICAL CONSEQUENCES FOR CENTRAL EUROPE

In retrospect, the political relation between the Allies is paradoxical. In view of the Soviets' steady pursuit of their revolutionary aim, one might have thought that the West would have been mistrustful. Instead, it was the Soviets who were mistrustful although, in view of the naivety of the West, for this there was scarcely any ground. But false sentiments, too, make history. The conflicting aims of the Allies among themselves not only influenced military planning but also led to many curious results in the political management of the war. In this connection, three problems are of special import within the framework of our theme: the Polish question; the plans for the dismemberment of Germany; and the establishment in Germany and Austria of the Zones of Occupation.

(a) The Polish Question

From the very first day of their unnatural alliance, the Polish question burdened relations between the Allies. Because of developments very varied in character, it became the neuralgic point of the alliance. In the course of the years the object of the tug-of-war between West and East thereby changed almost imperceptibly. While at the beginning it was a matter only of Poland's eastern boundary, later it concerned the freedom of the whole of Poland.

From the outset, the British Government, which in 1939 entered the war to make good its guarantee of the territorial inviolability of Poland, found itself in an unpleasant position since, even at the negotiations in the summer of 1941 about the resumption of Polish-Soviet relations, the Soviets allowed the British to be in no doubt about the fact that the annexation of the East Polish territories was an irrevocable fact.[52] Although the Polish *émigré* Government swore to its British hosts that, whatever the circumstances, it would see that the new allies renounced the acquisitions they had secured by force during the period of the Soviet alliance with Hitler, in their treaty of July 30, 1941, with the Soviet Union they could achieve only the colourless statement that the Russo-German treaties of 1939 were no longer valid.[53]

Outwardly the British Government still adhered for some time to its policy of non-recognition of the annexations that had been agreed by force, but as early as the spring of 1942 Churchill felt "under the pressure of events the impossibility of sticking firmly to the purely moral point of view"[54] and asked Roosevelt to acquiesce in recognising the Soviet boundaries of 1941. It is true that Roosevelt did not agree at once, though he did not definitely oppose it and subsequently left it to a great extent to the British Prime Minister to take the lead in the negotiations concerning Poland, which took a dramatic turn in the spring of 1943. When after their victory at Stalingrad the Soviets built up in Russia the "Union of Polish Patriots", they sought to make a break with the *émigré* Government in London. They were provided with a welcome opportunity to do so when the Germans made known the mass murder by the Soviets in the Katyń woods. From then on, the Soviet leaders backed only "their" Poles in Russia and the "Polish Workers Party" (PPR) which was founded at the same time to replace the Communist Party dissolved by Moscow in 1938.

Churchill immediately comprehended that the freedom of Poland was now at stake, but in an astonishing under-estimation of the Communist urge to expand, an under-estimation that could originate only at the twilight of the anti-Hitler coalition, he clung to the hope that the Soviets were concerned only with the parts of East Poland which they annexed in 1939 and not with the whole of the country. If the London Poles were to be reconciled to the Curzon Line as the eastern boundary they would be equally as acceptable to the Soviets as was the Union of Patriots which, from the beginning, naturally represented the Moscow point of view in this respect. It is in the highest degree odd to observe how at this point of time the same idea suddenly cropped up both in the East and in the West and based on fundamentally opposing starting-points of a compensation of Poland at German cost.[55]

After there had already been much talk of the detachment of individual German provinces, it seems that at the Teheran Conference Stalin for the first time suggested giving Poland the whole of German territory east of the Oder. What motives he had in doing so, apart from the intention of doing damage to hated

Germany, he never betrayed. But when one does not lose sight of the fact that, even at this time, he was counting on a Communist, or at least a Soviet-directed, régime in Poland, the idea suggests itself that he wished to spare his Polish emissaries the odium of a massive renunciation of territory without corresponding compensation, and that at the same time he also wanted to extend his own overlordship as far as the Oder.[56] In addition, he wanted to ensure that Poland became inescapably dependent on Russia if, by a similar type of annexation, it became fundamentally an enemy of Germany.

For precisely contrary considerations Churchill at once approved the proposal. He was motivated by the wish to preserve Polish freedom. If this were successful it would mean that the *émigré* Government in London would be able to return to Poland. Credulous, he believed that the new eastern frontier of Poland, which he wished to make palatable to the Poles in London by the compensatory offer, would be an adequate price for the Soviets. M. Ciechanowski, the Polish Ambassador in Washington, warned in vain of the proposal in respect of compensation, pointing out that the real intention of the Soviet Union was only to make Poland dependent on it and "possibly use it as a springboard for a far-reaching domination by the Soviets of Central Europe, particularly of Germany".[57] One year later, when in Moscow Churchill attempted to arbitrate between Stalin and Mikolajczyk, the Prime Minister of the Polish *émigré* Government, the British Premier believed that his policy had saved Poland. But soon even he had to appreciate that, through plans that had been thoroughly thought out, the Soviets' urge to expand did not allow itself to be halted at the Curzon Line.

At Teheran, Churchill stated that he did not wish to see the Soviet Union included among the "hungry" nations after the war. He failed to appreciate that a universal, revolutionary ideology such as that of the Soviet Communists cannot, by reason of its essential content, know the feeling of satiation so long as it has a hostile, non-"socialistic" environment. For this reason it was also an act of doubtful wisdom when, at Teheran, Churchill did not hesitate to meet Stalin's wish and agreed to the Soviet annexation of the northern part of East Prussia about

Königsberg, which, from the point of view of power politics, signified two things: the *de facto* recognition of the annexation of the Baltic States, and a northern encirclement of Poland permitting the grip that was strangling the country to become still tighter.

(b) Plans for the Dismemberment of Germany

There was a similar position when the plans for the re-shaping of Germany after the war were being discussed. Here, too, the three allies were in agreement on the main essentials, but the real interests of the West ought to have demanded a different policy.

It seems that Stalin, by nature a fierce hater, let himself, from 1941 to the beginning of 1945, be blindly guided by his bitterness towards Germany. This country, which had utterly invalidated his well-thought-out policy of the third man with the laugh on his side, whose workers had shown no shred of support for the "Fatherland of the Workers" but had readily taken part in the war against the Soviet Union – this Germany must be severely punished and permanently weakened. It was, therefore, agreeable for Stalin that, in January, 1943, Roosevelt and Churchill announced that their war aim was the unconditional capitulation of Germany, although Stalin was clever enough to realise that the public proclamation of this policy was a mistake, since it hardened Germany's resistance. This point of view affected the Western statesmen less since their minds were ranged in the moral category of a "crusade", and they wished at the same time to show their eastern allies that they definitely rejected the idea of a separate peace with Germany.[58] Here Hitler's abominable policy of mass extermination was clearly recoiling on the German people. Nazi Germany, with its frightful atrocities, contrived that throughout Europe the brutal enslavement methods of the Soviets should slip into forgetfulness, enabling the ill-assorted allies jointly to plan their policy for the punishment of Germany.[59]

It is unnecessary in these pages to trace in detail the development of the allied plans for the dismemberment of Germany since they were not subsequently realised.[60] The first prod was clearly given by Stalin, who, in December, 1941, elaborated before Mr. Eden, the British Foreign Secretary, his ideas about the treatment of Germany after the war.[61] At the beginning, the Western Governments were somewhat sceptical about the idea of a forced dismemberment of Germany, and they thought more of a support of separatist currents. Roosevelt was still warning in the spring of 1945 of a return to "the methods also promoted by Clemenceau".[62] But in the course of the year the flood of hate mounted irresistibly, nourished as it was by the reports of German atrocities in the occupied territories and by the grief of those who had to mourn a victim of the war. Little by little the flood overflowed the banks of political reason. Underground reports gave rise to thoughts of revenge and inspired in the minds of the politicians plans of a ferocity that could be engendered only in the era of a Hitler or a Stalin. Above all, the proposal put forward by the United States Secretary of the Treasury, that became notorious as the "Morgenthau Plan", under which highly-industrialised Germany, in spite of its population density, was to be transformed into a predominantly pastoralised country, achieved a dismal reputation.[63] Characteristically, the Morgenthau Plan also incorporated the idea of a partitioning of Germany, which was a permanent ingredient of the policy of a destruction of Germany that triumphed in both the World Wars and continued to find its effect when war had come to an end. It was of great significance for further developments that in this sphere the incongruous allies found a community of ideas, a community that otherwise usually existed only in the military realm. Because of this, the idea occurred that it might be possible to evolve a concordant policy for the treatment of Germany after the war. This seemed to all concerned of great importance, since they regarded Germany as a permanent danger to the world in the highest possible degree.

Had the Western Powers taken the Soviet urge to expand as seriously as it deserved, Germany, crushed, would not have appeared to them as the greatest danger for the future. Hitler, however, in his senseless war had brought Western Europe so near to the brink of defeat that the German danger seemed to loom above everything else. A sober consideration of future developments ought, at the latest in 1943, to have made the Western statesmen realise that after the war the Soviet Union would become the most powerful military Power on the Continent. Had the United Kingdom earlier on paid attention to the fact that sufficient strong States remained in Central Europe to be able to withstand Russia's sinister power, now more than ever it ought to have been made a concern to establish, or to preserve, healthy, robust secondary States between the Soviet Union and the Atlantic, since Russia was being driven not only by its traditional straining towards the west but also by a revolutionary impulsion. Every plan for the carving up of Germany betokened, apart from the related economic weakening of Central Europe, an offence against statesmanlike discernment.

This registering of disapproval of the wartime policy of the West towards Germany is not a matter of the application, as an afterthought, of standards the soundness of which could not be recognised at the time. In those days Churchill himself once gruesomely predicted a situation in which there would be nothing "between the white snowfields of Russia and the white cliffs of Dover" that could halt the Russians. He was also conscious of the fact that it was a matter of a comprehensive consolidation in Central Europe. His first hope was of a free Poland; his second, a strong, wide-stretching Danubian Federation. It is characteristic of Churchill's constructive thinking that, by proposing at Teheran the association of South Germany in a Danubian Federation, he himself wished to make the dismemberment of Germany serve to bring about a new structural system, full of vitality.

It is equally characteristic of Stalin, to whom otherwise every form of carving up Germany was a fit process, that he immediately opposed this idea of Churchill's. Stalin's arguments constituted a contradiction in themselves. He averred that a Danubian Federation would have no vitality, and in the same breath he expressed the fear that, with German help, a new Great Power would come into being. It is probable that Stalin's real objection came to light in his curt question as to whether perhaps Hungary and Roumania ought not also belong in this Danubian Federation.

74

For understandable reasons, the Soviet Head of State had not the slightest interest in such a consolidation of conditions in the Danubian area. Stalin passed lightly over the British Premier's tart counter-query as to whether he, Stalin, possibly desired a Europe composed of nothing but little States.[64] For him, the hour had not yet struck when he was in a position to lay his plans and aims openly on the table.

In general, contemporary literature has paid little attention to Stalin's motives in rejecting the Danubian Federation, since he himself, only a bare twelve months later, during Churchill's visit in October, 1944, swallowed his opposition. In this connection, however, the essential fact is overlooked that the Danubian Federation as now proposed by Stalin himself no longer deserved its name, since it envisaged Hungary's remaining aloof from the amalgamation of Austria and South Germany. Together with Poland and Czechoslovakia, Hungary was to form "a realm of independent, anti-Nazi, pro-Russian States". Churchill, in informing Roosevelt about the matter, in all probability repeated very precisely Stalin's ideas and words, without appreciating their complete context, when he wrote that Stalin now wanted "to see Vienna the capital of a federation of South German states including Austria, Bavaria, Württemberg and Baden."[65] It was not the new federation that was important for the Soviet Head of Government but the alluring prospect that this federation would be governed from Vienna. Hungary seemed to be in a position of imminent collapse; the capture of Vienna by the Red Army was at hand; and, in contrast to Berlin, there was no agreement about sharing the occupation of the Austrian capital with the Western Powers.

It is, therefore, not surprising that a good three months later, at the Yalta Conference, Stalin once more raised the question of the partitioning of Germany and emphatically pressed for a decision.[66] Had things gone the way the Soviet Head of Government wanted, it would have been decided, on February 5, 1945, to partition Germany at the line of the River Main into two States each separate from the other. Happily, the Western Powers did not feel sufficiently prepared for a decision of such magnitude, above all since the Foreign Offices in Washington and

ondon – to a certain degree in contrast to the Heads of Govern-
ent – doubted the wisdom of an enforced dismemberment.[67]
Thus Stalin could only achieve that the draft of the document on
Germany's capitulation included merely a non-binding noti-
fication of the partitioning, and an Allied Commission was set
up to "study the process".[68] The Yalta Conference ended without
a decision being expressed on the partitioning of Germany, and,
before it ended, Mr. Stettinius, the American Secretary of State,
inserted, without knowing it, a thorn into the heart of the Soviets
by asking what would be the effect of the dismemberment of Germany on reparation payments.[69]

c) Zones of Occupation in Germany and Austria

Since the war against Nazi Germany had taken on the character
of a crusade that could end only with the unconditional surrender
of the vanquished, early on an occupation of the whole of Germany was planned. The allied negotiations about the post-war
military occupation of Germany and Austria were conducted
entirely independently of the discussions concerning Germany's
partitioning. At no stage did the projected Zones of Occupation
tally with the *Länder* into which, in accordance with one of the
partitioning proposals, Germany was to be divided.[70] In so far
as the occupation of Germany was understood to be a military
measure to be taken during the first post-war phase and the dismemberment to be, on the other hand, a political measure for a
later stage of development this is not surprising.
Prior to the first negotiations, there was a grotesquely mistaken
appreciation of Soviet intentions on the part of the Allies. Far
removed from the idea that the Soviets, in conformity with their
revolutionary proclamations, desired to thrust as far as possible
into Europe, the experts of the Western Powers feared that the
Soviets had secretly resolved to make a halt at Germany's eastern
frontier and to leave the conquest of Germany to the Western
Powers. When during the Foreign Ministers' Conference in
October, 1943, in Moscow, Stalin enthusiastically intimated his
approval of the joint march of the Allies into Berlin – which was

the subject of an American toast – there was great satisfaction on the part of the Western experts.[71] The Western diplomatists' last doubt was certainly removed one year later, when Stalin assured the British Prime Minister that the Soviet armies would "press vigorously and continuously into Germany".[72]

Another view was taken by the American military experts. At the end of 1943, they were counting on the whole of Germany up to the Rhine being under Russian control by the time the Germans were defeated and considered that the Soviets would then certainly not be ready to let the other Powers occupy a part of the territory they had conquered. The American State Department had some difficulty in convincing the War Department that at least an attempt to lay down Zones of Occupation ought to be made.[73]

At first, both the British and the Americans made suggestions which, in view of the subsequent consequences of Germany's division into zones, still deserve attention even if they were discarded. There had been a number of instances in Europe over the last 150 years of occupation by military troops – in France, from 1814 to 1815, in Schleswig and Holstein, from 1864 to 1866, and in Germany, after the first World War. But the Occupying Powers had always been States having the same or similar social systems. Now, for the first time, a country was to be occupied jointly by States having contrasting social systems. It was obvious that danger would ensue if the States wished to align their respective zones in accordance with their own particular social systems.[74] Had the British proposal not to have the troops of each of the Occupying Powers stationed in one zone but to have the whole of the troops of all of the Powers spread over the whole of Germany been accepted, the danger of partitioning might have been arrested. Unfortunately, it was rejected by the Americans, on the one hand for political reasons, mainly on account of the difficulty of supplying the troops, and, on the other hand, with regard to the Soviets, in that it was thought that the Soviet Government would attach importance to concentrating the Soviet Armed Forces in one inter-connected area to prevent the unfettered contact of Soviet soldiers with the other Allied troops.[75] The proposal put forward by General Eisenhower, the American

Commander-in-Chief, to leave the occupation of Germany to the Anglo-American Supreme Command, enlarged by the addition of French and Soviet officers, seems to have come to naught for similar misgivings.[76] Nor, having regard to the Soviets, did the Western Governments follow Eisenhower's subsequent suggestion not, at least from the start, to divide at least West Germany up into zones.[77]

When in January, 1944, the British delegate in the European Advisory Commission put forward a first proposal for dividing Germany up into Zones of Occupation, the Soviet Union was treated "somewhat in generosity"[78], partly because London wished to save occupation troops and partly because thought was already being given to the cession of the eastern territories to Poland. According to British calculations, the Soviet Zone comprised 40 per cent. of the territory, 36 per cent. of the population, and 33 per cent. of the productive capacity of Germany within its 1937 boundaries. Nevertheless, it seemed to the Western diplomats a sign of moderation that the Soviets should declare themselves in agreement with this proposal without making difficulties.[79]

Certainly the Soviets had a little supplementary proposal to put forward, which in spite of its unpretentiousness betrayed that they, in contrast to the Western Powers, regarded the military occupation of a part of Germany not solely from the point of view of controlling the defeated adversary but that they had recognised the inherent possibility of a further extension of Soviet influence. They proposed the incorporation into the Soviet Zone of the island of Fehmarn, a spring-board to Denmark. M. Gousev, the Soviet envoy, did not let himself be disconcerted by the British delegate's pointing out that this island belonged to Schleswig-Holstein and that it must, therefore, fall within the British Zone. For months Gousev persisted in his demand, so that at last the British Foreign Office authorised its delegate to agree to it. It was only due to the stubbornness of the British diplomat that Fehmarn did not fall into Soviet hands.[80]

On a further five occasions the Soviet Government showed that, in contrast to the United Kingdom and the United States, it was intent on extending its sphere of military occupation as far as was possible. Only with difficulty can this be reconciled with the control functions of an Occupation Power.

In respect of Austria, the British draft proposal was to the effect that, together with Southern Germany, Austria should be occupied by the American Armed Forces,which were pressing forward in Italy. On the other hand, here, too, the Soviet counter-proposal envisaged a splitting-up into three zones so that the Soviet Union could occupy the eastern part of the country, thereby securing the opportunity to influence its policy.[81] On the other hand, while the Western Powers agreed at once to the further extension of the Soviet sphere of occupation, the United States, who, contrary to the British proposal, wanted to occupy the north and west of Germany, still continued for months to demur from participating in the occupation of Austria. The Americans wished to leave the remainder of the country entirely to the British, or at best to send a few soldiers to Vienna as a symbol. Thus unimportant, indeed burdensome, did the task of occupation seem to them. It was not until the American Government learned from the alarming Soviet procedure in Bulgaria that the influence of an Occupying Power stands in direct proportion to the number of troops it maintains in the country in question that it decided on a regular participation in the occupation of Austria.[82]

The Soviet desire for authority was again made manifest in the negotiations about the zonal and sector boundaries. At the middle of 1944, when the Soviet troops were still a long way from Austria, the Soviet delegate pressed for the early conclusion of a zonal agreement in order to ensure part of Austria for the Soviet Union. When, however, through the fault of America, the agreement was put off until the spring of 1945, the Soviets suddenly made difficulties. By that time the Red Army had occupied Vienna and large parts of Austria, and their Commander-in-Chief, Marshal Tolbukhin, began to feel himself master of the house. Churchill and the new-elected American President Truman had to intervene with Stalin in order to secure any agreement about the zones at all.

For Vienna, a joint occupation was planned. During the negotiations the Soviets tried to make the Vienna area as restricted as possible since, just as Berlin, the Austrian capital lay in the middle of the Soviet Zone. Besides this, they claimed as their sector the north-east, including the First District in which the most important Ministries are situated. In this case the Western Powers recognised the danger in good time and, through a special regulation in respect of this District ("Four Men in a Jeep"), saved the future Austrian Government from one-sided Soviet pressure.[83]

Still more significant were the two amending proposals put forward by the Soviet Government in respect of the zonal division in Austria. The British draft forming the basis of unification included for the apportionment of the whole of Lower Austria, including the northern half of Burgenland, to the Soviet Union. This would have placed the American troops in Upper Austria on the Czechoslovak frontier and the British troops in Southern Burgenland on the Hungarian border. The Soviet delegate promptly tabled two applications for amendment, which envisaged that Southern Burgenland and that part of Upper Austria north of the Danube were to belong to the Soviet Zone. Although the American delegate urgently recommended his Government not to agree, the Government expressed its approval, since "no military considerations of importance" contradicted it.[84] In this manner the Soviet Union was able to ensure for itself the control of the whole of the frontier between Austria and Czechoslovakia [85] and of that between Austria and Hungary and employ their Occupation Zone in Austria as a "cordon sanitaire" in front of these two countries, just as the Soviet Occupation Zone in Germany cut Poland off from the West.

In Germany, the Soviet Union's efforts to bring the maximum amount of territory under its military control were once again made manifest when it was a question of setting up a fourth Occupation Zone, for France. After lengthy resistance, Stalin registered his approval at the Yalta Conference, in February, 1945, but only after he had been given the assurance that the French Zone would be allocated out of the two Western Zones.[86] He would surrender nothing of the Soviet Zone. The same applied for the sectors in Berlin. Here, too, the Soviet Union succeeded in retaining its original share.

These examples show that at the negotiations over the Zones of

Occupation the Soviet Union applied a standard different from that of the Western Powers who almost unwillingly addressed themselves to the task. Clearly the West did not think of the possibility that the zonal frontiers could assume more significance than a mere administrative boundary. A British participant at the discussions has confessed: "It was not our expectation that the Zones would be sealed off from one another."[87] For the Western Powers, the Occupation Zones were in the first place just a technical institution. On the other hand, the obstinacy with which the Soviets fought over the extent and the special position of their Occupation territory indicates that, even from an early date, they regarded the zonal distribution from a different standpoint. Accustomed to their blunt conception of power, they perceived in the military occupation an instrument for political transformation. They had been able to gain experience in this realm in 1939–40 in the Baltic States.

How very much the Western Powers, believing in the durability of the alliance, mistook the Soviet policy can be measured by their well-known neglect to ensure unobstructed approaches to Berlin through the Soviet Zone. When the American delegate intimated to his Government the importance of this matter, he was coolly assured by the War Department that it was purely a "military matter" which would be taken care of "at the military level" when the time came.[88]

Chapter Four

THE THIRD PHASE: EXPANSION TO THE ELBE
(1944–1945)

> Unfortunately the Soviet Army was not in a position
> to afford the same help to the French and Italian
> Communist Parties (as that to the Yugoslav Com-
> munist Party).
>
> *From a letter from the Soviet Union's Communist
> Party Central Committee to the Central Committee
> of the Yugoslav Communist Party (1948).*

As we know from Mátyás Rákosi, the Hungarian member of the
Comintern, the foreign Communists in Moscow had been at work
on post-war plans for Europe ever since 1942.[1] The Soviet victory
at Stalingrad fulfilled the hope that the second World War would
not come to an end with the armies still deep inside Russia but in
Central Europe. To reach its desired goal the Red Army tried
with all its might to repel the troops of the Axis Powers as
quickly as possible. As soon as the course of the war provided the
opportunity, the Soviet Union once again resumed the propensity
to expand that it had been disavowing for years. With the might
of the Soviets their tanks carried Communism to Central Europe.
There is no ground for the belief that the Soviets had forsworn
the ideas of World Revolution during the war as their propaganda feigned, and that they did not return to a consideration
of such matters until after they had gained the victory. If from
1941 to 1945 they disavowed their revolutionary urge to expand,
it was only with their eye on the advantages attaching to the
alliance with the Western Powers. As far as they themselves were
concerned, the struggle against Germany and Japan was, as later
an American observer pertinently said, "only the first phase in
the ultimate struggle between Communism and capitalism."[2] This
American, who during the war had gone to Moscow with the best
of good will to help the Soviet allies, later summarised his ex-

periences in the words: "In my opinion, there can no longer be any doubt that Soviet leadership has always been motivated by the belief that Communism and Capitalism cannot coexist. Nor is there any doubt in my mind that present day Soviet leaders have determined upon a program pointed toward imposing Communism on those countries under their control and elsewhere creating conditions favorable to the triumph of Communism in the war against Capitalism which they consider to be inevitable."[3]

This change of opinion on the part of a high-ranking American officer is significant. In the West, where the honesty of the Soviet assurances had been believed, there set in a disenchantment that developed into a profound disappointment. They had grown accustomed to considering cooperation with the Soviets the normal thing and now had to realise that for the Soviets it was an exception. For years the West was not able to overcome this disappointment of 1944–45. Almost all the memoirs dating from this period written by Western politicians and diplomats bitterly accuse the Soviets of breaking the anti-Hitler coalition. They overlook the fact that the struggle against Nazi Germany was the sole content and purpose of that coalition. For this reason there existed in point of fact no ground for the West's disappointment in 1945 but only for remorseful appreciation of their own blind confidence.

The gradual awakening of the West and its reflecting on the danger inherent in Soviet policy came too late to prevent the sovietisation of those territories that were prostrate under the boots of the Soviet soldiery. The relations between the Powers that prevailed in the centre of Europe when the war came to an end remained determined for a long time.

1. THE "LIBERATION" OF SOUTH-EAST AND EAST-CENTRAL EUROPE

In the ten months from the middle of 1944 to May, 1945, in all the countries occupied by the Soviet Army the existing conditions were suppressed and governments in which there was a more or less strong Communist influence installed. The Communists also recognised the connection between military occupation and revolutionary transformation. Disregarding the fact that since 1941 Stalin had unflaggingly demanded a "second front", an American Communist writes: "Fear of the Soviet forces occupying hitherto capitalist countries was ... what motivated the Anglo-American invasion of Italy – a drive that was supposed (but failed) to reconquer the whole Balkan and South European areas ... This was also the motivating reason causing the United States and Great Britain, at long last, to launch the deliberately delayed second front ... The Anglo-American imperialists managed to check the revolution in France, Italy, West Germany, Belgium, Holland and Franco Spain ... Therefore the victorious Revolution was finally restricted to Czechoslovakia, Poland, Hungary, Roumania, Bulgaria, Albania and East Germany, involving about 100 million people." [4] A French journalist affirms: "Every country that might have been 'liberated' by the Red Army, whether it be France, England or Spain, would have suffered the same fate." [5]

For years, Stalin's policy had been aimed at transforming the largest possible parts of South-East and East-Central Europe into "socialistic" countries.[6] Now that the Red Army had occupied one country after another, it again proved itself, as in 1920–21 in Transcaucasia and in 1939–40 in East Poland and the Baltic, as the upholder of the Revolution. With the troops came the secret police and their reign of fear and terror was established. Whether the majority of the population or only a sizable minority wanted revolution was immaterial. For Stalin, "political power is the creator of social systems, not the other way around".[7] Of all European countries that have become Communist since 1944, only in Yugoslavia and Albania have the countries' own Communist parties provided an essential contribution to the establishment of the new régime.[8] In all others, the Soviet organs had to resort to force in making the "liberation from capitalism" its concern. With cold logical consistency, they immediately grappled with this task in every country into which they came.

(a) Poland

Poland is the largest, the most highly populated and geographically the most important country athwart Russia's European threshold. Preparations for the domination of it were made by the Soviets with especial care. Apart from the "Union of Polish Patriots" in the Soviet Union, on January 1, 1944, there had been established on Polish soil as further shock troops for Soviet expansion a "National Council of the Fatherland" (Krajowa Rada Narodowa – KRN). [9] For this purpose the Soviet leaders had sent to Poland at the end of 1943 Boleslav Bierut, the leader of the Polish section of the Soviet secret police, who assumed the chairmanship of the National Council. While the Union of Patriots was intended to form a counterweight to the *émigré* Government in London, the National Council entered into rivalry with the "parliament" of the Polish underground movement. In a declaration on January 11, 1944, the Soviet Government advocated a "strong and independent" Poland. Later, the West was to experience what the Soviets meant by that.

As soon as the Soviet troops advanced beyond the eastern part of Poland (which was immediately re-incorporated into the Soviet Union), the leaders of the Union of Patriots and the KRN joined forces to form the so-called "Polish Committee of National Liberation" (Polski Komitet Wyzwolenia Narodowego – PKWN), under the chairmanship of E. Osóbka-Morawski, a socialist of the Left. In a manifesto issued on July 22 from Cholm, the Committee recognised the imposed drawing of the eastern frontier, called for a vigorous extension of Poland towards the west, and, moreover, proclaimed that security could be provided against the "pressure of German imperialism" only by the establishment of a "great Slavic barrier", the foundation of which would be a Polish-Soviet-Czech agreement. [10] Three days later, the Soviet Government announced that it regarded the military operations in Poland as operations on the territory of a "sovereign, friendly and allied" State. [11] Yet one more day later, Molotov and Osóbka-Morawski signed an agreement in Moscow under which the Soviet Union handed over to the "Liberation Committee" the "complete management of all civil administrative affairs" outside the combat areas[12], thereby eliminating the *émigré* Government in London. The procedure recalled the Soviet tactics in the autumn of 1939 when Finland was attacked, except that in Poland there succeeded what miscarried in Finland: helping the Communists installed by Moscow and their fellow-travellers to gain control.

Now, however, the Soviet leaders came up against two difficulties. Neither the Western Powers nor the non-Communist underground movement in Poland wanted to reconcile themselves without more ado to the absorption of Poland within the Soviet camp. Already, two months previously, the Soviet ambassador Gromyko had failed when he had tried to get the American Government to acknowledge the pro-Soviet Poles as a legitimate Government.[13] Now the Western Powers once again came out in favour of the *émigré* Government led by Mikolajczyk. At this period Stalin was still concerned to save his face. He therefore, on August 3, received Mikolajczyk in the Kremlin, although he demanded of him that he unite with the Liberation Committee, which had in the meantime moved into quarters in Lublin. "Hereafter I intend to deal with only one Polish Government, not two."[14]

Nor could the Soviet leaders disregard without more ado the hostile mood of the great mass of the Polish people. General Anders, the Commander of the Polish *émigré* Army in Italy, can probably have characterised the views of his countrymen aright when in a talk with Churchill he said: "We cannot trust Russia, knowing her too well, and we are convinced that all Stalin's announcements that he wants a free and strong Poland are lies and impostures. The Bolsheviks want our eastern provinces in order that they may ruin us the more easily and enter more deeply into Europe to make her Communist."[15] Because of this mood, the non-Communist underground movement had long planned a great uprising for the moment of the Soviet invasion, which while ostensibly directed against the Germans was in the main to proclaim before all the world the Polish will to freedom. In this, the Soviet leaders had, understandably, no interest. When on August 1 the uprising broke out in Warsaw, the Soviet troops stood at "order arms" on the eastern bank of the Vistula, until the revolt was suppressed, with appalling devastation, by the

Germans. Since the non-Communist underground movement thereby lost its organisation and its finest brains, the Soviets had an easy time of it when they entered Warsaw in January, 1945.

Beforehand, however, Churchill made one more attempt to achieve that the *émigré* Government in London had a say in the matter. When in the middle October, 1944, he was in Moscow for talks with Stalin, he had Mikolajczyk follow on later for another discussion, to make use of the "friendly atmosphere" in the Kremlin. However, the conversation, about which Mikolajczyk later made a dramatic report [16], took a totally different course from what the Prime Minister had anticipated. From the outset, Stalin demanded that Mikolajczyk should take note of the existence of the "Committee of Liberation" and should recognise the Curzon Line. Without going into the first of these demands, Churchill declared that he had new hopes of an agreement. Mikolajczyk should reconcile himself only to the loss of the territories in the east of Poland, taking in their place East Prussia, Danzig and Silesia. But the Polish Prime Minister remained obstinate. He knew better than Churchill what was really the Soviet concern. Even, he said, if Poland accepted the exchange, there still existed no guarantee for the country's future independence. "And who is threatening Poland's independence?" asked Stalin, indignantly. "Soviet Russia perhaps?" Although Mikolajczyk did not venture to reply with "yes", the talk petered out unsatisfactorily.

Churchill, still labouring under the delusion that Poland's freedom could be secured by the recognition of the loss of the eastern territories, then most violently reproached the Polish Government leader. "If you do not accept the frontier", he threatened, "you are out of business for ever. The Russians will sweep through your country and your people will be liquidated." Side by side with the threatening, he promised that, if Mikolajczyk came to terms with Stalin and returned to Poland, he would soon have a British and an American ambassador there as a prop against the Soviet Union. In addition, he said, the United States would possibly give the new Poland a big loan, "perhaps, indeed, free of interest".

On his return to London, the ambitious Mikolajczyk, in no way overjoyed at the prospect of an existence in exile of unforseeable duration, suddenly switched his policy in another direction. He got the British Government to give him the promise in writing that Poland would be compensated with German territory "up to the Oder Line" for its losses in the east and, within its new borders, would receive a guarantee of its independence and integrity.[17] On this basis, Mikolajczyk tried to talk his Cabinet over to this change of course. Because of the mistrust of the majority of the exiled Poles, the attempt failed. The new *émigré* Government, which was formed at the end of November, after Mikolajczyk's resignation, by the Socialist Arciszewski, was characterised by a still harsher hostility towards the Soviets, so that from the beginning Churchill regarded it as an unserviceable implement for his attempts at settlement.

Meanwhile, however, the Soviet leaders did not allow themselves to be held up on their political path. On January 1, 1945, the Communist "National Council" proclaimed the Lublin Liberation Committee the Provisional Government. Roosevelt hastened to send a telegram to Moscow, asking Stalin to await the new conference that had been planned before recognising the Government, so as to be able still to alter the one-sided composition of the Government.[18] But the Soviet leaders, who looked on Poland as falling within their sphere of control, were not so inconsequential as to let the Polish Government they themselves had installed remain in suspension out of consideration for the West. On January 4, they gave it their formal recognition. The first Soviet satellite was born and went into its previously-calculated orbit.

Shortly afterwards, the winter offensive of the Red Army began. In rapid strokes the German troops were driven back, and every day saw the further extension towards the west of the Soviet sphere of domination. Within a few weeks, the whole of Poland was liberated – and oppressed anew. When, on February 4, the second "summit conference" opened in the Crimea, Poland was lying firmly in the Soviet grip.

Roosevelt and Churchill came to Yalta with the intention of relaxing the strong hold of the Communists in Poland and, in spite of Soviet occupation, of giving the country, for the freedom of which Great Britain had gone to war in 1939, the chance of independence. Since at this point of time the Soviet Government had no wish for an open conflict with its allies, it was prepared to meet them half-way, so long as the Soviet position of authority was not seriously affected. There thus arose a strange discussion lasting several days. The Western Heads of Government started by demanding the formation of a new Polish Government in which democratic *émigré* Poles, such as Mikolajczyk, should participate. Stalin, on the other hand, expected of the Western Powers their recognition of the Provisional Government. Once more "patriotic" motives had to bear the brunt of the reason for the Soviet demands. Throughout the annals of history, averred Stalin, Poland had been a corridor serving the attacking of Russia. For that reason the Soviet Union needed a "strong, independent and democratic Poland". Engrossed in the anti-Hitler coalition idea, Roosevelt and Churchill did not perceive Stalin's distortion of history. Neither in 1914 nor in 1941 was there an independent Poland that could have served as a "corridor", but, in both cases, with Russia's powerful participation, Poland was partitioned.

Stalin and Molotov's bargaining beat down bit by bit the dangerous demands of their Western partners. At first the Russians entrenched themselves behind their own creatures, Osóbka-Morawski and Bierut, declaring with a shrug of the shoulders that these two gentlemen insisted that Mikolajczyk was not Prime Minister. When Roosevelt and Churchill acquiesced in this, Molotov proposed that the problem be solved by the "addition" of a few of the *émigré* Poles. He regretted that there was nothing more one could do since the Provisional Government was very popular in Poland. Roosevelt finally gave the Soviet Government Head the decisive cue by asking when, in the latter's opinion, the Provisional Government would be in a position to hold free elections. Stalin, who clearly immediately recognised the chance, countered: It might be possible in a month, provided no catastrophes occurred on the front.[19] With that the problem lost interest for the Western Powers. Recognition of the Polish Government for so short a time now seemed of importance only in so far as the preparations for the elections themselves were concerned. It was, therefore, now easier for the Americans to desist from requiring the formation of a new Government and to be satisfied with a "recognition" of that existing. Churchill resisted somewhat longer and, indeed, demanded that the Allied ambassadors in Warsaw should be charged with the supervision of the Polish elections. But at this the two Soviet statesmen once more hid behind the creatures that were their products and declared that this assignment could not be decided on without the concurrence of the Poles.

At the end of the conference the following resolution was adopted.[20] Molotov, together with Averell Harriman and Sir Archibald Clark-Kerr, the ambassadors of the Western Powers in Poland, were to discuss "with members of the present Provisional Government and with other Polish democratic leaders from within Poland and from abroad" a "reorganization" of the Polish Government "on a broader democratic basis". The resulting "Polish Provisional Government of National Unity" was to hold free elections "as soon as possible". Independently of this, however, it was to be recognised by the Western Powers, who desired "to be kept informed about the situation in Poland" through their ambassadors. At the same time, Poland's "shifting towards the west" through recognition of the Curzon Line and a "substantial accession of territory in the north and west" was proclaimed.

The realisation of this last resolution, which entirely accorded with the Soviet temper, was taken in hand by the Soviet Government before it was passed. As early as February 5, Bierut announced, after a visit to Moscow, that the Provisional Government had made a start with the incorporation of the German eastern territories.[21] In March, Polish voivodes were organised in the German eastern territories. On the other hand, in regard to the carrying out of the remaining agreements reached at Yalta, the Soviet Government was in no hurry. At the discussions in Moscow, Molotov made all conceivable difficulties. At first he refused to invite any Poles at all. Not once did his gaze rest with sympathy on Mikolajczyk. At the same time, in order to have no disagreeable witnesses of the deportations and the executions which at this time attended the setting up of the totalitarian régime in Poland, Molotov refused to allow Western observers to go to Poland.[22]

The Soviet terror in Poland reached its first climax at the end of March with the arrest of a 14-man delegation of the remnants of the Polish underground movement headed by General Okulicki, the last commander of the underground Army. The delegation had been invited to Moscow by the Soviet political police, allegedly to discuss the formation of a unified Polish Government on the basis of the Yalta resolutions. After the talks had been successfully concluded, they were to be given the opportunity of going to London to discuss the matter with the *émigré* Government. Although the delegates had had their personal security guaranteed in writing, they were arrested at the deliberations with the Soviet members, and in June they were brought before a Moscow court, most of them being sentenced for "espionage" and other crimes.[23]

Unconcerned about the expostulations of Roosevelt and Churchill, who from the beginning of March had been pressing for the realisation of the Yalta resolutions, the Soviet Government took a further step, on April 2, to make Poland, under Communist direction, dependent on the Soviet Union by signing in Moscow with Osóbka-Morawski a pact of friendship and mutual assistance.[24] Shortly afterwards it made another attempt to secure the recognition of the still unchanged Polish Government by demanding that the Government be invited to the inaugural conference of the United Nations at San Francisco. But with this step Moscow had gone too far. Truman, who after Roosevelt's death had become United States President, sharply demanded of Molotov during a conversation that the Soviets keep to the Yalta agreements. Shortly before, one of Truman's advisors had recommended that it was better to have a trial of strength now rather than later if the Soviets wished to bring the whole of Eastern Europe under their control.[25]

Nevertheless, the Soviet Government knew how to delay reorganisation of the Polish Government still further. Not until some weeks after Germany's capitulation did Stalin, at the end of May, declare to a personal envoy sent by Truman that he was prepared to accept Mikolajczyk and three other Polish democrats into the Government. At the same time he set his visitor's mind at rest by assuring him that all talk of a sovietisation of

Poland was nonsense.[26] At last, in June, more than four months after Yalta, the new Polish Government, in which Mikolajczyk was deputy Prime Minister, was in being. But after, on July 5, the United States and the United Kingdom had recognised the new Government, it found the matter of free elections, which should actually have taken place one month after Yalta, no longer called for speed. Eighteen months were still to go by before elections were to take place for the first time. In the meantime, the Communists had got their hands firmly on all positions of authority.

(b) Roumania

In Roumania, in the summer of 1944 the situation was completely different from what it was in Poland, since the Roumanian State was intact and, just like Finland, it had from the very first days fought on the German side in the war against the Soviet Union. There was, however, similarity in one respect: the population entertained fears just as did the Poles. As early as February, 1943, shortly after Stalingrad, Mihai Antonescu, the Roumanian Minister for Foreign Affairs, took steps for the first time to warn the Western Powers of the danger of a Soviet invasion of Europe and advised them urgently to make a special peace with Germany. At a conversation with Hitler in April, 1943, Jon Antonescu, the Roumanian Head of State, suggested to him also to end the war with the Western Powers so as to be able to carry on the war against the Soviet Union to a successful conclusion.[27]

Since Roumanian ideas produced no results on either side, in the second half of the year the Government initiated a new policy aimed at piloting Roumania out of the war but, with the assistance of the Western Powers, sparing the country the looming fate of being occupied by Soviet troops. This idea could not, however, harmonise with the Western conception of alliances vis-à-vis the Soviet Union. At the beginning of November, 1943, the Roumanian Government, after putting out a feeler via Ankara, received a message from the British Government to the effect that, in accordance with the resolutions made a short while before at the Moscow Foreign Ministers' Conference, proposals for peace could be accepted only if addressed to all three allies – thus to the Soviet Union also – and containing an offer of unconditional surrender. It appears, however, that the Roumanian statesmen could not believe this message to be the last word. At the end of December, they informed the Western Powers that Roumania was prepared to surrender unconditionally as soon as there had been an invasion of the Balkans by the Western Powers directed towards Roumania, and if Turkey had entered the war on the side of the Allies.[28]

At this moment, however, matters took a surprising turn. The Soviet Government secretly informed the Roumanian State leaders, via Stockholm, that it desired to enter into contact with a view to ending hostilities. Since, in accordance with agreements, the Western leaders had informed their Soviet allies about the Roumanian peace feelers, it is obvious that the astonishing step taken by the Soviets represented a reaction to the Roumanian attempt to explore the situation. Unconcerned about their alliance with the West, the Soviets wished to secure the decisive influence in Roumania for themselves, in conformity with the Soviet Balkan programme of November, 1940. For this reason they kept their negotiations with the Roumanians secret from the Western Powers and tried to win the Roumanian Government over to their side by modifying the conditions the Allies had laid down.[29] To allay the suspicion of the Roumanian State leaders, Molotov expressly declared, on April 2, 1944: "The Soviet Government declares that it is not aiming at securing any part whatever of Roumanian territory or at changing the social system existing in Roumania."[30]

The precautionary measures taken by the Soviets proved, however, unnecessary. On May 5, 1944, the British Government put forward a proposal to the Soviet Government that South-East Europe should be divided up into particular zones, serving at first military operations only. Roumania was to fall within the Soviet sphere of operations, Greece within the British. While the Soviet Government immediately agreed, the American Government at first withheld its acquiescence. Not until Churchill had expressly made it clear that it was not a matter of political spheres of interest did Roosevelt, without the knowledge of the State Department, concur, and even then for three months only. The Western Powers thereby gave up all claim to a participation in the military occupation of Roumania, for which at this time both the State leaders and the Opposition were hoping. They left the country to Soviet "influence".[31]

Nevertheless, the decisive step was taken by the Roumanian leaders themselves. When in August the Soviet armies opened up a fresh offensive, which broke the Roumanian powers of resistance within a few days, on August 23 King Michael dismissed the Antonescu Government, summoned a new Government under the leadership of General Sanatescu, and issued a proclamation to the effect that Roumania was no longer at war with the Allies. The significance of this step cannot be too highly estimated. With one stroke the gateway to the Balkans lay open to the Soviet troops. Not without reason did Stalin later bestow on the King the Soviet Order of Victory.

The new Government, to which the leaders of the four Roumanian parties, including the Communist Patrascanu as Minister without Portfolio, belonged, entertained the hope that from the very first day the Allies would cooperate with so "democratic" a Government. The hope was, however, not realised. Instead, the Soviet Union delayed the signing of the armistice until, by the beginning of September, it had completed the military occupation of the whole of Roumania except for Siebenbürgen.[32] Keeping in mind the agreement about the Balkan zones, the Western Powers did nothing to assist Roumania. Since the armistice agreement bound the country not only to place money, transport, power, fuel, food and other things at the disposal of the Soviet Supreme Command but also simultaneously to pay reparations amounting to 300 million dollars, the Soviet Union disposed from the outset over very powerful means for exerting pressure.[33]

At the same time, however, a start was made with the transformation of the country internally. In 1944, the Roumanian Communist Party was very weak. Its membership was estimated to be scarcely a thousand. For this reason the Soviets supported with all their means a supplementary organisation, the so-called "Ploughmen's Front", headed by one Petru Groza. Up to then this had had only local importance, but it was now extended to cover the whole of Roumania so as to be able to do as much damage as possible to the democratically-disposed National Peasant Party, headed by one Juliu Maniu, a man of high repute.[34] They also saw to it that, together with Groza and another Leftist party calling itself the "Union of Patriots", the Communists and the Social Democrats formed a "National Democratic Front" (FND).[35] Sanatescu was caught in the pincers between the FND and the "Allied Control Commission", which was in reality a Soviet organ. When the FND demanded a share in the Government, Marshal Voroshilov made a protest about an alleged procrastination in complying with the armistice conditions. Sanatescu was obliged to dismiss his Government and to form a new Cabinet in which the FND was strongly represented. Nor did the development end there. Through vehement attacks on M. Penescu (National Peasant Party), the Minister of the Interior, the Communists secured the fall of this Government, too, a few weeks later.

The new Prime Minister, who took up office on December 2, was General Radescu, whose appointment as General Chief-of-Staff the Soviets had already insisted upon because of his well-known hostility towards the Germans. Apparently they hoped he would gradually play Roumania into the hands of the Communists. But the General was their greatest disappointment. He ordered the Communists to disband their armed militia, advocated a postponement of the land reform demanded, and combated the terrorism and the local Communist dictators, who, under the protection of the Red Army and the Soviet secret police, had been installed in the towns and villages. After Ana Pauker and Gheorghiu-Dej, the leading Roumanian Communists, had returned from exile in Moscow, the situation soon came to a head. When the authorities tried to intervene against the Communist intriguing, the Soviet Commandant protested that the Government wished "to suppress the will of the people" or "to favour the Fascists". The Communist State Secretary in the Ministry of the Interior took a stand against Radescu, and when the latter wanted to dismiss him he refused to go.

In February, 1945, it came to an open clash. After Radescu was no longer given a hearing in his country's censored Press, he attacked the Communists, particularly Ana Pauker, this "alien without God and Fatherland", at public gatherings. After the Yalta Conference, Radescu was able to maintain his stand for only a few more weeks. The Soviet Commandant deprived him of the Army by abruptly occupying its headquarters and having the Roumanian troops in the capital disarmed. At the same time, on February 27, the Soviet Deputy Foreign Minister Vishinsky, who in 1940 in Riga had already passed his test as the ridder of an unpalatable Government, made his appearance in Bucharest. He rudely ordered King Michael to dismiss Radescu, alleging the latter incapable of providing for law and order, and to entrust the formation of a National Democratic Front to Petru Groza.

By March 6 the new Government was complete. This time the Communists took over the Ministry of the Interior themselves. As they were also given the Ministry of Justice they held in their hands all the instruments necessary for terrorising the country. Maniu and Bratianu, the best-known democratic party leaders, were excluded, but the renegade Liberal Tatarescu became Minister for Foreign Affairs, in spite of his former close relations with the "Iron Guard" and Hitler. In as short a time as fourteen days after the formation of the Government, a land reform, as the first socialist measure, was proclaimed.

The Western Powers were exasperated about the Soviet action in Roumania, representing as it did a clear-cut infringement of the Yalta resolution that provision was to be made for free elections and democratic governments in the countries that were liberated. But Churchill felt himself tied to the agreement about the spheres of interest in the Balkans that awarded Roumania to the Soviets and he refrained from making a protest.[36]

(c) Bulgaria

It is true that Bulgaria was one of Germany's allies, but, in contrast to Roumania, it had never taken part in the war against the Soviet Union and had made use of the alliance with the Reich only to occupy a number of adjacent districts in Yugoslavia and

Greece. Bulgarian assistance to Germany consisted solely in allowing German troops to march through Bulgaria to Yugoslavia in the spring of 1941 and, later on in the war, in permitting German troops to use the Black Sea ports of Varna and Burgas.

From May, 1944, under the imprint of the allied successes, Bulgaria gradually broke with the Axis Powers. Political prisoners who had been arrested primarily at German behest were allowed to go free, and anti-Jewish measures were for the most part lifted. On August 17, a few days after the upheaval in Roumania, M. Bagrianov, the Bulgarian Prime Minister, spoke before the National Assembly of his people's yearning for peace, adding that the "great Slav brother" showed understanding for Bulgaria's position and would lend a helping hand.[37] Intermediaries were despatched to Cairo to negotiate with the Western Powers about an armistice. On August 23, Bagrianov announced that Bulgaria had "withdrawn from the war".

It seems that the Bulgarians were unaware that an Allied agreement in respect of Bulgaria had been in existence since June, 1944. At that time the agreements about military operations in South-East Europe had been extended to include Bulgaria and Yugoslavia. Although Bulgaria was not at war with the Soviet Union, it was placed within the Soviet Union's sphere of operations.[38] A bare four years previously, in a secret protocol, the Soviet Union had secured also from Germany confirmation of the Soviet interest vis-à-vis Bulgaria.

After the upheaval in Roumania, which within a few days carried the Red Army through the Dobruja to the northern frontier of Bulgaria, the Soviet Union was confronted with the question of how it should profit by its political chances. It solved the problem in the simplest fashion by declaring war on Bulgaria, on September 5, thereby for the first time making, unprovoked, an attack preceded by a normal declaration of war.[39] The Bulgarian Government's reply consisted in immediately enquiring about conditions of peace from the Soviet Legation and in declaring war on Germany, on December 6. But that was, of course, no use to the Soviet Union, whose wishes included the overthrow of the Bulgarian democratic régime.[40] On September 8, Soviet troops marched into Bulgaria, meeting with no resistance. Simultaneously the Moscow radio called for an uprising against the "dominating group". The following day a coup d'état in Sofia brought to power the "Patriotic Front".

The "Patriotic Front" was an idea of Dimitroff, who was one of the Bulgar Communists who had lived for years in Russia. He was General Secretary of the Comintern.[41] As an anti-constitutional Opposition, the "Patriotic Front" mainly embraced the Communists, the Leftist landowners headed by Pettkov, and the Zveno Officers' League, under Colonel Damjan Veltchev. Close ties had existed between the "Patriotic Front" and the underground movement supported mainly by Communists and which combated the Bulgarian Government and its organs. Now, therefore, the young partisans came down from the mountains, distributed arms, and staged demonstrations in order to assist the "Patriotic Front", in whose Government the Communists played an important role. It is true that, as in Roumania, an officer, Colonel Kimon Georgieff, was allowed the premiership, but one of his deputies was a leading Communist, and, above all, here, too, the Communists were able immediately to get the Ministries of Justice and the Interior into their hands.

The armistice with Bulgaria, signed on October 28, 1944, in Moscow, by representatives of the Red Army and the Allied Supreme Command Mediterranean Area, assured to the Soviet Union the exclusive influence in Bulgaria.[42] The Communists had already, in September, started to indulge in their acts of terrorism, protected by the Red Army. The three Regents, 22 former Ministers and 28 parliamentary deputies were sentenced by special courts and executed. One official statement confirms that 2,138 sentences of death were carried out in the six months up to March, 1945. Even the members of the last Government, which had declared war on Germany, were sentenced to terms of imprisonment, either for life or for many years. It was clearly wished to eliminate all resistance. At the same time, Jugov, the Communist Minister of the Interior, managed to get the police apparatus permeated with Communists. In many provincial towns and villages, Communists and partisans took over the positions of public authority.

The seizure of power by the Communists was urged forward so

swiftly and brutally that the remaining partners in the "Patriotic Front" soon became the opponents of the Communists. But the latter knew ways and means of getting rid of dangerous confederates. When Dr. G. M. Dimitroff, the General Secretary of the Landowners' Union, publicly aired the view that Bulgaria ought to seek the friendship not only of the Soviet Union but also that of the Western Allies, he was forced, in January, 1945, to retire. The same happened to M. Pettkov, his successor, who also became involved in contention with the Communists. A few weeks later he had to resign the general secretaryship of the Landowners' Union, and then, in protest against the methods used by the Communists in this electoral campaign, he surrendered his ministerial office also.

(d) Yugoslavia and Albania

Yugoslavia and Albania were the only Balkan countries in which the Communists had played an authoritative role even before being invaded by Soviet troops. Since, however, from the beginning Tito had by no means acted independently of Moscow, the development in these countries also belongs to our theme.

In the years prior to the war, Tito was in Moscow from 1935–36, when he worked in the Balkan Secretariat under the direction of Wilhelm Pieck, the German Communist.[43] At the end of 1937, he was installed, at Moscow's instigation, as General Secretary of the Yugoslav Communist Party. Before he finally returned to Yugoslavia, he translated the "History of the Communist Party of the Soviet Union" which had just been published and which became in a short time the handbook of Revolution for Communists all over the world.[44]

When in the summer of 1941 the Russo-German war began, Tito quickly showed that he understood something of Communist tactics. Supported by the not inconsiderable Partisan Army he had gathered around him a few months previously when Yugoslavia collapsed, he made the offer of a joint effort to the other resistance groups in the country, amongst which was that headed by Colonel Mihailović. But the cooperation was of short duration, since there was much distrust on both sides. As early as November, 1941, Tito made a basic change of front. From then on, his main targets in the struggle were his internal opponents, and he let the war against the German Occupation recede into the background. He drove all non-Communist forces into the enemy camp in order to pave the way for undivided sway for himself in Yugoslavia. At the same time, in the little Serbian town of Užice, not far from the Bosnian border, he made a first attempt to proclaim a "People's Republic". This, however, collapsed after a few weeks.[45] At the beginning of 1942, Tito's partisans in Montenegro undertook a second venture of this kind by setting up a dictatorship in the region of Mount Durmitor, and, indeed, on February 8, he went so far as to proclaim Montenegro a Federal State of the Soviet Union.[46] Here, too, the experiment quickly came to grief.

This self-willed procedure of Tito certainly stands in marked contrast to the tactics of concealment which, with an eye on the Grand Alliance, the Kremlin was enjoining on all Communists in those days. He was therefore reproved by Moscow and told to subject his tactics and actions to a "serious overhaul".[47] Tito did not feel himself called upon to use the methods of the "three-cornered war" which since the 1930s had been tried out by the Chinese Government in the fight against the Japanese and the Kuomintang. In November, 1942, he so far yielded to criticism in that he had a formally non-party "Anti-Fascist Council of the National Liberation of Yugoslavia" (AVNOJ) set up at Bihać in Bosnia, though this did not completely satisfy Moscow, since it seemed too much a counter-Government to the Yugoslav *émigré* Government in London.[48] Tito continued the fight against Mihailović although in the meantime the Colonel had been appointed Minister of War by the *émigré* Government in London.[49] But Tito was lucky. Since, during the 1942–43 winter, Mihailović more and more clearly avoided accepting orders from London, the Communist leader's star rose in the West also. This did not, however, prevent him from registering at the end of 1943 massive protests against the British landing in the Balkans. At the same time AVNOJ openedly turned its back on the *émigré* Government which had temporarily moved to Cairo, and proclaimed its own Executive Council a Provisional Government.[50]

By 1944, Tito had so strengthened his power that the British Government, which regarded Yugoslavia as falling within the British sphere of interest, believed it necessary to come to grips with him. After Churchill had got Stalin to confirm the British interest in Yugoslavia, in August the British Prime Minister invited Tito to Naples for a talk, in the course of which he asked Tito whether he wished to introduce socialism into Yugoslavia after the Soviet pattern. Tito's reply, that Yugoslavia because of its peculiar circumstances could not without more ado become Communist, seemed to leave possibilities for the future open.[51] Since Tito, at the next discussion with Dr. Subašić, the new Prime Minister of the *émigré* Government, declared himself in agreement with the recognition of King Peter and an amalgamation of the two Yugoslav Governments, Churchill was satisfied with the outcome, and Mihailović was now finally allowed to be dropped. It seems certain that Tito's tactical change of front took place in closest agreement with the Soviet leaders.[52]

In the summer of 1944, most of the mountain and forest regions were already in the hands of the Partisans. The lowlands and the towns were liberated in two phases – Serbia, Macedonia and the greater part of Bosnia and Dalmatia in the autumn of 1944, the remaining parts of the country to the north and east not until May, 1945. Here we are concerned only on the fringe with the fact that rivalry broke out between the Soviet Army and Tito's troops. What is more important is that the "National Liberation Front", the name of which was altered at the time to the classic designation of "Popular Front", was able throughout the country to form its "People's Committees", dominated from the outset by the Communists. The Communists also held the Army and the police firmly in their hands. A leading member of the Communist Party named Ranković built up the secret political police (OZNa), which soon had at their disposal an extensive network of agents.[53]

Impressed by Tito's position, Churchill, during a visit to Moscow in October, 1944, had already conceded that the Soviet and the British interests in Yugoslavia should be in the relation of 50 : 50.[54] However, the next year it was soon seen that a relationship of this composition was not possible. The democratic politicians who, returning from exile, had joined the Yugoslav Government, were obliged to confirm that they had no power and were simply not consulted by their colleagues. Tito and his people were firmly determined to surrender nothing of their power and to re-shape the country according to the principles of the realisation of which they had been dreaming for years. How far they wished to go in the full flush of victory is seen by Tito's invitation to the Soviet Ambassador to look upon the Yugoslav Communists as "representatives of a future Soviet Republic and not as the representatives of a foreign State." [55]

There is no direct connection between Tito's successes in Yugoslavia and the Communist conquest of Albania. In 1942, at Moscow's instruction, the Albanian Communists had to subordinate themselves to Tito, and from then on the events in the two countries ran parallel with each other. When Tito had to form his "National Liberation Front", he also ordered Enver Hoxha's Albanian Communists to set up a "National Front", which, however, in Albania remained even more clearly a mere façade.[56] Here the Albanian Abbas Kupi, a true factionist of ex-King Zog and the West, played a similar role to Mihailović. During the years 1943 and 1944, he was caught in the pincers between the Albanian and Yugoslav Communists. Since British help was not forthcoming, he was unable to hold his ground. In May, 1944, in Berat, the "National Liberation Committee of Albania" (LNC) declared itself the national Government, under Hoxha's leadership.[57]

When in the autumn of 1944 the German troops evacuated Albania, the Partisans and the LNC moved in after them. By November they were in Tirana. By this time Kupi was so weak that there remained nothing for him but flight. He rowed in a boat across the Adriatic to Italy.[58] After the victory, Enver Hoxha re-christened the "Liberation Front" the "Democratic Front", without anything of the Communist domination being changed.

(e) Hungary

Hungary had taken part in the war against the Soviet Union on the side of Germany though it did not declare war on the Western

Powers. Therefore, when the German defeats in the east forecast the change in the course of the war, the Hungarian leaders of State soon turned to the Western Powers with a request to arrange for an armistice. Since the Regent, Admiral Horthy, and M. Kállay, the Prime Minister, clearly recognised the Soviet danger, they repeatedly tried to ensure Hungary's freedom in the only possible way – by urgently entreating the West to send troops to Hungary.[59] When the Western Powers referred the Hungarians to the Soviet Union, the Hungarians followed this advice only hesitantly, and then tried to get Moscow to accept the condition that, apart from Soviet troops, British and American troops should also participate in the occupation of their country.[60] However, the armistice agreement, which was finally signed on October 10, 1944, in Moscow, never entered into effect, since the Germans arrested Horthy and his Government, occupied the country, and handed the Government over to the "Arrow and Cross" men, the Hungarian Fascists, who carried on with the fighting.

Hungary had already played a part in the joint deliberations of the Allies, on December 1, 1943, at the Teheran Conference of the Big Three. When, in connection with the plans for the dismemberment of Germany, Churchill put forward his pet idea of a Danubian Federation, Stalin, suspicious, asked him whether, in such a combination, Hungary and Roumania also should not be drawn into the association. The Soviet Prime Minister emphatically urged that Hungary, Bulgaria and Roumania should continue to exist as independent States. Apparently he had immediately realised that what Churchill had in mind was a sort of cross-bar on the Danube that could be directed only against the Soviet Union, as, indeed, Churchill allowed to be glimpsed when he asked Stalin whether the latter could possibly have in mind a "Europe of little states, all disjointed, with no larger units at all".[61]

For Hungary, as for Yugoslavia, an equal division of interest for both sides was envisaged in the agreement about spheres of military operations in the Balkans, discussed between Churchill and Stalin in October, 1944, in Moscow.[62] When, in December, 1944, after the conquest of part of Hungary, the Soviets formed a Provisional Government, Moscow formally held to this agreement by appointing not a Communist but General Béla Miklós to be Prime Minister. However, here, too, in the train of the Soviet troops came the secret police and a number of Hungarian Communists from exile. These were enabled forthwith to rebuild their party apparatus, with enormous material assistance from the Red Army.

In Hungary, just as in other countries, the Soviet tactics were aimed not at the immediate realisation of a domination by one single party based on the Soviet prototype. Instead, an instruction was given for the formation of a four-party régime. Besides the Communist Party there were to be the traditional Small Farmers' and Social Democratic parties, as well as a "National Peasant Party", the so-called village investigators, whose job, like that of Groza's "Ploughmen's Front" in Roumania, was thought of as being to prejudice the conservative Farmers' Party to the greatest possible extent. Since the Communists took their task very much to heart, in the spring of 1945 their agitators could be seen riding about the countryside in Soviet army vehicles attending to the constitution of the afore-mentioned four parties, which were then amalgamated to form the "National Committee of Liberation".[63]

In the first Government, the Communists left the Ministry of the Interior to Ferenc Erdei, of the National Peasant Party. With him it was, however, in good hands. He was more nearly inclined to the Communists than he was to his own party adherents, and he allowed the police to fall completely under Communist control. In place of the Ministry of the Interior, the Communists had retained the Ministry of Agriculture, because they hoped to gain sympathy for a drastic land reform, which was certainly necessary in Hungary. As early as March, 1945, Imre Nagy, the Minister of Agriculture, issued the appropriate decrees, and a start was made with the greatest haste in carrying them out.

Apart from the continuing measures of terrorisation which the Communists were in a position to take under the protection of the Soviets, in the summer of 1945 they pursued two aims in the field of domestic policy. They attempted to tame the Small Farmers' Party and to overthrow the Social Democrats. The former attempt was as complete a failure as the latter was a success. The Hungarian Social Democrats, who earlier on had already been weakened by corruption, had just as little success as the trade unions had in warding off Communist infiltration. By the time their leader, Károly Peyer, had returned from the German concentration camp at Mauthausen, it was already too late. At the Budapest communal elections, held during the summer as a try-out for general elections, the Social Democrats put forward a joint list of candidates with the Communists. They had capitulated.

However, the result of these elections now cast all Communist calculations to the winds. In the certain expectation that in a large city such as Budapest it was impossible for a Peasant Party to win, they had themselves advocated free elections. The Small Farmers' Party, however, received 51 per cent. of the votes. Thereupon the Communists lost their liking for free elections. Marshal Voroshilov, the Soviet Commander-in-Chief, had the Small Farmers' Party leaders brought before him, and suggested to them that for the parliamentary elections they draw up a combined list of all four parties. He offered them 40 per cent., then 45 per cent., and finally 47.5 per cent. of the seats if only they would acquiesce in his proposal. Nevertheless, the Party's Executive Committee decided by a majority to put up their own candidates. Not without more ado did Voroshilov submit to this. Instead, he told the Small Farmers' Party that, irrespective of the election results, the four-party coalition must remain in being. Only then, for the second time, did he sanction free elections.

The new election results provided yet another surprise. Although it was the Communists who had proclaimed the land reform, they had to be satisfied with 17.7 per cent. of the votes, while the Small Farmers secured 57 per cent. It was the greatest victory ever achieved since the war by a democratic party in a Soviet-occupied country. Nothwithstanding this, their victory was stolen from them. The promise that the four-party coalition would be continued after the elections now provided the basis for the appropriate manipulation. The Communists abused the promise, which had been extorted by blackmail, by a barefaced – though successful – trick. At the government negotiations, in November, 1945, they announced that they would not take part in the Government if they were not given the Ministry of the Interior. It was, of course, only due to the support of the Soviets that this impudent demand could be carried out.

Imre Nagy, the originator of the land reform, was now Minister of the Interior. He extended the Soviet influence over the police. And with that, the Communists considered they had achieved enough as a first step. The Small Farmers' Party was able to console itself with being able to fill the post of Prime Minister.

(f) Czechoslovakia

Czechoslovakia was the only European country which, at the time when it was occupied by the Red Army, had a contractual alliance with the Soviet Union. The "Treaty of Friendship, Mutual Assistance and Cooperation after the War" had been signed on December 12, 1943, in Moscow by the former President of Czechoslovakia, Dr. Eduard Beneš, as President of the Czechoslovak émigré Government, which, like the Polish émigré Government, had also found asylum in London. Even before the war, Beneš was pro-Russian and with an almost friendly disposition towards the Soviets, above all having regard to the menace of Nazi Germany. He considered it necessary to lean towards the Soviet Union in order to guarantee the security of his country.[64] However, the alliance with Moscow was made easier for him through his belief in the possibility of a lasting cooperation of the so different "democracies" in the east and the west.[65] Moreover, at the time the treaty was concluded, shortly after the Teheran "summit conference", he foresaw that in the course of the war the Red Army would succeed in reaching Central Europe and, therefore, Czechoslovakia also[66], and he wanted to adjust himself to this position in good time. The negotiations in Moscow and the contents of the treaty that was concluded seemed to him right. Stalin repeatedly assured him in every way that the Soviet Union would neither interfere in Czechoslovakia's internal affairs nor claim any part of Czechoslovak national territory – as, for

106

example, the Carpatho-Ukraine, which had been allocated to Czechoslovakia in 1919 at St. Germain.[67] Therefore, on his return from Moscow, Beneš, in a talk with Churchill, signalised the Russian situation as "very hopeful".[68]

In spite of this, when in the autumn of 1944 the Red Army entered Czech territory, the Soviet promises soon showed themselves to be a delusion. The first thing the Soviets took in hand was blackmail. In the twinkling of an eye, new officials friendly to the Soviets were installed in the Carpatho-Ukraine; anti-Communists were arrested and carried off; and the delegates of the *émigré* Government were obstructed in the carrying out of their duties. After the voice of the people had been suppressed in this fashion, the Soviet radio stations began to quote telegrams to Stalin in which inhabitants of the Carpatho-Ukraine allegedly declared that it was "the eternal dream of Ruthenia to live in one family with the Ukrainian people".[69] When M. Fierlinger, the Czechoslovak Ambassador in Moscow, made a protest to the Soviet Government on behalf of his Government, he received a peerless reply: "As we have promised you, and as it is stipulated in the Soviet-Czechoslovak treaty, we are not entitled, and we do not wish to interfere in your internal affairs. Therefore it is difficult for us to help you in solving your problems in the Sub-carpathian Ukraine." In an exchange of letters with Beneš, Stalin declared, with a shrug of his shoulders: "As the question was raised by the population of the Subcarpathian Ukraine itself, it will be necessary to solve it." [70] The solution consisted in Czechoslovakia's having, in June, 1945, to surrender the province to the Soviet Union, with Molotov asserting that "an age-old dream of the much-afflicted people" [71] of the Carpatho-Ukraine had thereby been realised.

With the formation of the new Czechoslovak Government, too, the Soviet Government transgressed the principle, laid down in Article 4 of the 1943 treaty, of "non-interference in the internal affairs of other signatory Powers". Since the Red Army managed to reach Czechoslovakia far earlier than did the armies of the Western Powers, the Soviet Government was able to have Beneš return to his homeland from London via Moscow. However, in the Soviet capital Beneš had placed before him, by Klement

Gottwald, the Czech Communist leader, not only a complete Government programme but also a full list of Ministers, in which the most important positions of authority were reserved to the Communists. Protected by the Soviets, the Communists were able to fill from the very first day the posts of Minister of the Interior, to whom the police were subordinate, the Minister of Information and Education, in whose province lay propaganda and scholastic affairs, and the Minister of Agriculture, by which they hoped to make themselves popular through the parcelling-out of the country in the Sudeten German areas.[72] Zdeněk Fierlinger, a former Social Democrat who had been converted to Communism during his period of office as Ambassador in Moscow, was nominated Prime Minister. Beside him, as Deputy Prime Minister, was Klement Gottwald, the official Party Chairman and former member of the Comintern. Similar demands were made on behalf of the Army. Here the Soviets had ready, among others, General Svoboda, the Commander of the Czech Brigade in the Soviet Army. Their estimate of Beneš was proved to be right. Instead of protesting against the massive interference in his country's domestic affairs, he accepted the list and continued on his way.[73]

But even now the Soviets did not allow him to return to his country. Beneš was detained with his Cabinet for a month in Košice in Slovakia without contact with London and without communication with the advancing Soviet troops, who in the meantime had everywhere installed, as communal administrations, Communist-dominated "People's Committees", after the pattern in other countries. The Soviets presumably wanted first to ensure that they were able to occupy the whole country before allowing Beneš and his Government to come to power.

In April and May the American troops, who crossed the Czechoslovak border on April 18, had the possibility of thrusting forward deep into Czechoslovakia, on to the Moravia, as their Commander, General Patton, intended.[74] But the chance was missed. Once again the Soviet concealment tactics, which had for so long lulled the West into a feeling of security, proved themselves successful. With a simple protest, the Soviets succeeded in nailing the American armies down on the line Carlsbad-Pilsen-

Budweis [75], from where they had quietly to look on while the Czechoslovak capital was occupied by Soviet troops.

In the Czechoslovak Government, which took up its activities in Prague in May, the Communists had sufficient power at their disposal to ensure their authority. Nosek, the Communist Minister of the Interior, saw to it that the police, and particularly the "National Security Corps" (SNB), were systematically interspersed with Communists. In the Army, too, the Communists penetrated swiftly and thoroughly. The radio was dominated by Kopecký, the Communist Minister of Propaganda. The country was plunged into an ecstasy of revolution, in the course of which the Communists especially profited from the expulsion of the Germans from the Sudeten region to whip up chaos, bewilderment and ferocity to a climax.

In 1945, the Communists in Czechoslovakia could have snatched the whole of the power had they wished.[76] If they desisted from doing so, it was certainly not out of any feeling of humanity or with regard to others who thought differently. Since Gottwald, the Communist leader, had tarried so long in Moscow, it may be assumed that he acted in closest accord with the Soviet leaders when in 1945–46 he evoked the impression that there are also Communists "temperate and patriotic".

(g) Austria and Germany

When in April, 1945, the Soviet troops reached Austria, everywhere they did what they had been accustomed to doing – set up a Government corresponding to what they thought proper. Without concerning themselves in the least about their allies' request to postpone this step, at the end of April they appointed Dr. Karl Renner State Chancellor. Nor did they forget to instal as Minister of the Interior Karl Honner, a Communist trained in Moscow. Another Communist, Johann Koplenig, who had become Vice-Chancellor, made haste in a public speech on May 13 to intercede for the establishment in Austria of a "genuine People's Democracy".[77]

The Soviets clearly felt themselves masters of the country. They looked upon the 74-year-old Renner, an upright Social Democrat, as a friendly advertisement, as they did Radescu and Beneš. Renner had been hoodwinked by the story that his appointment had been made in agreement with the Western Powers, so that he was forced to assume that all over Austria nothing stood in the way of his activity. In reality, however, the Western Powers had no thought of acknowledging without more ado the Government installed by the Soviets, above all since, in spite of urgent remonstrances in Moscow [78], their Missions were prevented from flying to Vienna. For months it was uncertain whether the country would not break up into a western and an eastern part as a result of the Soviets' despotic procedure.[79]

In Berlin the situation was quite different from the very beginning, since at the time the city was taken no new German Government was envisaged. However, in that part of Germany occupied by them, the Soviets felt themselves just as much master of the house as they did in Austria. This was already shown by the unconcern with which they handed over the whole of the territories east of the Oder-Neisse Line to Poland without asking their allies, although no agreement had been reached at Yalta as to the amount of territory to be ceded to Poland. Nor can one perceive much regard for the Western Allies in the Soviet actions in Berlin in the first weeks after the city's capture, particularly as far as the internal political arrangements were concerned.

Just as they did in the case of Czechoslovakia and Hungary, the Soviet leaders early on evolved, for Germany, too, particular tactics for the political sphere. As in the former countries, they did not aim at an immediate sovietisation. For executing their policies, they despatched to Germany at the end of April a band of trusted Communists, headed by Walter Ulbricht. During the journey, the group was precipitately greeted by Soviet officers as the "new German Government".[80] On arrival in Berlin, Ulbricht gave his minions the job of setting up district administrations – usually with a Social Democrat or bourgeois burgomaster, but with reliable Communists to superintend the police, personnel matters and popular education. He appended the classic directive: "It is surely quite clear: it must look democratic, but we must hold everything in our hands." [81]

With this, Ulbricht formulated a recipe that may rank as a maxim for the policy of all Communist parties in the Soviet-occupied countries. The Soviet leaders, who were doubtless responsible for this instruction, had good grounds for still continuing for some time their concealment tactics, which had stood the test so well during the war.

2. GROWING RESISTANCE IN THE WEST

The Western Powers, who had been drawn into the war to rescue the freedom of Europe from Hitler, could not permanently look quietly on while great parts of the Continent fell into subjugation by another dictator, but it was a long time before they fully recognised the new danger. So far as Germany is concerned one must certainly not level reproaches at a man like Churchill if he regarded the second World War as "all one and as a Thirty Years' War" [82] of the British, French, Russians and Americans against Germany, since it was Hitler who had conjured up this unholy coalition. But, looking at the matter objectively, it is to be maintained that hatred of Nazi Germany, combined with the delusions in regard to the Soviets, for a long time diverted the Western Powers from recognising the Soviet danger. During the war it was only a question of friend or foe. "Characteristically", writes a British historian, "for years having thundered against Stalinism, Churchill during the war concentrated the whole of his forceful personality and tremendous energy upon defeating Stalin's most deadly enemy, and thereby, with American aid, he opened the gates of Eastern Europe to the Russian invasion". [83]

The Western Powers' mistrust was first aroused by the Soviet attitude towards Poland. In the Polish question, however, two circumstances took place which favoured the Soviets. The British Government held the Soviet demand for the eastern districts of Poland justified, and therefore considered that the opposition of the *émigré* Government was stubborn nationalism and showed so little understanding for it that the leaders in Moscow ranged themselves against the *émigré* Poles in London. In addition, Stalin's argument that, for reasons of security, the Soviet Union

111

was dependent on a "friendly" Poland had an illuminating effect, though there was no venturing to get quite clear what a Russian Communist who regarded the whole non-Communist world as hostile meant by a "friendly" State. Rather, the Western leaders at first preferred to make the theme of the Soviet need for security, which was the mainspring of Moscow policy, their own [84], and, for the rest, placed their trust in the future.

Still, the Polish example warned them to be careful. Churchill would have been no good trustee of British interests had he not in the spring and autumn of 1944 given thought as to how the Balkans, or at least a large part of South-East Europe, could be rescued from incorporation within the Soviet sphere of power. In spite of the urgent appeals of some of the countries affected, Churchill saw no possibility of helping through the despatch of Western troops, particularly after his project of a Balkan landing had finally been buried at Teheran. The American Government showed itself uninterested in the Balkan questions. Roosevelt was wont to smile sympathetically at the zeal manifested by Churchill. For him the main thing was that America did not become enmeshed in the obscure, horrible Balkan entanglements.[85] Thus Churchill found himself alone and having to rely on political means when he addressed himself to aiding the Balkan States as best he could.

He seized at the classic medium of spheres of influence, camouflaged as spheres of military interest, for to the Americans "power politics" was an abomination. He left Roumania and Bulgaria to the Soviets and claimed Greece and Yugoslavia for Great Britain and the West. When this "Balkan Agreement", which had been sealed during Churchill's visit to Moscow in October, 1944, became known after the war, it was severely criticised, particularly by the South-East European *émigré* politicians and the Americans. Disappointed and enraged, they saw confirmed that the Soviet Union had only occupied and sovietised those countries left to it voluntarily by the West – just as it had the Caucasian countries a quarter of a century before.

Nevertheless, closer examination does not support this attitude. As will presently be seen [86], only in the case of Greece has the

Balkan Agreement held good for the West. Neither in Yugoslavia nor in Hungary has it been able to prevent incorporation within the "socialist" camp. The agreement was merely nothing but a desperate attempt to save one more part of South-East Europe without effective means. Today it must be affirmed that the significance of the Balkan agreement vis-à-vis the political fate of South-East Europe is overrated. The agreement was "merely a recognition of the military situation", as one expert has said.[87] Only if the Western Powers had been prepared, and in a position, to occupy militarily other Balkan countries beyond Greece could they have obstructed the Soviet Union. The opportunity to do so existed, at least in Czechoslovakia and Yugoslavia. It was, above all, the American military leaders who were not prepared to do so. Far from every political consideration, they saw only the task of defeating Germany as quickly and as thoroughly as possible.

Moreover, the reproach that, in the Balkan Agreement, the West delivered the countries over to the Soviet Union without, so to speak, reservation goes too far, inasmuch as Churchill expressly recognised a preponderant – though not an exclusive – interest in these States on the part of Moscow. Otherwise the curious listing of percentages of influence (for example, Bulgaria 75 per cent. Soviet influence and 25 per cent. Western influence) is not to be understood. By no means did the British Premier wish to leave these countries to Soviet domination without some barrier in between. By laying down the percentages he wished at least to achieve that in the new Governments the Communists could not eliminate all free elements from the very beginning.[88] He did not suspect that apart from this it was in conformity with Soviet tactics to allow counterfeit multi-party régimes of the "National Front" type to develop.

Just as the Balkan Agreement, the Yalta Conference, too, is usually overrated. One American expert has rightly affirmed that none of the critics of Roosevelt and Churchill has yet proved that either of them "granted anything (to the Russians) that they were in a position to withhold".[89] Compared to the relationship between the respective military strengths and the new partitioning of the spheres of influence in Europe, as they were a natural development moulded by the course of the war, the results of the Crimea conference are almost negligible. Another American historian has coined the formula: "Thus concessions at Yalta inevitably reflected the powerful position of the Soviet Union..." [90] With an attentive perusal of the conference protocols, it is found that both sides, while still not keeping their fingers off the other's sphere of influence, already at bottom recognised them. Apart from the tedious negotiations about Poland, which have so frequently been described [91], the discussion concerning a "Declaration on Liberated Europe" mainly deserves notice in this regard.

This Declaration, which had been drafted by the American State Department, provides the best testimony that in the spring of 1945 the Western Powers by no means awaited the development in the East and the South-East of Europe completely without misgivings. Apart from the Polish and other *émigrés*, Averell Harriman, the American Ambassador in Moscow, had also warned his Government in good time.[92] The American State Department thereupon drew up a plan to preserve the freedom of the liberated countries by purely political means and, if possible, without military intervention. In essence, this plan envisaged the establishment of a "Provisional Security Council for Europe"[93], or, as it later came to be called, an "Emergency High Commission for Liberated Europe". [94] This organ, composed of representatives of the United States, the Soviet Union, the United Kingdom and France, was to help in the solving of problems such as the return home of certain *émigré* Governments, the formation of provisional Governments, the maintenance of order, and the early holding of elections.[95] In other words, the American State Department, which had, indeed, never recognised the Balkan Agreement's "spheres of military operation" as political spheres of influence, did not want to leave to the Soviet Union the "ordering" of the occupied territories but wanted to take an active share in it itself.

The idea was, however, a miserable failure. At the preliminary discussions of the American delegation, on February 4, 1945, in Yalta, Roosevelt spoke, seemingly without lengthy consideration and talking-over [96], against such a "large" body, and, completely misapprehending its task, said that he himself envisaged periodic meetings of the Foreign Ministers. The kernel of the American proposal was thereby settled, to the great disappointment of Mr. Stettinius, the United States Secretary of State.[97] There remained the "Declaration on Liberated Europe", which contained the same idea in declaratory form. Here the "Emergency Commission" was at first replaced by "Special Commissions"[98] of the four Governments, then still more vaguely by "appropriate machinery".[99] In this form, Roosevelt placed the document before the Conference on February 9.

The following manipulation of the Declaration provides a spectacle savouring of tragi-comedy. Stalin and Molotov at first proposed a small supplementation under which the Great Powers were to bind themselves to support, in the countries in question, persons "who took an active part in the struggle against German Occupation".[100] Stalin thereby hinted what Molotov quite openly said to his colleagues the following day: the purpose of the supplementation was to prevent "recurrencies similar to those in Greece" (where a Communist attempt at insurrection was being combated by British troops).[101] In other words, a free rein was to be given to the Communist underground movements. After the Soviet attempt to achieve this amendment by making use of the element of surprise had failed, as an alternative Molotov proposed to the Western Foreign Ministers a second amendment: that the last remnant of the "Emergency High Commission", the "appropriate machinery", should now also be struck out and replaced by "mutual consultation" of the Great Powers.[102] In comparison to the imputations contained in the first supplementary proposal, this second amendment Stettinius and Eden considered an advance and intimated their agreement. Thus the last teeth had been drawn from the American plan. What remained was a piece of paper.[103]

At this time the Western Powers ought to have decided to "roll back" Communism, to obstruct the sovietisation of East-Central and South-East Europe. For this, however, neither the leaders of State nor public opinion were prepared, since thoughts were still ranged in the mood of the "Great Alliance". The common front into which Hitler had forced the West and the East turned out to be in favour of the East, in view of the geographical conditions and the steadiness with which the Soviets pursued their aims. Since the West could neither employ force nor wished to threaten with force, there remained only political and diplomatic means, as applied in the cases of Poland, Yugoslavia and the "Declaration on Liberated Europe". These means soon proved themselves unserviceable. As early as February and March, 1945, the Soviet Government showed, by handing over the Oder-Neisse territories to Poland and by overthrowing the Radescu Government in Roumania, that it regarded the Soviet-occupied part of Europe as its sovereign territory in which it would govern and administer without regard to the Western Powers.

It is questionable whether the development would have taken a different course had the idea of the "Emergency High Commission" not been thrust on one side by Roosevelt in view of the Soviet attitude towards the "Declaration on Liberated Europe", it can with certainty be assumed that Stalin would nevertheless not have agreed to this direction and that the West would have had to put up with it, just as they had to do so in the extensive re-drafting of the Declaration, only in that case the responsibility for later events would have been clearer. However, the "Declaration on Liberated Europe", too, has, at least to a certain extent, served the purpose of showing the world where the fault lay.[104]

For the West, the Declaration represented a standard of measurement by means of which the development in the countries in question could be assessed. As little as the "Declaration on Liberated Europe" helped the countries concerned, it served to emphasise the painful process of recollection in the course of which the West, in 1945 and 1946, gradually regained awareness of the Soviet danger. What the Soviets, and with their help the Communists in Poland, Roumania and Bulgaria, have done, stands in such clear contrast to the spirit of the Yalta agreements that the Western Powers have not been able to preserve their belief in Moscow's loyalty, even with the most generous interpretation.

It is no accident that, a few months later at the Potsdam Conference, it was precisely over Roumania and Bulgaria that the bitterest controversy developed.[105] Following the "Declaration on Liberated Europe", the Western Powers could at least have expected to be heard before decisive changes took place in those countries. That, instead, the Soviets set up completely despotic puppet régimes was a clear violation of the spirit of this Declaration, and was so considered by the Western Powers. For that reason, at Potsdam the new American President Truman was obliged to refuse recognition of the Governments [106] and called for free elections.[107] Moreover, on the basis of the Yalta Declaration, the Western statesmen were easily able to reject Stalin's attempt to dismiss concern about the freedom of Bulgaria and Roumania as interference in the domestic affairs of these countries.[108] They had a clear legal entitlement to concern themselves with the conditions in South-East Europe, and they had become sufficiently suspicious to view with distrust Stalin's assurances that he had no desire to bolshevise any other countries.

3. THE BLOODLESS CONQUEST OF CENTRAL GERMANY

Although the period of the unnatural alliance between West and East was rapidly drawing to a close, in the summer of 1945 the Soviet Union was able to contrive one more bloodless conquest, fraught with the gravest consequences, at the cost of the Free World. In July, the Soviet troops were able to push forward towards Thuringia and the western parts of Saxony-Anhalt and Mecklenburg, thereby extending the Soviet sphere of domination still further towards the West by some 125 miles.

To enable this new Soviet success to appear in the right light it is necessary to cast a glance at the detailed circumstances attendant on the military occupation of Germany. It is uncontested that, at the end of 1944 and in the spring of 1945, the troops of the Western Powers could have thrust forward more quickly and farther than actually happened. Two circumstances seem to have prevented the Western leaders from seizing the chance afforded by the respective military strengths: the overrating of the German power of defence, which in certain respects was increased through Hitler's senseless Ardennes offensive, and the illusion that the West-East alliance could be continued beyond the war. S. Fuller, the British war historian, correctly describes the situation at the time when he says: "The war, in fact, had ceased to be a strategical problem, and having entered upon its purely political course, the race was no longer between armed forces, but instead between two political systems: on the one hand that of the Western Allies, and on the other that of Russia. Which of these two would dominate Eastern and Central Europe – this was the question?"[109] Unfortunately the Western leaders did not early enough recognise this question posed by history.

By contrast, the Soviet leaders were completely clear about the prospects and dangers these months offered. The ideological basis of their policy had never, even during the war, permitted the war's primary aim, the defeat of Germany, to be confused with the actual aim, the expansion of Communism and Soviet power. For that reason, as soon as the war "ceased to be a strategic problem" and entered on a "purely political course", the power politics point of view and the inevitable distrust of the "capitalist" world once more gained the upper hand. This was reflected particularly clearly in the Soviet reaction towards the West with the first feelers in respect of a German peace. Whether the Soviet leaders now feared that, now that Nazi Germany was beaten, the Western Powers would continue the war against the Soviet Union – possibly with German help – or whether they now wished to prevent, through a premature armistice between Germany and the Western Allies, being cheated of parts of the fruits of victory, at any rate their reaction was so sharp and insulting that it caused the Western Governments to be conscious of the first inroad into the illusion that the cooperation could last.

While Stalin addressed himself to remoulding the victory over Germany into a victory of socialism over capitalism, he called for further energetic support from the Western Powers and bitterly reproached them when they started negotiating with the S.S. General Wolff about the capitulation of the German troops in the south. In a message to Churchill, Stalin, using the tone of conscious admonition, spoke of the "duties and rights of an ally"[110], which he himself had nevertheless continually infringed. He bitterly complained of the "more than strange and unaccountable" attitude of the German soldiers who delivered into the

118

hands of the Western Allies towns like Osnabrück and Mannheim without a struggle when the Red Army had to fight desperately for "obscure" little villages.[111]

Nevertheless, Stalin's anxiety that, through accepting a German capitulation on the Western Front, the Western Powers wished to anticipate him by occupying Central Germany with Berlin was unfounded. General Eisenhower, the Western Allied Commander-in-Chief, had no perception of the political importance of the capture of the German capital. On March 31, 1945, he declared over the radio, in regard to Berlin: "That place has become, so far as I am concerned, nothing but a geographical location und I have never been interested in these."[112] The British Field Marshal Montgomery believes that the Western Allies could have captured Berlin, Vienna and Prague before the Soviets, provided their commanders had given them appropriate orders. But there were no orders since the rosy-hued haze of the war coalition still prevented Western politicians and military men from seeing clearly.

Only at one place did it come to a regular race between the Western troops and the Red Army. After the Soviets had succeeded in encircling Berlin in the second half of April, they pressed feverishly on through Mecklenburg in the direction of Lübeck. Apparently they wanted to reach Schleswig-Holstein before Montgomery, probably for the same purpose for which, at the discussions about the Zones of Occupation, they wanted to bring the island of Fehmarn within their sphere: so as to be able, via the German bridge, to "liberate" Denmark as well and bring it under their wing. For the Soviets the aim was doubtless important. As they showed with the occupation of the Danish island of Bornholm and their obstinate refusal to evacuate it again, they tended at that time to regard the Baltic as a Red inland lake. Churchill, however, promptly recognised the danger. "It is thought most important that Montgomery should take Lübeck as soon as possible", he wrote. "There is no reason why the Russians should occupy Denmark, which is a country to be liberated and to have its sovereignty restored."[113] Montgomery received an additional army corps and reached the Baltic before the Red Army.[114]

119

Apart from this special case, the Western Allies made no particular efforts to press forward into Germany more quickly than the Soviets in order to secure possessions. It was without political intentions that, in the course of the operations, the Western troops, favoured by the fact that the Wehrmacht defence was always directed preponderantly towards the East, advanced in part far beyond the zonal boundary that had been envisaged for later military occupation, so that in May, 1945, Thuringia and parts of Saxony-Anhalt and Mecklenburg also came under their military control. Had the Western Powers, as the Soviets, at this time adjudged success or failure by the strengthening or the weakening of their social systems and by the extension of their sphere of influence, they ought not to have evacuated these Central German regions. At the time, however, their thoughts were ranged on different levels.

Although Churchill later lamented the evacuation of Central Germany as a "fateful milestone for mankind"[115], it seems that no serious consideration was given to preventing the Soviets from carrying out this bloodless conquest. As early as April 18, Churchill assured, when the problem was first outlined: "I am quite prepared to adhere to the occupational zones."[116] It was only repugnant to the British Premier to leave to a partner such as the Soviet Union, so saturated with the idea of power politics, the massive prize of Central Germany without equivalent return. Of the equivalent return from the Soviets worth striving for, Churchill could only gradually form a clear picture. At the middle of April, it was still primarily a matter of the establishment of the Allied Control Council in Berlin and of a participation of the Soviet-occupied Zone in feeding West Germany.[117] At the end of April, when the Soviets were arbitrarily setting up a Government in Vienna, when they were chaining Poland to themselves by contract and delaying the reorganisation of the Government, when Tito was treating the Western Powers with impudence through his ruthless venture in Venezia Giulia, and when the hope of an unfettered development of events in Bulgaria and Roumania was proving more and more vain, in Churchill's eyes the importance of the value of Thuringia as a security in Allied possession grew. On May 11, to Truman he expressed

120

the hope that in no case would the Americans first recede from their positions before another conference of the Heads of Government, and added protestingly: "Mr. President, in these next two months the gravest matters in the world will be decided."[118] The following day the tone of his warning heightened. In another telegram to Truman, in which he coined the expression "Iron Curtain", the Premier pointed out that Poland threatened to be cut off from the West by a broad band of many hundreds of miles. "Surely it is vital now to come to an understanding with Russia, or see where we are with her, before we weaken our armies mortally or retire to the zones of occupation."[119]

But the new American President Truman was just as impervious to such ideas as his predecessor. Not for years had America looked askance, full of aversion and scorn, at the struggle of power politics in Europe, now to plunge into these controversies itself. Instead of making use of a security in their own possession, the American Government preferred to continue in amicable cooperation with the Soviets, and Churchill's advice had to be rejected because, as Truman wrote, it "would be highly disadvantageous to our relations with the Soviets".[120] Thus easily did American policy wish to continue the phantom illusion of the East-West alliance.

That being so, in this case there was a reason of great moment for cooperation with the Soviet Union. At the first meeting of the Allied Commanders-in-Chief, on June 5 in Berlin, the Soviets had declared, in a manner not to be misunderstood, that the Allied Control Council for Germany could not be established before the troops of the Western Powers had been withdrawn to the zonal boundaries that had been laid down.[121] It therefore looked for the Western Powers as though the realisation of a common policy in respect of Germany depended on their retreat. Presumably the Soviets, although they offered the Control Council as an award, had at least as much interest in that realisation as the Western Allies. At the time, Robert Murphy, Eisenhower's political adviser, expressly put forward in a report the view that the Soviets considered the Control Council as "necessary and its operation as redounding to their interests".[122] But the threat had its effect. So as not to let cooperation in Germany run aground at the start, the Western Powers decided on with-drawal.

However, when in the first days of July they relinquished their positions in Central Germany, the Western Allies yielded not only to the Soviet pressure. At the same time they secured two advantages, the importance of which should not be underestimated. In Austria the Red Army had to surrender substantial areas to the West[123], and at the same time the Soviets evacuated the agreed sectors in Berlin and Vienna in favour of the Western troops. Had the Western Powers hesitated in Thuringia, Stalin would probably have made them wait in Berlin and Vienna. However, the Western Powers rightly attributed great importance to participating in the occupation of the German and Austrian capitals, in which, after the experiences with Warsaw, Sofia and Bucharest, it was intended that independent Governments should be established.

In these circumstances it is difficult to agree with Churchill when he says that at that time the West had allowed the "best, and what might prove to have been our last, chance of durable world peace composedly to fade away."[124] If there ever was such a chance, it was folly not to have seized it much earlier. With the threat of denying Thuringia to the Soviets one would scarcely have been able to get the Soviet leaders to deny their belief in their world mission and accordingly to allow the countries occupied by them to develop freely. The Western prize of Central Germany was confronted by the Soviet prizes of Berlin and Vienna. The compromise to hold to the agreements on the zonal boundaries and the joint occupation of the capitals was an appalling disappointment for the many thousands of Germans in Thuringia and Saxony who believed themselves to be safe and who now fled west in the wake of the American troops. Politically, it was not unfair.

With the bloodless conquest of Central Germany the third phase of the Soviet expansion came to an end. The Red Army stood in the heart of Europe, and we see today that Montgomery was right when, three weeks before the Potsdam Conference, he wrote in his diary: "The immensity of the problem of the future of Germany, and of Europe, to be settled at the Big Three Conference is becoming clear. So is the divergence between the views of the Western Allies and the Russians as regards the solution. It remains to be seen whether a workable solution can be achieved. It is far more likely that eastern Europe up to the line from Lübeck to Trieste will fall under solely Russian domination and will remain so for many years." [125]

Chapter Five

CAUTIOUSNESS IN VICTORY
(1945)

> Of all the deadly weapons with which the Communists
> are threatening democracy today, patience is by far
> the most dangerous.
>
> *Mogens Lauesen in "Freiheit ohne Furcht"*

The Soviet successes in the third phase of the expansion exceeded
by far not only in extent but also in significance those in the
first two stages. By conquering the Transcaucasian republics the
Soviet Union had subjugated some seven million beings, and by
the annexations of the first years of the second World War about
20 million. In 1944–45, the Soviet empire increased by approximately 90 million persons, even if only some 1.5 million of them
were directly Soviet citizens. The first phase of the expansion
brought with it 200,000 square kilometres, the second more than
400,000 square kilometres. The fresh annexations in 1945 in
Europe were of modest proportions, bringing with them a bare
20,000 square kilometres, but the satellite empire with which
Moscow at the same time furnished itself comprised approximately 1,000,000 square kilometres.

However, more significant than the acquisition of territory and
people were the prospects for the future. While in the first two
phases of the Soviet expansion it was possible to speak of a restoration of the territorial extent of the former Czarist empire,
now the Soviet Union incontestibly extended beyond the Russian
borders and busied itself with building up a Communist empire.
Through the establishment of a "socialist camp", the territory of
the "capitalist camp" was simultaneously, and for the first time,
unmistakably restricted. From now on it was possible to speak of
the "progress of socialism". At the same time, the Soviet Union,
as the guiding force of the "socialist camp", had by the end of
the war gained, from the geographical point of view, an "ideal

sally-port"[1] for the conquest of the remainder of Europe. Within the space of a few years the Soviet Union had been elevated to being the dominant Continental Power, and its victory over the once mighty Germany was bound to fill its dependants with self-importance, its enemies with fear. When after a time the American troops withdrew[2], there remained in the whole of Europe no further serious obstacle to prevent Soviet expansion as far as the Atlantic.

From the Muscovite point of view Europe has always represented a peninsula of the land-mass of Eurasia. Now, since the Red Army had occupied half of this peninsula, and also above all held half of Europe's heart in its power, the day could not be far distant when the Red Flag would be waving over Paris and Rome. Only a few dozen miles separated the Red troops from Hamburg and the North Sea and, thereby, entrance to the Atlantic. The map must have presented to the Soviet leaders a magical attraction also to attempt to break down the last bridgehead of "capitalism" in Europe so as to complete the victory of the Revolution on the European continent.[3]

1. THREE DISCONTINUED ATTEMPTS AT EXPANSION

For the full description of the Soviet expansion, at this point mention must be made of three attempts made by the Soviet leaders, partly during the last year of the war and partly directly the war had come to an end. The countries in question – Greece, Finland and Turkey – lay on the fringe of the Soviet empire that was now developing, but they differed from each other in that each stood in a completely different relationship to the Soviet Union. Greece, as the Soviet Union itself, had been attacked by Germany; Finland had made use of the German attack on the Soviet Union to continue the struggle in Karelia that had been broken off in 1940; while Turkey had remained neutral in the decisive phase of the great war. Nevertheless, these varying attitudes formed no obstacle to the Soviet urge to expand: they merely influenced the choice of means.

In Finland, the Soviet Union wished to assert its military superiority. In Turkey, menace and intimidation were intended to induce the effect. In Greece, where an external influence had led to the conflict with the West, use had been made of the Communist underground movement. In all three cases, however, the attempts at expansion were given up after a time, and everywhere probably for the same reasons. The Soviet intentions had come up against determined resistance; the mind of the world public had become altered; and a further open pursuit of the aims might have exposed the policy of the Muscovites. To prevent a fresh conflict breaking out prematurely, the attempts were broken off and the aims postponed.

(a) Finland

The Soviet leaders thought to find on their north-west flank a suitable starting-point for their efforts at expansion in the circumstance that, from 1941, Finland had "continued" the war against the Soviet Union, broken off the previous year, so as to regain lost Karelia. When at the beginning of 1944 the Finnish State leaders sought an opportunity to withdraw from the war, the Soviet Government had transmitted to them a list of six conditions the acceptance of which would in all probability have brought the entire country into Soviet hands.

Although in the meantime Great Britain had declared war on Finland, the Soviet Government apparently considered it necessary, in its actions against this adversary, to pay regard to the sensitivities of the Western Powers. Perhaps they also disguised their intentions so as to deceive the Finnish leaders. The snares were hidden less in the actual peace terms, which called for a return to the 1940 boundaries. More damaging was the demand to intern the German troops which were in the country before initiating peace negotiations. If Finland were not in a position to do so, the Soviet Union offered to help. Since it was possible that the Finnish Army could not accomplish this task, the leaders of State would have had to reconcile themselves from the beginning with the occupation of substantial parts of Finland by the Red Army [4], added to which the country was to be burdened with reparations amounting to 600 million dollars, payable within five years. Since at the same time Karelia's important industries would have been lost, this condition, too, exceeded Finland's capacity[5], giving rise later to a comfortable excuse for measures of violence.

The Finnish leaders of State were confronted with a difficult decision. On the one hand, they knew the war was lost, and they were being pressed by Sweden and the United States to conclude peace. On the other hand, they realised that the Soviet conditions meant not only the territorial loss of certain districts but possibly the loss of freedom throughout the country. The Government heroically decided to continue the struggle, even though the outlook seemed so hopeless. On April 12, M. Linkomies, the Prime Minister, declared at a secret session of the Finnish Parliament: "After mature consideration of the conditions placed before it, the Government has unanimously come to the decision that they are inacceptable ... since acceptance of the conditions would, in the opinion of the Government, most seriously jeopardise our independence and freedom..."[6] After the Parliament had unanimously concurred in the Government decision, on April 19 the Soviet Union was informed that Finland regretted not to be able to accept the conditions.

The Soviet leaders replied to this announcement some weeks later, in June, by making a heavy attack on the Karelian peninsula. From the military point of view, this offensive, which was carried out with the employment of a tremendous quantity of aircraft, artillery and troops, had little purpose. Finland could never represent a menace to the Soviet Union, but as soon as the Red Army had reconquered the Baltic region it was sooner or later forced to cease the struggle. The Soviet troops employed in Karelia were, however, missing during the offensive in the Baltic States. Naturally all this was well-known in Moscow, too. If, nevertheless, Finland was attacked on such a massive scale, it may be suspected that the Soviet leaders – as, moreover, Allied Intelligence also confirmed – had decided "to swallow up Finland".[7]

The first days of the Soviet offensive were attended by great successes. Vyborg, the Karelian capital, was taken, the Finnish troops were forced a long way back, and the situation could once more be stabilised only by accepting German assistance (Ryti-Ribbentrop pact). Nevertheless, resistance and continuation of the war proved to be the right thing. When at the end of August new armistice negotiations were initiated, the Soviet Union imposed conditions which, though hard, permitted the country to retain its freedom and independence.

There were, in particular, two concessions made by the Soviet Government that made it possible for the Finnish Government to accept the new conditions. Instead of demanding the immediate internment of all German troops, they now set a date, even if an early one, for their withdrawal. It seems that this moderation, which saved Finland from being invaded by the Soviets, was traceable to the influence of Great Britain and the United States.[8] Reparations amounting to 300 million dollars were now demanded, half the amount called for in April. In addition, the date of payment was extended – again at British insistence[9] – from five to six years. The territorial demands were, in general, not new: Karelia, and the Arctic region of Petsamo, with its valuable nickel deposits. The only thing that was new was that, instead of Hangö, the Soviets insisted on having made over to them for fifty years the so-called Porkkala region, thus succeeding in being in direct proximity to the capital. These losses were painful, though not mortal.

Since Finland, apart from the Far North, remained spared military occupation, here, too, the Soviets were unable to instal their instruments of terror.[10] Nevertheless, the situation remained dangerous for a time. As chairman of the Allied Control Commission, the Soviet Government despatched to Finland Zhdanov, the stage-manager of the Esthonian revolution in 1940. It needed much circumspection and determination to steer the country clear of the dangers of the initial post-war period, but once the Finnish politicians realised that the Soviet Union shrank from the odium of a military intervention they skilfully utilised the room for action by taking pains to fulfil the armistice conditions while warding off every interference in internal affairs.

The tactics also proved their worth, since at the first post-war elections, on March 17, 1945, the Communists achieved a surprising success. To meet the Soviets, a "Popular Democrat" named Pekkala, who had switched over from the Social Democrats, was commissioned to form the new Government, and the Ministry of the Interior was given to a Communist named Leino. The latter at once attempted to emulate his prototypes by building up a "State police", which uncovered "conspiracies" and made many savage arrests. But since the Finnish Democrats believed themselves safe from Soviet intervention, they did not let them have their own way but placed obstacles in the way of false confessions being extracted under torture from the arrested persons. They managed to keep the constitutional State intact.[11]

(b) Greece

In Greece, a strong resistance movement under Communist leadership had sprung up during the German and Italian occupation. Like Tito's partisans in Yugoslavia, they did less battle in the last years of the war with the enemy occupation Forces than they did with the non-Communist resistance groups. Here, too, the aim was clearly Communist domination after the war had ceased. At the same time, when provisional Governments under Communist leadership were set up at Moscow's direction in the other countries of South-East and East-Central Europe, the Greek organisation E. A. M. followed suit. On March 26, 1944, a "Political Committee of National Liberation" (PEEA) was established "in the Greek mountains", and Georgios Siantos, who for decades, with interruptions, had led the Greek Communist Party, became "Minister of the Interior".[12]

The British Government, which in view of the Mediterranean passage had always looked on Greece as a neuralgic point, at once recognised the danger that a situation similar to that in Poland was developing. When a few days later the Greek troops stationed in Egypt tried by a large-scale mutiny to overthrow the *émigré* Government, whose constitutionality was being emphatically contested by the partisan Government, Churchill gave orders that the insurrection should be suppressed by force.[13] On May 4, the British Prime Minister directed his Foreign Secretary to recapitulate briefly for the Cabinet the "brutal issues" which had developed between London and Moscow "in Italy, in Roumania, in Bulgaria, in Yugoslavia and above all in Greece".[14]

From that moment the problems in the various Balkan States were just as interweaving for the British Government as they had been for a long time for the Soviet leaders. At the same time, herein, too, lies the origin of the division of the Balkans into spheres of interest that, at British suggestion, was decided on during the following weeks. Using this traditional medium of diplomacy, Churchill's primary wish was to ensure British influence in Greece.

This step produced results in Greece. At the end of July, 1944, a Soviet Mission put in its appearance at the headquarters of the Communist-led Resistance, and fourteen days later the provisional Government (PEEA) expressed its readiness to participate in the *émigré* Government with five representatives and to disband the "Political Committee of National Liberation".[15] Gnashing their teeth, the Greek Communists were obliged to concur in Moscow's direction, although more than half of the country was in their hands.

The great strategy of the Revolution took first place. Clearly the Soviet leaders had reflected that setting up of the spheres of interest in the Balkans was a profitable transaction. There were 7.5 million Greeks compared with 22 million Roumanians and Bulgars, not to speak of the 16 million inhabitants of Yugoslavia, the shepherding of whom into the Socialist fold could be left to Tito.[16]

In the early days of October, British troops landed in Greece in order to ensure the return of the *émigré* Government and to prevent the sovietisation of the country. Now matters could be clinched. If the Communist partisans allowed themselves to be disarmed, Greece would be saved from revolution. Otherwise, civil war would break out. For weeks on end the Communist Resistance was able to delay the disarmament. On December 2, their Ministers laid down their governmental offices. The next day the insurrection started.

Had the uprising been successful, Greece, just as the other countries in South-East Europe, would have been transformed into a

"People's Democracy". At first sight the Communists' chances looked favourable. The Government had nothing with which to oppose their Armed Forces. Solely the British troops could double the rebels' stakes. But so doubtful was it that the British Government would intervene that M. Papandreu, the Greek Prime Minister, immediately resigned. Although General Scobie, the Commander-in-Chief of the 5,000 British troops, called upon the rebel forces to evacuate Athens and the Piraeus at once, during the night of December 5–6 they attempted in a coup d'état to occupy the government buildings in Athens. The attempt miscarried, but it did so only because of the presence of the British.

Almost at the same time as the E. A. M. leaders decided on the coup d'état, Churchill had ordered General Scobie from London "to act as if you were in a conquered city where a local rebellion is in progress".[17] Thereupon, in place of the Greek police the British Guards had taken the government buildings over into their protection. Apparently the rebels were not prepared for this. They did not dare to attack the British soldiers. For some days a curious situation developed. It seems as if the rebels hoped that the British Government would yield to Soviet pressure and pay regard to world opinion, which was reacting very sensitively to a bombardment of Athens.[18] However, the British made use of this pause to have reinforcements brought over from Italy and concentrate their scattered forces at certain important points so as to be armed against an attack. When in the night of December 16 the E. A. M. troops at last attacked, they had missed their opportunity.

At the turn of the year, Churchill and Eden, who had personally hurried to Athens, initiated a series of political and military steps to preserve Greek freedom. The non-Communist members of the Resistance were appeased by the installation of a Regent and a Republican Prime Minister, General Plastiras.

At the same time, the rebels, counter-attacking, were repulsed by the British troops. At the middle of July, 1945, an armistice was concluded, in accordance with which E. A. M. had to vacate large parts of Central Greece. One month later the rebel leaders concluded a sort of peace treaty with the Government, under which they undertook to surrender their weapons and to disband their troops, while the Government decreed an amnesty in respect of all "political" offences committed since December 3.

The first attempt at incorporating Greece into the Soviet sphere had been frustrated. While the Greek soldiers had been fighting against their countrymen and the British soldiery, the Soviet troops had remained stationary on the country's northern boundary. The Greeks benefited neither by deliveries of arms nor by a public promise on the part of the Soviets although they were bleeding for the common cause of Socialism. As in 1936, in the Spanish Civil War, the Soviet Government found it inexpedient to aid their like-minded comrades to victory. At this time an open conflict with Great Britain did not fit in with Stalin's ideas. When, however, during these weeks he met Churchill at Yalta, he could not suppress getting in on the side a biting remark about the British procedure. It was in connection with the aforementioned discussions on the "Declaration on Liberated Europe". After Molotov had proposed the amendment whereby the political leaders of the resistance movements should receive Allied support, Stalin sarcastically let fall that Churchill need have no fear that Molotov's proposal was destined to be applied in Greece.[19] This notwithstanding, there was a sombre menace couched within his words as he added that a "very dangerous" situation would have developed in Greece if the British Prime Minister had allowed forces other than his own to go into the country. The next day Molotov publicly stated that the purpose of the proposal was "to prevent occurrences similar to those in Greece".[20]

(c) Turkey

In contrast to Finland and Greece, Turkey had managed to remain neutral up to the spring of 1945. The Soviet Union, in particular, had repeatedly urged Turkey to enter the war, but when at length, at the end of February, Turkey declared war on Germany and Japan the step had no military value, only political significance. It mainly led to the fact that Turkey also received an invitation to attend the inaugural meeting of the United Nations.

Turkey had for a long time harboured a pronounced mistrust of the Soviet Union, based in essence on apprehension of the unswerving wishes of the Russian in regard to the Straits and parts of Eastern Anatolia. As early as the autumn 1939, the Soviet Government had tried to get Turkey to conclude a pact of mutual assistance (on the Baltic pattern), which envisaged, among other things, a joint defence of the Dardanelles.[21] Turkey's refusal seems to have embittered the Soviet leaders. The following year Stalin and Molotov repeatedly complained of "Turkey's domination in the Straits", and, indeed, when in the middle of 1940, through the publication of the German White Book No. 6, the Anglo-French plans for a bombardment of Baku became known, the Soviet Union recalled its ambassador from Ankara for a time. Towards the end of 1940 the Soviets were once more pursuing the idea of a Turco-Soviet pact of mutual assistance, which, like the Hangö clause in the peace treaty with Finland which had been concluded a short while previously, envisaged the establishment of a Soviet military base on the Straits "on the basis of a long-term lease".[22] When the Russo-German war broke out in 1941, the Soviet Government was concerned to keep Turkey neutral, and it therefore assured Turkey in a Note, dated August 10, 1941, that it had "neither aggressive intent nor demands in regard to the Straits", and was prepared "carefully to observe the territorial integrity of the Turkish Republic".[23] However, the distrust was too deeply rooted to be overcome by such paper assurances. As a result of long historical experience, the Turkish leaders of State knew that Russia had always regarded the Straits as one of the goals most worth striving for, and in times when the Russians were strong they had been moved by an uncontrollable desire to expand up to the Bosphorus. It was, therefore, with mounting anxiety that Ankara watched the development of Soviet power in the last stages of the war.

It meant no great surprise for the Turkish Government when, on March 19, 1945, the Soviet Union terminated the Turco-Soviet neutrality pact of 1925, advancing the very pregnant reason that, after the far-reaching changes of the second World War, it no longer corresponded with the new conditions, and was in need of serious improvement.[24] Since the note of termination was not at first burdened with demands, Turkey politely replied, at the beginning of April, that the Turkish Government would examine with attention and the necessary good will the Soviet proposal awaited.[25] But Turkish anxieties grew when a savage campaign against Turkey was unleashed in the Soviet Press and at the same time rumours could be heard about Soviet territorial demands in Eastern Anatolia.[26] The war of nerves lasted more than two months, and then, on June 7, Molotov summoned the Turkish Ambassador to him and apprised him of the conditions for the conclusion of a new treaty. These conditions were such that, without reference to his Government, the Ambassador at once rejected them.[27]

Molotov had made two demands. They were: an adjustment of the Turco-Soviet frontier, and the ceding of military bases in the Straits.[28] Whether beyond this there was a demand, as Radio Ankara reported[29], for the formation of a "democratic" Turkish Government is unclear. In any case, to Turkey these demands, despite the threats which accompanied them, seemed wholly inacceptable. The districts of Kars and Ardahan, the return of which was demanded by the Soviet Union, had belonged to Turkey up to the Turco-Russian war of 1878. In 1921, they had been returned to Turkey by a treaty which Moscow now wished to abrogate. As a reason for this, Stalin at Potsdam merely said that the Soviet Union was justified, when entering a treaty of alliance, to fix the boundaries it would thereafter be obliged to defend.[30] This was openly-proclaimed hypocrisy since nowhere was there any third State which could violate the Soviet-Turkish frontiers. The Soviet Government was merely coy at confessing its power politics in all crudity. But the Soviet demand for the cession of military bases on the Bosphorus and the Dardanelles appeared still more dangerous. After what had happened in the Baltic countries the Turkish people understandably feared that such footholds could form a basis for the sovietisation of Turkey.

From the very first moment Turkey was determined to resist. Since, however, it did not feel capable of engaging in a trial of strength with the heavily-armed Soviet Union, it sought support from the Western Powers, particularly from Great Britain, where the people were loudly condemning the Soviet demands. In the middle of July, M. Saka, the Turkish Foreign Minister, returning from the United Nations inaugural conference at San Francisco, made a pause in London. After a talk with Mr. Eden, he announced that the regulation of the rights of passage through the Straits was not a bilateral Turco-Soviet affair but something that concerned all the signatories of the Treaty of Montreux. He publicly proclaimed the joint Turco-British standpoint. At the Potsdam Conference, which opened a few days later, Churchill took up a decisive position on the side of Turkey and, indeed, managed to get Stalin to yield in the frontier question. On the other hand, in regard to the Straits Stalin once again protested that "a small state, supported by Great Britain, held a great state by the throat and gave it no outlet". But the only concession the Soviets were able to secure in the matter was the assurance that in future the Dardanelles would be accessible to the whole world.[31]

The Western Powers were very careful not to meet the Soviet wishes to any further extent since shortly beforehand Stalin had shot a bolt from the blue which shed a harsh light over the scene of world politics. By enquiring about the apportionment of the Italian possessions in North Africa, he gave notice of Soviet interest in the Mediterranean.[32] This highlighted for the Western Powers a new direction of Soviet expansion, from the Black Sea via the Bosphorus to the Near East. All the less could their inclination be to allow a free rein for the Soviet claims on Turkey. Without going any more deeply into the course of the future negotiations, the Soviet threats and demonstrations, and the combined resistance of the Turks, the British and the Americans, it can be affirmed that the offensive against Turkey was repulsed.

2. THREE DISCONTINUED REVOLUTIONS

Besides their military strength and the respect reposing thereon, when the war came to an end the Soviet leaders held in their hands a second trump that they could throw on to the table in the gamble for Europe. During the war, the Communist parties in some of the West and South European countries had acquired an importance far exceeding what it had been in pre-war days. Since the Soviet Union, if it wished to avoid an open conflict with the Western Powers, was unable to assert its military potential beyond the limits of its sphere of control, the idea of exploiting the strengthened Communist parties in these parts of the Continent suggested itself. The prior conditions seemed favourable. There is a ring of truth in the report of a British Communist: "In the early days after the war it was believed in Moscow, and so in the various Communist parties, that nothing could stop France and Italy from in time falling into the hands of the Party ..." [33]

In the main, the strength of the Communist parties is to be perceived in their fusion with the partisan organisations, which in many respects conformed to the Communist doctrine. In accordance with the theories of Lenin and Stalin, it was to be expected that as soon as danger threatened the "Fatherland of the Workers" the European proletariat would join its own "struggle for freedom" with that of the Soviet Union to make good its position. Even if this hope was nowhere fulfilled in Central and Western Europe in the form of a large-scale uprising, nevertheless a trace of it was actively present in the resistance movements. Without losing their credibility, the Communists in Western Europe, after the revolutionary changes of 1941, comprehended with astonishing rapidity how to switch over from sabotaging the war effort of the West in favour of Germany to resisting sullenly German domination. With almost equal rapidity they were able to assume a leading role in the secret underground organisations. In this connection their cooperation in secret political operations and their rigid command stood them in good stead. In particular, however, their fanaticism for underground activity, with all its dangers and privations, made them more suitable than most other politicians.

Above all, the Communists had one great political advantage. While for the bourgeois politicians the forcing of all non-Fascist parties to cooperate in the underground meant a revolution of their ideas, it was a familiar phenomenon for the Communists.

For them, the resistance movements were ideologically a continuation of the Popular Front régimes of the pre-war days, both
as regards their own position in the partisan organisations and
the aim they set themselves – namely, combating Fascism. But
they also found their old Popular Front tactics of use in following
the partisan life. While they held their own cadres as tightly as
possible together, and indeed formed special resistance groups out
of them, at the same time they managed to infiltrate the non-
Communist underground movements with their most reliable
party-followers. In France, as in Italy, they succeeded in occupying the key positions in the military underground organisations.[34]
They would not have been true revolutionaries had they not
recognised the opportunity that lay therein and seized it. So far
as circumstances permitted, even during the German occupation
they made preparations for a local assumption of power by committees strongly resembling the Russian soviets of 1917.

(a) France

At the time of the Allied invasion in 1944, France's Communists
were so strong that it was often feared that they would utilise
to stage a coup d'état the period of chaos between the time the
German troops retreated and de Gaulle's Government arrived on
French soil.[35] In point of fact, Communist partisans did occupy
temporarily certain districts of France, exercising, as in Yugoslavia and Greece, the executive power.[36] As a result, after de
Gaulle had arrived in Paris, in August, 1944, the disarming of the
partisans bands had, as in Greece, to undergo a decisive trial of
strength. On October 29, de Gaulle ordered the dissolution of the
bands "for the maintenance of public order and in regard to the
international reputation of France".[37] On November 7, Duclos,
the Communist party leader, declared that the legislative power
lay exclusively in the hands of the Resistance, that the Provisional
Government must restrict itself to a "trustee administration", and
that disposal over the "patriotic militia" should be left to the
local "liberation committees".[38]
Civil war seemed to stand before the door. But, just as in Bel-

gium, Denmark and Italy, this was spared to France, at least in the well-known forms. It was Maurice Thorez, for years the leader of the French Communists, who at the turn of the year brought with him from Moscow the new policy. Since he had deserted in 1940, Thorez had been one of the prominent members of the Comintern in the Soviet capital, and he was certainly well-informed about the Soviet leaders' tactics and aims. All the greater, therefore, was the surprise when, following amnesty at the end of 1944 shortly after his return, he gave, in contrast to Duclos, his word of honour to subordinate himself to the Provisional Government. At a meeting of the party's central Committee at Ivry in the second half of January, he spoke out in favour of the dissolution of the "patriotic militia" [39], and with this, the danger of a bloody collision between the Resistance and the de Gaullist Forces was eliminated.

Since at the same time Thorez demanded that France must hurry to the front at least a million fighting-men, it seems possible that the Soviet leaders' concern was as swift a victory over Germany as possible. Many also think that de Gaulle engineered the change of direction when, in December, 1944, together with M. Bidault, his Foreign Minister, he went to Moscow and concluded a pact of friendship and mutual assistance with the Soviet Union. This treaty was doubtless welcome to the Soviet leaders, not only because in it France undertook not to conclude a separate peace with Germany, "in order to prolong Germany's aggressive policy", but also because of the assurances for the future. The partners bound themselves to give each other mutual assistance should there be a new threat on the part of Germany and, beyond that, "to participate in no alliance or coalition directed against one party or the other".[40] The treaty had advantages for the French Communists, too, since they must to some extent profit from the lustre of the new comrades-in-arms. Nevertheless, the Communist change of course cannot thereby be satisfactorily explained. For the Soviet leaders a Communist France would have been infinitely more valuable than a pact of mutual assistance. If they desisted from the attempt to transform France, as Yugoslavia, into a "People's Democracy", there were other reasons for the decision, about which we shall speak later.[41]

Henceforward the Communists in France, just as their comrades in Italy, pursued a different policy. While they made use of the "purging" of the country of collaborators for inconspicuously, if effectively, liquidating accounts with their opponents[42], outwardly they comported themselves, entirely in the sense of the Soviet tactics of concealment, as peaceful and correctly-thinking democrats. Taking a long view of affairs, this policy offered good opportunities for three reasons. Because the Comintern had been dissolved, the Communist Party could give itself out as a national French party. Indeed, because it had earned great merit in resisting the German occupation, it could claim to be, in particular measure, the "party of the French renaissance". And, because at that time, in contrast to its first heyday in the 1930s, it also had the advantage of being one of the government parties from the beginning, it no longer seemed a party of obstruction or negation.[43] In association with the powerful trade union movement CGT, the leading positions in which had been occupied by the Communists even during the German occupation[44], and with the Socialist Party, which at the end of 1944 had no inclination for a fusion with the Communists[45], the road to a seizure of power by legal means seemed to be clear.

Fortunately the French Communists made mistakes. In November, 1944, they received from the Socialist Party an offer to form a Socialist Unity Party. They did not make it clear that the reason was, perhaps, that they wanted first to demonstrate in an election their numerical strength or that they did not yet consider their cadres mature. After the communal elections at the end of April, 1945, at which they achieved important successes, they approached the Socialists with the same offer.[46] Léon Blum, the old Socialist leader, hesitated for a moment and then refused. After the success of the Communists at the election the merger would have been equal to a defeat.

The Communists did not, however, throw in their hand. They now addressed themselves to competition for election votes at the coming parliamentary elections. To this end they assumed a disguise that bordered on self-defamation. Indeed, to lull the bourgeois classes, Thorez set himself against the miners' demands for higher wages.[47] The results of the elections of October 21,

1945, brilliantly justified these tactics, since the Communists became the strongest party in the country. With 26 per cent. of the
votes, they came before the Socialists and the MRP, the new
Catholic Party of the Centre. It was still more significant, however, that, with 152 Communists and 142 Socialists in Parliament,
the Left now had a clear majority. The Communists immediately
repeated their offer to the Socialists and suggested the formation
of a joint Government with Thorez as Prime Minister.[48] It was
a magnificent triumph.

It was due to the Socialists that the Communists did not achieve
their goal. Once more Léon Blum interposed his authority. Under
his leadership the Socialists forced a coalition of three with the
Catholic MRP. The outcome of the government negotiations also
showed that the Communists had underestimated the opposing
forces. De Gaulle, strengthened by the massive vote of confidence
which he had received in a referendum on election day, withheld
from the Communists the three most important Ministries – those
for Foreign Affairs, the Interior, and War – of which they had
demanded at least one. He declared that Communists did not
come in question for offices on which the sovereignty of the State
depended.[49] After a dramatic debate in Parliament they had to be
content with the Ministry for Armaments and the Ministries
concerned with economic affairs; but they had the satisfication of
seeing Thorez, the 1940 deserter, become Minister of State.[50]

How fluid the situation in France was, was seen a few weeks
later in the struggle over the new Constitution. Their new alliance
with the Communists was the signal for de Gaulle's withdrawal.[51]
His successor was the Socialist, M. Gouin. In the months that
followed, the political picture in France was determined by the
cooperation of the two Socialist parties, which also gave the draft
of the Constitution its decisive characteristics. Although the triple
coalition had been preserved, the MRP were more and more
forced into opposition by this development. In April the bourgeois
party finally rejected the Constitution.[52] When soon afterwards
it was put to a popular referendum, the majority did not follow
the "yes" cry of the Leftist parties but rejected the draft. Thereupon there had to be new elections. This time, too, the Communists
showed up well, but they were outstripped by the MRP, and as a

result of the decrease in the Socialist votes the Left lost their majority.[53] The spell was broken. The attempt to secure power by legal means had miscarried.

(b) Belgium

The position in Belgium differed from that in France in that here during the war two resistance groups, one Communist and one led by army officers, had emerged. But the development after the liberation took a different course. Here, too, the Communists attempted to make their private army gain the upper hand, but they gave up the attempt when ordered to do so by the Western Allies.[54]

After the rapid liberation of the country at the beginning of September, 1944, the *émigré* Government, led by Hubert Pierlot, returned to Brussels from London. To adjust its composition to the changed political conditions it was broadened, whereby the Communists, for the first time, received two seats in the Cabinet. Confident in the strength of the armed resistance groups, the Communists adopted an aggressive attitude from the very first moment. In spite of their participation in the Government, they avoided their share in bearing the responsibility for decisions. As in France they terrorised parts of the country by persecuting their political opponents as well as real collaborators, made savage arrests, and intimidated property-owners by requisitioning. After the Government had tolerated the business for some weeks, in November it ordered the members of the Resistance to surrender their weapons.

The reply of the Belgian Communists, just as that of their comrades in France and Greece, was open disobedience. Assemblies to protest were summoned, and in the provinces there were new acts of violence. When the Government suppressed the protests by forbidding them, the Communist Ministers resigned, and Lalmand, the Party's General Secretary, gave the signal for uprising and a general strike with the cry "Liberate the country from the Government by every suitable means!" The Belgian Communist Party subsequently based this decision in the classic fashion by declaring that the vote to disarm their resistance groups had been dependent on "whether we shall once more have the old apparatus of State manned and controlled by the rich ... or a new apparatus of State manned and controlled by the representatives of the people". Since these words represent an unmistakable repetition of Lenin's war-whoops of 1917, the Communist aims in attempting a coup d'état are fairly clear.[55]

The Government police forces were numerically superior to the armed *milices patriotiques*. Apparently the Communists had not calculated that the Allied troops would be employed against them. But Pierlot had ordered the disarmament at the express order of General Erskine, of Great Britain, and General Eisenhower, the Supreme Allied Commander. While the Government Chamber conferred special powers, British soldiers, at Pierlot's request, took over, as shortly before in Athens, the protection of the government buildings. There were only a few clashes. As early as November 29 the general strike was called off, and on December 2 Erskine could publicly announce that the planned march on Brussels from the mining area of the armed Communists had been prevented by the intervention of the British troops.

From then on the Belgian Communists followed the same course as their French comrades. At the first opportunity they once more joined the Government. This opportunity was given them in February, 1945, when Pierlot was overthrown and a new Government was formed under the Socialist Van Acker. Even before then, they made an approach to the Socialist Party for a "fraternal exchange of opinions". In the Government crisis they proposed a "democratic coalition", and in August they discussed with the Socialists an "election community", which was to ensure a "democratic majority" in Parliament. But the Socialists rejected these approaches, and the first Chamber elections, which took place in February, 1946, showed that, in spite of the increase in the number of votes, the Communists remained far behind the Christian Socialists and the Socialists.[56]

(c) Italy

In Italy, during the German occupation the Communist Party, just as in the other West European countries, had had a massive impetus given to it, but in underground activity there had developed keen competition in the form of the Action Party. Only in North Italy did the Communists, in association with Pietro Nenni, the Socialist, have it their own way. After the coup d'état against Mussolini and the capitulation of Badoglio in the autumn of 1943, they also attempted to seize power for themselves there. But the attempt failed because Hitler had the Wehrmacht march into Italy, and the Communist resistance fighters had to return into the inaccessible mountains for two more winters, where, as in Yugoslavia and Greece, they installed local dictators in some areas.[57] Perhaps it was of great importance that the liberation of Italy did not take place from the north but from the south.

In the south, Marshal Badoglio had at first remained Head of Government after the Italian change of front. In his Government none of the six parties which had reformed following the twenty-one years of Fascist oppression was represented. Moreover, the parties themselves had not been prepared to enter this Cabinet, but required as a prior condition the relinquishment of the Crown by Victor Imanuel, whose cooperation with Mussolini they could not forgive. Since Churchill, however, held his protecting hand over the King and his Marshal, the parties' protests remained fruitless until the spring of 1944.

It is interesting that the impulsion for the alteration in Italy's internal politics emanated from Moscow. On March 13, 1944, the Soviet Union, as a complete surprise, recognised Badoglio's Government. Two weeks later, Palmiro Togliatti, the Italian Communist leader, returned to Italy. Like Thorez, he had been for years in Moscow, where he had played an important part in the direction of the Comintern. Within a few days he thrust the rudder in reverse. As early as April 1, the Communists suddenly declared that, independently of the King's attitude, the six parties ought to enter the Badoglio Government.[58] Since the other parties could not dissociate themselves from this invitation, shortly afterwards the first Party Government, in which besides Benedetto

Croce and Count Sforza Togliatti took up office as Minister without Portfolio, was formed.

Moscow subsequently asserted that the surprising recognition of Badoglio was based on the fact that the Soviet Government had not been sufficiently informed by the Western Powers about the development in Italy.[59] In diplomatic language, this indicated Moscow's intention to have a hand in this development as opportunity offered. Probably having a hand in Italian politics was also intended to serve the sudden change adopted by Togliatti after his return' from Moscow. The goal was reached. Through the temporary supporting of the Monarchy, the Communists ensured a key position for themselves and compelled their participation in all Governments until far beyond the end of the war. As Government partners, they were, as in France, "socially possible", but under cover of their new dignity they misused their power in combating their opponents. As in France, the suitable pretext was offered by the "purging" of Fascists from public life, particularly as Togliatti was Minister of Justice and in this capacity could quite officially appoint Scoccimarro, the leader of the Communist Underground, to be head of the department responsible for the "purging".[60]

During 1944, the Leftist tendency in Italy grew continually more pronounced. Togliatti and Nenni grew ever more intimate, and, indeed, agreed the establishment of a joint leadership for the two parties. So popular was the idea of a new social shaping of the country that even conservative circles were enthusiastic about a basic reorganisation. Without difficulty the Communist-Socialist block secured the support of the trade union movement. As in France it seemed scarcely possible to halt the development towards a Leftist régime.

In this situation it must have been attractive for the Communist leaders, when North Italy was liberated in the spring of 1945, to turn to use the strength of the armed resistance groups there. At first it looked as if they would give way to the temptation. Even during the fighting in Italy the Communist Resistance in North Italy had disobeyed the orders of the Government and the Allied Supreme Command and at the same time had tried, after the example of Tito, to bring into subjection the other underground organisations. Now, as soon as the country had been liberated, the Communists attempted to seize power. Since almost everywhere the local liberation committees were under their influence, they were able to occupy innumerable key positions. Without any shedding of blood they secured control of large areas, where the usual Communist terror immediately started up. The Communist militia assumed the role of the gendarmerie; "people's courts" condemned their opponents and had them executed in the twinkling of an eye; and the population were oppressed by dispossessions and requisitions.[61]

The situation was ripe for a coup d'état against the Rome Government, but the uprising failed to materialise. When in the summer of 1945 the Allied Supreme Command and the Government demanded the disarming of the partisans and the dissolution of the "people's courts" and the special police, Togliatti continued to delay these measures for some time, although finally giving way. In Italy, too, the retreat was sounded for the Revolution, if not for all time. The Communists apparently retained many weapons in secure hiding-places[62], awaiting a more favourable opportunity after the withdrawal of the Allied troops, for which from then on they called unceasingly.

Meanwhile it paid the Communist Party to cooperate in the Government, although they received none of the three most important Ministries – Foreign Affairs, Internal Affairs, and Defence. Regard for them grew to such an extent that by the turn of the year, 1945, their membership had reached 1.7 million[63], and they were therefore the largest Communist Party after that of the Soviet Union. This success was apparently connected with the cautious line steered by Togliatti in lagging behind the Socialists for a time with social demands and prating more of national unity and human dignity than of radical reforms. Not once did the heads of important Ministries – for example, that of Finance – make use of the Communists to propose and execute major social reforms. The Italian Communists themselves have asserted that, as a result of the Allied occupation and the opposition to the Rightist parties, important reforms would not at that time, in any case, have been possible. Even if this excuse contains a kernel of truth, it in no way explains why at least the attempt was not made. It is not difficult to perceive the true reason. In order to draw near to power by legal means, it was necessary to gain the confidence of the masses other than those falling within the working-classes who traditionally stand to the Left.[64]

But the Communist calculations proved in Italy to be just as wide of the mark as in France. It is true that at the communal elections in April, 1946, the Communists gained the victory not only in Rome and Turin but also in Florence, Naples and many other cities, so that, apart from the trade unions, from then on the communal administrations were for years their best support in large areas of Italy.[65] But the peak had been topped. In Italy, as in other countries, suddenly the mood began to change. The people started resisting the Communist terror. The dreams of a better world faded away, and little by little the longing for order gained the upper hand. By November, 1945, the Liberals, exasperated by the Communist terror, had overthrown the Government of Parri the Actionist and helped de Gasperi, the Christian Democrat, to become Prime Minister. Then, at the parliamentary elections in June, 1946, it was seen that a government led by the Catholic Centre Party corresponded to the development of the country's mood. The Christian Democrats were by far the strongest party and the Communists dropped to third place, behind the Socialists. Thus there vanished for them, for as long as one could see, the hope of being able to secure power by legal means. The longing of the people for orderly conditions and their attachment to religion triumphed. There is no contradicting a Communist author when he writes: "Powerful forces were at work to prevent Italy from becoming a People's Democracy, as so many countries in Eastern Europe were doing."[66]

3. AUTHORITY IN DISGUISE: PEOPLE'S DEMOCRACY

After setting up in Russia the first Soviet State, the Communists had the idea that every further "socialist" country would be a constituent part of the "Union of Soviet Socialist Republics" until this Union finally embraced the whole world. When the Constitution was being drafted this expectation played an im-

146

portant part. In the name of the State, every allusion to its geographical position and to its origination in Russia was intentionally avoided. By the selection of the form of State, too, a new way was sought which would facilitate the Soviet States newly arising to join up with the Soviet Union.

It was precisely for these reasons that, during the discussions about the Constitution in 1920, Stalin urged a federation of States as loose as possible. In a letter, later suppressed, to Lenin he wrote: "For nationalities formerly living in the old Russia one can and must regard our type of federal State as a very suitable means for international unity ... This does not, however, apply for the nations not belonging to the old Russia. These latter had set up their own States and lived as independent nations. If they were to become Soviet States, for example, a future Soviet Germany or a Soviet Poland, Hungary or Finland, the force of circumstances would compel them to take up some sort of inter-State relations with Soviet Russia. Since, however, they possess their own State, an Army of their own and finances of their own, they will not immediately agree to federation with Soviet Russia, as, for example, the Bashkir or Ukrainian Republics, since for them such a Soviet federation represents a restriction of their self-determination and an attack on their independence. I do not doubt that for these nations the most acceptable form of composition will be a federation of States (a union of independent States)." [67]

In the first two phases of the Soviet expansion there was adherence to the rule that every "socialist" country was a constituent part of the Soviet Union. The Transcaucasian republics, Eastern Poland, the Baltic States and Bessarabia were annexed, either immediately or a short time after their subjugation, although in part in the form of new Soviet republics. In the third phase of the expansion of Communism, direct annexation played but a minor role. Apart from East Asia and the re-incorporation of the territorial gains of 1939–40, it was limited to additional Finnish districts, the northern part of East Prussia, and the Carpatho-Ukraine. However, in these cases the imperialistic form of direct annexation, without the intermediate stages of a federalist system, was still openly used, particularly with the incorporation of the northern part of East Prussia which, in 1946, became a constituent part of the Russian Socialist Federal Soviet Republic, with the title "Oblast Kaliningrad". On the other hand, in by far the majority of the cases, the new "socialistic" countries remained as seemingly independent States, connected with the Soviet Union only by inter-State treaties. Similarly, the transmitting of the Soviet pattern of government to these countries was also rejected. The Communists were satisfied with getting into their hands the most important means of State power, and in general they permitted a multi-party régime a more or less formal existence.

The idea of a tactical compromise with other political groups, which is the rudiment of the popular democratic conception, was familiar to the Communists all over the world – at least from 1920 – for Lenin, in his screed against "Leftist extremism", had deprecated the orthodox combating of the Communist theory as a "children's complaint". From that time the Communists had always tried to follow Lenin's advice and also, as occasion offered, to support a political opponent "as the strap supports the person hanged".[68] Even when numerically they were in a minority they had infiltrated into trade unions, cooperatives and other organisations, establishing a *"Komfraktion"*, a comrades' political group, and trying with their combined minority to influence the direction of the whole.[69] When in the 1930s the Comintern proclaimed the policy of the "popular front", it was nothing more than an application of these tactics in international politics. In the course of the years the methods became more crafty and cynical. For our purpose here it is especially important to remember that, even before the war, Dimitroff, the General Secretary of the Comintern, publicly advised the Communist parties to introduce themselves subtly under national or democratic disguise into Western society like the wooden horse of Troy.[70]

There is a good deal that speaks for the fact that Dimitroff also took a substantial part in elaborating the popular democratic notion, which, according to Rákosi, the Hungarian Communist leader, was tackled as early as 1942 on Soviet instructions by the East European Communists living in exile in Moscow.[71] At that time Dimitroff was the most powerful non-Russian among the

Comintern leaders, and, by reason of his own past as a revolutionary and of his origin in one of the countries in question (Bulgaria), he was able to claim a certain authority. We are also accidentally informed that, just at this time, Dimitroff instructed the Communist parties in all the countries which found themselves at war with the Axis Powers to introduce a policy of the "National Front".[72] How this advice was followed has already been described.[73] There is unmistakably a link between this instruction and the later "People's Democracy", which is also confirmed indirectly by the author mentioned several times when he writes that the "People's Democracy" is an application of the Comintern tactics and, in fact, the "anti-Fascist front" policy outlined by the seventh Congress of the Communist International in 1935.[74]

In this connection, consideration must, however, be given to the fact that meanwhile the tactic of "common front Governments" had been further developed. In 1940, Mao Tse-tung, in his basic work on "China's New Democracy", described it in detail, thereby also influencing the theoretical ideas of the Soviet leaders.[75] Characteristically, he had taken as a starting-point Lenin's screed against "Leftist extremism", which recommended Communist participation in parliaments. Mao now developed this thesis by declaring that direct participation in governments is even more useful than entrance to parliaments, since the Communists could thus prepare, in the simplest and most logical manner, the ground for their seizure of power. They could sabotage the policy of the other Ministers, infiltrate their agents into key control positions, and secretly put their own party in the way of securing means of power. In other words, they could employ all those methods with which, for two decades, the Communists all over the world, helped by the "*Komfraktions*", had attempted to guide the democratic organisations.

Mao's revolutionary proposals were intended for the countries in which the Communists formed a minority, as was, indeed, the case in most of East-Central and South-East Europe. But there was one great difference. From the beginning, the "*Komfraktions*" in the post-war provisional Governments in this area were not dependent on themselves but had the support of the Red Army and – which was more important still – the sinister help

149

of the Soviet secret police. Thus they could always make their will prevail [76] and degrade the other Ministers to the role of supernumeraries. Gradually all opponents and fellow-travellers who were not wholly tractable were removed "in slices", in accordance with a recipe which Rákosi cynically described as "salami tactics".

As this account shows, "People's Democracy", even in its initial stages, had nothing in the least to do with Western conceptions of democracy. In December, 1948, Dimitroff, in his lecture at the 5th rally of the Bulgarian Workers' Party, expressly confirmed this fact by propounding the thesis: "The People's Democratic State is a State of the period of transition. It is called into being to safeguard the development in the direction of socialism." [77]

At first the Western Powers allowed themselves to be deceived by the fact that the multi-party governments of the popular democratic type apparently conformed to their own demand that in all the liberated countries there should be formed provisional Governments "representative of all democratic elements in the population". In the afterlight, it is perceived as one of the ironies of history that it was just this demand, which was naturally intended to prevent the elimination on the Soviet model of the bourgeois forces, that made the West's temporary deception easy for the Soviets. And it was deception from the very beginning. In most of the countries of East-Central and South-East Europe, the Communists were only a comparatively small group, and the other parties had little inclination to cooperate with them since they saw in them only Moscow's agents.[78] However, under the compulsion of the Soviet occupation, which was replete with all the means of the Soviet secret police, the democratic parties were obliged to enter the all-Party Governments, in which from the outset the Communists laid claim to the most important positions of authority, something after the formula: "a maximum of actual Communist control should be combined with a maximum of apparent freedom." [79]

Dimitroff's concept of People's Democracy as a "state of the period of transition" is also applicable insofar as the popular democratic pattern always left elbow-room for a swifter or a slower "development in the direction of socialism". Nevertheless, it was nowhere laid down when the goal should be reached or, for example, that all popular democracies had to make equally rapid progress in this direction. Here the "period of transition" could be shorter; there, longer. In point of fact the tempo of sovietisation varied. Nevertheless, it does not seem to have depended, as one would have imagined from the Marxist theory, on the degree of industrial development in the respective countries but on the geographical and political distance from the West. While the process was carried out very rapidly in, for example, Roumania, the Soviet Zone in Germany lagged behind for a long time. This circumstance caused many observers to believe that the Soviet Union did not at first consider its Zone of Occupation in Germany as being logically part of its new empire. The new concealment tactics of the Soviets had results similar to their campaign of deception during the second World War.

4. THE MOTIVES OF THE NEW BREATHING-SPACE

It is, perhaps, one of history's most consequential decisions that, presumably under the authoritative influence of the cautious Stalin, the Soviet leaders decided, in victory, not to make use of the propitiousness of the hour but to let the tide of Revolution indulge in a fresh ebb so as first to secure what had been won. Stalin's mode of thinking had never fallen along the lines of banking all on one card. Whether in the winter of 1944–45 he got the Politburo to decide expressly not to confront the West in a head-on fight we do not know.[80] The Soviet leaders' cautious reticence in the period that followed indicates a decision of this nature.

The policy of the Soviet leaders and the European Communists in the final stage of the war and the first phase of the post-war period cannot be correctly apprehended if one does not keep in mind that, despite the formal dissolution of the Comintern and the many differences in tactics, it was a matter of policy cast in one mould. Broadly this consisted in holding and safeguarding what had been won and, moreover, in making Europe a convenient sally-port for Communist infiltration, without, however, through an all-too-public process, arousing resistance that could jeopardise all successes. This policy conformed to the discontinuance of the attempts at expansion and the forgoing of serious attempts at coups d'état in the Western European countries. It also conformed to the new form of Soviet expansion through the establishment of nominally independent "People's Democracies".

The behaviour of the Soviet Union in Finland, Greece and Turkey follows a common pattern. When the Soviet Government so moderated its armistice conditions for Finland in the course of a few months that the freedom of the country remained intact, it clearly took account of the war alliance with the Western Powers, an alliance it did not wish to terminate earlier than was necessary.[81] The Soviets probably feared that the Western powers, who in 1940 wanted to rush aid to Finland, would four years later not have contemplated in silence the subjugation of this valorous people. In Greece, the Soviet Government, for reason of political prudence, felt itself bound by the Balkan Agreement. But this Agreement forbade them only a military occupation and not an attempt at a Communist coup d'état. Here, therefore, the Soviet leaders were obliged to leave to the E. A. M. resistance movement the attempt to incorporate the country into the socialist sphere. It is characteristic that this attempt was undertaken before Great Britain had assembled a substantial number of troops in Greece. Indeed, Moscow had not reckoned that the British would let it come to an armed clash. In the case of Turkey it is even more clear that the Soviet Union surrendered its aim, or postponed it, when it was forced to realise that success could be achieved only by the employment of military force. Thus the danger of a larger war would have arisen. For the Soviet Union this was too great a risk.

By and large the discontinued attempts at expansion in Finland, Greece and Turkey provide a starting-point for a more pertinent answer to the question as to whether, through the Balkan Agreement or at the Yalta Conference, the Western Powers have "made a present" of countries to the Soviet Union. The Soviet Union clearly let itself keep aloof from the Communist infiltration of a country only when it had reason to fear it would become involved in a serious conflict with the West, and not only on paper. Whether this fear was justified so far as Finland was concerned must remain undecided. In Greece it was certainly so, and in Turkey it was probably that the Soviets would have become involved in conflict with Britain had they made an external attempt to bring those countries into their sphere of control. Both these three countries occupy a special position compared to the broad stretch of land from Lübeck to Sofia, the occupation of which by the Red Army the West, after their strategic plans had once been laid down, could no longer prevent. The limits of the new Soviet empire stretch exactly as far as the Soviet line of advance in 1945. Apart from the special case of Yugoslavia, they did not go farther and, apart from the special case of Austria, they did not recede.

The Soviet tactics will be still clearer if the comportment of the Communist parties in the remaining parts of Europe is noted. One must guard against the false conclusion that by the time the war had come to an end these parties could have acted independently of Moscow. For example, Western eye-witnesses in Greece thought that the Communists had engineered their uprising on their own. They drew this conclusion mainly from the persistent silence maintained by the Soviet Government during the struggles that ensued.[82] But it has already been indicated[83] that such a lack of subordination to the Soviet leaders (who, moreover, maintained representatives in Athens) is simply unthinkable. Up to the secession of Tito, it would be unique in the history of modern Communism. To be able to accept so daring an idea, other evidence than the mere silence of Moscow, which indicates agreement rather than condemnation, must be adduced, since in the Soviet world condemnations are usually vociferously proclaimed.

It is inconceivable that the Soviet leaders, who during the war also maintained constant contact with the Communist underground leaders, should have voluntarily shirked the issuing of definitive principles precisely at the moment of historical crossroads. Rather the precisely similar comportment of the partisan organisations in all the Western European countries is indicative of central direction. At the same period of time the Communist

153

underground fighters in Greece, France and Belgium opposed disarmament. They wanted to retain their weapons in order to throw them in the balance during the political shaping of their countries. Certainly this inclination also lay at the root of the elementary sentiment that it is the task of partisans to establish a "new order" and to prevent a return to the old forms. But the possibility of guidance from Moscow is not to be avoided.[84]

Common direction from Moscow is quite clear with the resultant discontinuance of partisan opposition to disarmament. Thorez brought with him from the Soviet capital the pertinent order for the French Communists, thereby nullifying the policy that Duclos had publicly proclaimed up to then. Similarly, in Italy it was Togliatti returning from Moscow who issued the watchword to refrain from violence. Both were well experienced in the policy and tactics of the Comintern. They were the confidants of the Soviet leaders. It is not necessary to search hard for the reasons for the change of direction. Without doubt it was that the troops of the Western Powers would not have tolerated the transformation of France and Italy into People's Democracies under Communist domination, but, if necessary, would have advanced against the Communists with all their military array. Thus attempts such as these would not only have been condemned to failure but they would also have jeopardised the West's war alliance with the Soviet Union. Indeed, it may be that the Soviet leaders' own groundless mistrust of the West played a part in that in this case it caused them to be blinded by the possibility of a joint German-Allied attack on the Soviet Union. Soviet propaganda subsequently attributed to the Americans such intentions at that time.

Under these circumstances the period of transition promised better success for the tactics of seizure of power by legal means. In any case, through the war Communism had received more impetus in the west of Europe than in the east. There is much that speaks in favour of the fact that the Soviet leaders believed that their vision of the demise of capitalism in Europe would be realised in the chaos of the post-war times without their assistance. Thus the Communists were relegated to legitimate means, whereby they unanimously sought to follow Mao's recipe pre-

154

scribing not only having a hand in parliaments but also participating in governments. The Communists forced their way into the Cabinets in France, Italy, Belgium, Germany and the Scandinavian countries. But their procedure was evolved as on a long-term basis. In order to prevent an anti-Socialist common front developing in the summer of 1945, they desisted – once again together in France, Italy, Germany and Scandinavia –[85] from a merger with the Social Democrats for which in the early days of the war the conditions had everywhere been favourable.

The introduction of a stage of People's Democracy in the East-Central and South-East European countries, probably intended to be followed later on by direct Soviet annexation[86], takes the same line. Communist revolutionary dogma includes a theory whereby every State has to suffer at least two revolutions before it can become completely socialistic.[87] Although the success of the Bolshevist revolution in Russia itself had contradicted this rule, the Soviet leaders seem to have adhered to it in 1944–45.[88] But the principle can no longer have had any great weight, since with the annexation of the Baltic States, for example, it had not been observed either. Rather is it to be imagined that concealment of the new imperialism was the decisive reason.

At first sight it seems astonishing that the Soviet Union, precisely at this moment when it was reaching out beyond the borders of the Czarist empire and proceeding to build up an empire the constituent parts of which were more difficult to clamp to the Soviet State than the former acquisitions, relied on the logical form of direct annexation. Nevertheless, it was in very truth a matter of compulsion. So long as the Soviet leaders had World Revolution clearly inscribed on their banners they could, with a bold face, defend before the world every extension of their sphere of domination. However, as soon as, for tactical reasons, they disclaimed that the Soviet State was endeavouring to "export" its ideology by military force, they had to count on the appetite for expansion being measured by the standards of normal States. They had, therefore, to make a differentiation. While the territorial acquisitions of the first two phases of the expansion could be given out as a restoration of the area formerly occupied by the Czarist empire, the Soviet Union by its new conquests in 1944–45 was threatened with the odium of a new imperialism.

To avoid this odium it invented the disguised form of government of the "People's Democracy", which rendered a twofold service by veiling Communist dictation and not letting the mistake of a wide support among the population make its appearance.[89] The disguise was important for three reasons. In the first place, in the long discussions on "Trotskyism" it had become clear to the Soviet leaders that Communism was more acceptable to highly developed people if it was not linked with a clear subjugation to Moscow's command. During the war at the latest they must also have seen that aversion to a genuine "satellite" relationship penetrated down into the ranks of the best Communists. Indeed, Tito's remonstration with Moscow began in his partisan days.[90] Secondly, Moscow shunned the slur of "colonialism", in regard to the Asiatic and African peoples too, to whose strivings for liberation the attention of the Communists had already been drawn by no less a person than Lenin. Thirdly, the Soviet Union rightly conjectured that the Western Powers would certainly not have accepted so easily the annexation of Poland, Roumania or Czechoslovakia as the changing of these countries into popular democracies.

Probably the anxiety of a sudden change of political course on the part of the West was decisive. Indeed, the Soviet leaders would assuredly have been able to cope with all other difficulties if only they had not had to fear that the West would suddenly interfere in Czechoslovakia, Hungary or Bulgaria. As we have already seen [91], there were already tendencies to that end exciting anxiety some time before the end of the war, and the Soviet leaders must have known that the establishment of a Communist empire could only have been interpreted as a challenge in the "capitalist world". For the West it was not easy, at the end of the second World War, to become reconciled to Soviet annexations which at the beginning of the war had aroused their condemnation, particularly with the renewed oppression of the Baltic peoples, which was now taking place in still more shocking circumstances.[92] In addition, the Kremlin must have told itself that the Western Powers, too, knew how little the Eastern and

South-East European countries, in which there was almost no industrial proletariat, had to offer the Communists in the way of land for providing food.[93]

Since the Soviet leaders, for a time in contrast to the Western Powers, were continually clear about the forced antagonism between West and East, they had to fear a massive reaction of the West if they overtensed the bow. All their successes would, however, have been jeopardised by a premature conflict. They therefore held themselves back in war. They held firmly in their hands the territories their troops had occupied, but they did nothing beyond that, and they instructed the Communists in the remaining parts of Europe to keep to legal paths. These new tactics determined, too, their behaviour in Central Europe.

Chapter Six

THE STRUGGLE FOR CENTRAL EUROPE

(1945–1946)

> The Russian totalitarian political aggression has split
> Europe.
>
> *Dr. Kurt Schumacher, Bundestag, Nov. 15, 1949*

Soviet policy at the conclusion of the second World War embodies
a bewildering number of individual features that cannot easily
be arranged so as to present an overall picture. It is possible that
Averell Harriman, the United States Ambassador in Moscow,
gave the best description of it when at the beginning of April,
1945, he affirmed, in detailed reports to the State Department,
that the Soviet policy was following three parallel lines: 1. Cooperation with the United States and the United Kingdom in a
world organisation – the subsequent United Nations and its
Security Council; 2. Establishment of a security ring by dominating the neighbouring countries; 3. Infiltration in other countries
by the Communist parties there.[1] This clear-sighted enumeration
of the salient points exposes the blindness of the Soviet leaders,
who believed that their imperialistic efforts and the Communist
infiltration could be reconciled with the maintenance of the
profitable alliance with the West.

At that time the Kremlin was seemingly a victim of its own
philosophy – the firm belief that the extension of Communism was
proceeding in accordance with a historical law, before which the
world had to bow. Accordingly, the West would have to reconcile
itself to the Soviet expansion, and, as the Soviet Government
declared thirteen years later[2], would have to continue, "on the
basis of a level-headed recognition of the position which had
developed out of the war", the (for Moscow) "beneficial cooperation". There is no reason to doubt that the Soviet leaders desired
this cooperation. It was precisely in accordance with their ideas

that, after an exertion like the second World War and the successes thereby gained, it needed a new period of "co-existence"[3] and peace – a peace which, in accordance with Lenin's classic words, certainly had to play "the role of a pause for breath and the gathering of forces for new battles".[4] For the sake of co-existence the Soviet Government also accepted the – to it – strange idea of a United Nations and World Security Council, veiled its imperialism under the mask of the "People's Democracy", and did not pursue its desire for conquest so far that a serious conflict with the West was bound to result.

The area in which Soviet imperialism directly came up against the Western Powers – Central Europe – had first and foremost to become the crucial point of these ideas of co-existence. After the war had run its course, it was no accident that the West and East did not meet at the frontier of a country but in the middle of two – Germany and Austria. This fact, however, contributed towards accelerating the inescapable choice between cooperation and discord, since here it must quickly be seen whether the West came up to Moscow's expectation of continuing the alliance "on the basis of a level-headed acknowledgment of the facts" or whether the Soviets were prepared to adjust themselves to the West's basic political idea of the restoration of order, freedom and well-being. For some time this alternative remained concealed, since the dissimilar allies were able to continue their cooperation in at least one sphere after the war: they were able to lay down common principles for the punishment, stripping of power and placing in bondage of the defeated enemy – in short, for the negative side of their policy. However, the more it seemed necessary to develop a positive policy as well for Central Europe, the clearer was seen the fundamental difference between their aims. The partitioning of Europe was manifest.

1. SOVIET POLICY TOWARDS GERMANY PRIOR TO POTSDAM

In the spring of 1945, the world was celebrating the collapse of hated Nazi Germany. For the most part, only what was expected is to be perceived. After years of bloodthirsty battling against the

Reich, when the struggle was over the world could take in nothing but the triumphal finale: how the armies advancing from the West and from the East crashed up against one another over Germany like two tremendous waves, burying beneath them the autocratic régime of violence. There was exultation over the victory and disregard of the tragedy. On the other hand, many people in Europe, familiar for years with the Soviet peril, felt with a shock how the abyss was yawning beneath their feet. Their reaction to the irruption of Soviet power into Europe was mass flight towards the West. Without wholly comprehending the historic event, they saw the Continent breaking in two and sought safety on the side to which they were drawn by their mode of thinking and living.

An observer outside of Central Europe could also watch the calamity with a keen eye, if he did not allow himself to be deceived by the Soviets. For example, as early as April, 1945, Mr. Harriman, the American Ambassador, pointed out that the Soviet Union's revolutionary urge to expand was not dead[5], and some weeks later prophesied that the Soviet attitude would be based on the principle of power politics in their strictest and most primitive form. During a visit to Washington, he alarmed the American politicians by warning that by the end of next winter "half, and maybe all, of Europe" might be Communist.[6] Churchill similarly displayed a clear eye when in the last days of April, in a message to Stalin, he made a bitter reproach about a new partitioning of the world: "There is not much comfort in looking into a future where you and the countries you dominate, plus the Communist Parties in many other States, are all drawn up on one side, and those who rally to the English-speaking nations and their Associates or Dominions are on the other."[7]

Above all, Churchill also realised that the Soviets equally wished to incorporate into their sphere of control and philosophy those parts of Germany and Austria that, like Poland, Roumania and Bulgaria, had been occupied by them. In an exposé for Eden he drew up on May 4, he said of the line up to which the Red Army could advance that it was "what in fact would be the Russian frontier", and he enumerated: "Thus the territories under Russian control would include the Baltic provinces, all of Germany to the occupational line, all Czechoslovakia, a large part of Austria, the whole of Yugoslavia, Hungary, Roumania, Bulgaria, until Greece in her present tottering condition is reached." At the same time the British Prime Minister gave an account of the consequences: Poland, buried deep in Russian–occupied lands; all the great capitals of Central Europe including Berlin and Vienna in Soviet hands. "This constitutes an event in the history of Europe to which there has been no parallel, and which has not been faced by the Allies in their long and hazardous struggle." [8]

Eight days later Churchill coined the phrase that for years was destined to become the symbol of the forced partitioning of Europe. In a message on May 12 to the American President, he spoke for the first time of the "Iron Curtain" that was drawn down upon the Soviet front in Europe.[9] "There seems little doubt that the whole of the regions east of the line Lübeck-Trieste-Corfu will soon be completely in their hands." In the same telegram there is talk of "this enormous Muscovite advance into the centre of Europe", and the British Premier poses the dread question: "What will be the position in a year or two, when the British and American Armies have melted and the French has not yet been formed on any major scale, when we may have a handful of divisions, mostly French, and when Russia may choose to keep two or three hundred on active service?"

Churchill rightly prophesied that Stalin no longer wanted to hand over any part of the countries he held in his possession "like an avaricious peasant" [10], nor even the parts of Germany and Austria that he was able to dominate with his troops only by virtue of the right of occupation. As soon as it was in any way possible, Stalin despatched his viceroys into the regions occupied – in Germany and Austria, just as a few months later into North Korea also.[11] But the prospect of being able to gain the whole of Western Europe for Communism allowed the eyes of the Soviets to wander prematurely beyond the boundaries of their Zones of Occupation. Their Zones seemed to them bridgeheads [12] for the conquest of the whole of Germany and Austria. Since the capitals of the two countries lay in the middle of the Soviet Zone of Occupation, the opportunity to bring the countries wholly within their control clearly seemed favourable.

The reason for the surprising change in the policy of the Soviets towards Germany which made its appearance in the spring of 1945 is obviously to be sought in this hope of theirs. If they wished to gain the whole of Germany, a dismemberment of the Reich was only an obstacle. Far more profitable did it seem to have in Berlin, encircled by Russian arms, a central administration exposed, unprotected, to Soviet influence, if little by little the Western Powers disbanded their Armed Forces. It was shortly after the Yalta Conference that the Soviet Government changed its song about a dismemberment of Germany to German unity. The Western Powers first learnt of this through a Soviet Government announcement on March 26, which put forward the view that the dismemberment of Germany was not considered "obligatory".[13] World opinion was made privy to the change in Soviet policy in Stalin's Victory Speech of May 9, in which he said: "The Soviet Union is celebrating the victory, even if it is not disposed to dismember or destroy Germany."[14] Since the existing Yalta resolution about the dividing-up of Germany, which had been drafted under Soviet pressure, had remained secret, with this declaration the Soviet Union could for a time pose as the protagonist of German unity.

Views diverge as to the reasons for the change of course in the Soviet policy towards Germany. Stalin himself, when he was later asked, could proffer only the threadbare explanation that he had supposed that the United States and the United Kingdom were against dismemberment.[15] Since this interpretation was clearly intended to conceal the truth, it can be suspected that Stalin had something to hide. For this reason it is not sufficient to explain the Soviet abandonment of the dismemberment of Germany, which they had previously been so urgently demanding, by the fact that in the meantime the Soviet Union had found it possible to weaken Germany substantially.[16] Therefore in contemporary literature the view has persisted that Stalin was pursuing aims that reached farther. The main view put forward is that the Soviet leaders wished, through the preservation of German unity, to ensure reparations deliveries from the whole of Germany and have some influence on the Ruhr, Central Europe's greatest industrial area.[17] Thus interpreted, the new Soviet policy

162

seems a reply to the acceptance, decided on at Yalta, of making France one of the occupying Powers. At the latest after de Gaulle's visit to Moscow, Stalin knew that the French Government was advocating the dismemberment of Germany and particularly wished to separate from it the Saar Territory, the Rhineland and the Ruhr.[18] Since West Germany and the Ruhr would then have been outside the scope of Soviet control, many writers seem to find it plausible that the Soviet Government sponsored the unity of Germany as a counter-move.

Probably, however, one must not seek the Soviet motives only in the economic sphere. In the Soviet ideas concerning power, economy is always merely a means helping the achievement of political ideas. In view of the chaotic situation in which the whole of Europe found itself at the end of the war and the hopes that Communism was able to harbour at the time in respect of France and Italy, it is to be presumed that the Soviet policy towards Germany was also made to serve the Communist conquest of Europe.[19] Following a thorough investigation into the Soviet attitude, a French historian has come to the conclusion [20] that the new 1945 policy towards Germany was "offensive". "The leaders in the Kremlin...", he writes, "sensed that the spring of 1945 represented one of the greatest hinges of history." Pointing out that at that time Germany had been replaced by the Soviet Union as the leading Power, that the Americans wished to withdraw from Europe as quickly as possible, and that the Communist parties everywhere in liberated Europe were powerful and active, he continues: "Why in this situation divide up Germany? Why not try to incorporate it wholly within the Soviet sphere of influence, perhaps as the first phase of a future extension as far as the Atlantic? Once the security of the Soviet State had been guaranteed, the revolutionary impulses became apposite once again. Devastated, chaotic Germany was once more a trump in the world-wide game of the Politburo."

If one accepts this interpretation, which fits most easily into the Soviet leaders' ideological ideas [21], the individual trends in Soviet policy dovetail without difficulty into an overall picture. Through the expulsion of more than 10 million Germans and through excessive reparations that in part could serve more to destroy

Germany rather than to restitute Russia, the chaos in Central Europe could be intensified and the German people made ripe for social upheaval. At the same time, through the "denazification", which provided the Communists, as the protagonists of Fascism, special opportunities, it was possible to bring about a social revolution in Germany as in South-East Europe, and in France and Italy, too. Finally, through its participating in the control of the whole of Germany, the Soviet Government could see that in the Ruhr, the industrial heart of Central Europe, nothing took place against its wishes, whether it be a matter of wanting dismantlings or perhaps, later on, of attempting to secure the Germans for the Soviets by foregoing (as at Rapallo) further reparations.

These motives were particularly evident in the Soviet attitude to the question of German central agencies, whereby two phases are to be distinguished: in May, the insistent demand for the dissolution of the "Dönitz Government" and in July, 1945, at Potsdam, the supporting of the establishment of German central agencies.

The sharpness of the Soviets attacks against the Western Powers is not to be explained by the fact that Dönitz had been installed by Hitler and had selected his Cabinet members from among the leaders of the Third Reich. A sentence about the "Dönitz Case" in the May 20 edition of "Pravda" is revealing. The Moscow party organ spoke of "reactionary circles in the Western countries" which were hostile to the "creation of a new Europe", and then continued: "These circles consider the preservation of Fascist States and nuclei a prior condition that the democratic forces of the freedom-loving peoples do not triumph."[22] In accordance with Stalin's linguistic parlance, this sentence means that the Soviet Government demanded the dissolution of the "Dönitz Government" because it was afraid that, with the support of the West, it could be an obstacle to the triumph of the Communists in Europe.

After the years of struggle against Nazi Germany, the Western Powers naturally did not think for a moment of making a Government composed of National Socialists useful to them in the sense of the Soviet charges. They never intended to gain a political advantage over the Soviet Union by preserving the

Dönitz Government, which was in the Western Occupation territory. In view of the enormous hatred that Germany and the Nazi régime had incurred through the persecution of the Jews and other peoples, such a consideration was out of the question. Only a successful uprising against Hitler might have provided Germany with the opportunity of retaining a recognised Government after the capitulation.[23] Herein probably lies the international significance of the frustrated attempt of July 20, 1944.

Up to shortly before the capitulation, the Allies reckoned – and this is often overlooked – with the continuation of a non-Nazi Reich Government.[24] Since the details of the dismemberment of Germany had not been decided and the Zones of Occupation had not been thought of as independent territories[25], the Allies wished, in administering Germany, to utilise the existing German central organs, as is clearly to be seen in the draft of the Instrument of Surrender.[26] Only in the final weeks before the capitulation did they realise that theirs was a false idea. The Reich had fallen into such a disintegration that they themselves had to take over the government and the administration of Germany. In all haste, therefore, a new Instrument of Surrender was drawn up, from which all mention of German authorities was omitted[27], and the original Instrument of Surrender was changed[28] into that "Declaration regarding the Defeat of Germany and the Assumption of Supreme Authority with respect to Germany"[29] in which, on June 5 in Berlin, the Allies proclaimed, on in international law a doubtful foundation[30], their assumption of supreme power.[31]

After the members of the "Dönitz Government" had been arrested and disbanded, the Soviet organs did not await further decisions of the Allies at the Potsdam Conference but hastened to set up, in the territory they controlled, new German agencies which they called ambiguously "German administrations on the territory of the Soviet Occupation Zone".[32] Just as in other countries of their newly-acquired sphere of jurisdiction, they took care from the beginning only too obviously to keep out the leading Communists. It sufficed for them that the most important administrations destined for realising the great reforms profoundly affecting the social conditions were headed by reliable Communists trained in the Soviet Union. The administration for agriculture and forestry was taken over by Edwin Hoernle and that for popular education by Paul Wandel, a former teacher at the Comintern school. The Soviets had an especial interest in land reform and school reform.

For the leading Communists there were at this time other tasks. While in the other Zones political life was curbed rather than advanced, the Soviets placed value on founding in their Zone not only the first German administrations but also the first German political parties. In doing so they proceeded on the same lines as in, for example, Roumania and Hungary. Just as side by side with Maniu's National Peasant Party Groza's "Ploughmen's Front" had been set up, or side by side with the Small Farmers' Party the so-called "Village Investigators", so in the Soviet Zone of Germany the formation of a bourgeois block was prevented by the simultaneous establishment of the Christian Democratic Union (CDU) and the Liberal Democratic Party (LDP), which, as in Hungary, were directed by the Communists.[33] The original intention was to create immediately a Socialist Unity Party out of the Left wing. In the summer, however, there came a direction from Moscow to found at first, as in France and Italy, a Communist and a Socialist party, and then to form an anti-Fascist block of the four parties.[34] With the zealous cooperation of the Communists, this democratic façade was set up in accordance with the standing directions of the Soviet command, but it was still some time before the democratic politicians who had a hand in this were able to see clearly beyond the façade character of this party system. The generals and other officers who, in the "National Committee", had placed themselves at the disposal of the Soviets so as to form a counterweight to the Communists[35], remained, insofar as they themselves had not become Communists, excluded from it all.

It is hardly possible sufficiently to imagine the steadiness with which the Soviets pursued their aim in Germany. For years German Communists had been trained in the Soviet Union for their tasks. Before they were brought back to Germany they were given precise instructions. The direction of the overall policy was assigned to Walter Ulbricht, who quite early on had been the link between the German Communist Party (KPD) and the Soviet

166

secret police[36] and who had subsequently become an important figure in the KPD's "Foreign Committee".[37] The Soviet leaders also sent to Berlin two Deputy Ministers, who had had special experience in the field of enforcing the final triumph of the Communist system. After the capitulation, A. Vishinsky, the Deputy Minister for Foreign Affairs, who had organised the seizure of power in Latvia and Roumania, made his appearance in Berlin as "political adviser" to Marshal Zhukov, the Soviet Commander-in-Chief.[38] Zhukov's deputy for all civilian affairs and deputy chief of the Soviet Military Administration was A. Serov, one of the most senior heads of the so-called State Security Service and First Deputy Minister for State Security. In June, Wilhelm Pieck turned up in Berlin with fresh instructions from Moscow. As early as the 1930s he had belonged to the leading circles of world Communism as head of the Comintern's Secretariat. When on June 10 Zhukov published his decree about the licensing of political parties, the clarion call for the founding of the KPD was ready for the Press[39] and was published two days later. The SPD followed on June 17, the CDU on June 25, the LPD on July 5, and on July 14, a bare ten days later, the formation of the "anti-Fascist-democratic" Common Front (Antifa) block of the four parties could be announced. The "National Front" system was ready even before a Government had been formed.

The Soviets' procedure in their Zone of Occupation took the same lines as their activity in all the other countries they had occupied in the course of their warring activities. They regarded the Zone as merely a part of their newly-acquired empire, just as they had, for example, Hungary and Roumania. Everywhere they adopted the same measures. The artificial establishment of a multi-party system by which the bourgeois or agrarian camp was split up, led to the formation of a "National Front", in which the Communists, thanks to their direct link as agents of the Occupying Power, took over the leading roles, while at the same time all forces and persons who attempted to resist this pattern of overlordship were ruthlessly persecuted.[40] Then, supported by this system of compulsion and fear, a start was made with a policy that broke the backbone of the till then leading political and economic sections

167

the countries in question, thereby ushering in the transition to cialism in the Communist sense.

In the Soviet Zone of Germany two events in the spring and summer of 1945 showed with particular clarity that the Soviets regarded this territory as part of their sphere of control in which they could rule and administer according to their will without taking all too much notice of the circumstance that Germany was to be administered jointly by the Great Powers. In the spring they handed over to Poland the German provinces east of the Oder and Neisse, without even informing the Western Powers of the fact. Certainly the Allies had expressed their agreement in principle that Poland should receive a large part of Eastern Germany, but precisely at the moment when at Yalta the Heads of Government had been quarrelling about the extent of the Polish annexations, the Soviets had commissioned the Osóbka-Morawski Government to administer the whole of the territories as far as the Oder-Neisse Line. Before the Western Powers had become aware of what was happening there, Polish voivodes had already been organised. The German eastern territories had been withdrawn from four-Power administration.[41]

In a second case also, in the summer of 1945, the Soviets treated with indifference the wish of the Occupation Powers to develop a common policy for Germany by undertaking in their Zone a momentous measure, again without informing the Western Powers. Shortly after the Potsdam Conference, they issued orders in their Zone, as a first socialist measure, in respect of a land reform which Kurt Schumacher signalised as a measure "senseless from the economic angle, endangering the lives of millions, and to be explained only as power politics".[42] A first step in the direction of making the Soviet Zone a separate State was thereby taken. Since in the intoxication of victory the Soviets regarded the whole of Central Germany as their booty, it seemed to them unnecessary to await the Allied Control Council's common decisions, valid for the whole of Germany, as had just been envisaged at Potsdam. The text of the land reform law was delivered direct from Moscow. German collaboration in it consisted in its being translated from Russian into German by a former pupil of the Comintern school.[43]

The incorporation of the Soviet-occupied Zone in Germany within the spheres of Soviet power and ideology is concealed by two facts which cannot apparently be reconciled. At the Potsdam Conference in July and August, the victorious Powers outlined their common policy towards Germany, and on this occasion it was precisely Stalin who advocated central organs for the whole of Germany. If these did not materialise, the fault lay not with Moscow but with Paris. The "Political and Economic Principles" agreed on at Potsdam by the three Heads of Government for the treatment of Germany in the initial period of Allied Occupation seemingly represented a complete programme the detailed execution of which could be left to the Allied Control Council. In the political sphere, the June 5 Declaration laid down that supreme governmental power was to be exercised by the Allied Commanders-in-Chief. The principles set forth were: the complete disarmament and demilitarisation of Germany; the passing of judgment on war criminals and the elimination of former Nazis; the development of political life; that educational and judicial matters were to be "on a democratic foundation"; and that the German nation should be made convinced of the fact of the nation's military defeat.

The economic programme envisaged the destruction of the German war potential; the breaking-up of the monopolies and cartels; and a concentration of the economic life on agriculture and the peaceful industries for domestic needs – an echo of the Morgenthau Plan. To the Control Council was given the task of evolving common principles in regard to the production and distribution of industrial products, agriculture, wages and prices, the import and export programmes, currency and taxes, transport matters, reparations, and dismantling. Measures were immediately to be taken to re-establish the means of transport and to increase coal and agricultural production. It was the Control Council's task to see that Germany's economy was rigidly controlled.

At first glance this cataloguing of a policy vis-à-vis Germany seems all-embracing. A closer study, however, confirms that, apart from the most primitive measures of revitalising the defunct economy, it was but a collection of destructive ordinances. In view of the hatred that, after years of warring, could now be let loose, one cannot wonder at this. The German people were expressly apprised of the fact that the "fanatical resistance of the Nazis ... had made chaos and misery unavoidable", and it was clear that the Allies considered a rumbling stomach a good political mentor. In this there was unanimous agreement, and it is in the highest degree remarkable how the "capitalist" Western Powers lent themselves in their treatment of the defeated enemy to methods of State control and political leading by the nose such as is customary only in totalitarian countries. They certainly thought to ensure a development for the good by talking at certain places of "democratic principles". It was still some time before it dawned upon them that the Soviets bestowed their own interpretation on this concept. It cannot for a moment have been difficult for the Soviets to register their accord.

What now, however, was the position surrounding Germany's political and administrative unity? Although we are not at present as well informed about the course of the Potsdam Conference as we are about the Big Three's meeting at the Kremlin, all the signs indicate that the idea of dismemberment, which only six months previously had been the subject of such animated discussion at Yalta, at Potsdam played no longer a role. It is true that an American taking part in the Conference has reported that the American papers did include an appropriate proposal[44], but Truman himself has testified that before Potsdam he himself visualised an all-Germany which in the course of time was to receive its own Government in Berlin.[45] Apparently the American plan of dismemberment was no longer discussed.

On the other hand, the establishment of a new central Government on the Austrian model does not seem to have been sponsored by any participant. At the second session Churchill put forward the idea of "a unified Government of all four Zones".[46] Since, however, none of the other reports, in general more reliable, go into the matter, or even hint at it, it is doubtful whether there was an official proposal for the early establishment of a German

170

central Government. Rather does it appear that the American draft, which expressly deprecated a new German Government [47] for the initial period, was accepted without lengthy discussion after the Foreign Ministers had been consulted.[48] At all events, the decision of the Conference was in agreement with the American proposal that "no German central Government should be set up for the time being", although a system of "central German administrative departments" were to operate "under the direction of the Control Council" in the fields of finance, transport, foreign trade and industry.[49]

There has since been much speculation as to whether the establishment of these central administrations (which were later vetoed by France) could have solved in Germany the task that the newly-formed Government in Austria accomplished with success: cautiously to secure the detachment of the Soviet Zone of Occupation from the Soviet sphere of control.[50] In this connection, the ever greater distance from those desperate years has led to the fact that still only this possibility is seen, though not the other way round – a misuse of the central authorities so as to draw the whole of Germany into the Soviet sphere of jurisdiction.[51] However, because of the steadiness with which Moscow pursued its aim, there is reason for presuming that the Soviet ideas were moving in the direction of agreeing to the institution of central authorities, which, indeed, was only a logical consequence of the dramatic change in their policy towards Germany in the spring of 1945. Just as the multi-party system and the "Antifa Block", which had been built up in the German capital in the greatest haste, could have proved as effectual for the whole of Germany as it did for the Soviet Zone, so also could the "German administrations on the territory of the Soviet Zone" serve the Allied Control Council equally as well as the Supreme Allied Command. At least they could have provided a basic stock.[52] That the establishment of German authorities was not announced until some time after the Potsdam Conference caused mistrust. It was expressly asseverated in this connection that they did not represent any "forestalling" of all-German administrative agencies. It is true that from the beginning the administrations in the Soviet Zone were by no means a collecting-point for Communists, though some key positions were manned by trained Communists whose operation in all-German administrative departments might have provided starting-points for the Soviets.

In this connection it must be remembered that the Soviet leaders had had some experience in making use of foreign institutions. As so much that was methodical, the function of "driving-belts", or "transmissions", had also been accorded lavish treatment in Soviet theory. After Lenin had coined the idea, it had been illustrated by, above all, Stalin. The proletariat dictatorship can be realised only via the "transmission" of the great mass organisations[53], – which means to say, by their infiltration by Communist groups. This system had been endorsed early on within the framework of the Comintern, even on the international level.[54] Subsequently in Iran and Korea the Soviets attempted to make the territories they occupied starting-points for the conquest of the whole of the countries. It is improbable that, precisely in Germany, they should have had more modest aims. One underestimates the Soviet leaders' keenness of vision if one imagines that in 1945 they had overlooked the ability of all-German institutions to serve as "transmissions" of Communism, to say nothing of letting them be used as "levers" for prising the land between the Elbe and the Oder out of Soviet control.

Since the Americans had given notice of early withdrawal and Communism received a tremendous impetus throughout Europe, the Soviets assuredly calculated that they would rather gain the whole of Germany than lose "their" part. Perhaps their chances were better than has since been imagined. The American General Bedell Smith, who at that time was Ambassador in Moscow, has expressed the view that his countrymen were politically too naive in those days to be able to hold their own against the Russians within the compass of all-German institutions.[55] If one recalls the extent to which, in the initial phase of the Occupation, the Western Occupation Powers, too, encouraged the Communists, whom they considered the best anti-Fascists, and allotted key positions to them[56], this opinion does not seem wholly wide of the mark.

In any case, anyone who approaches an international problem with such determination and clarity of aim as the Soviets had no need to be afraid of institutions such as the Allied Control Council and the German administrative agencies. At best they could use them to serve their own ends; at worst they could be made to miscarry, as was later the case with the Control Council. Since it was not intended that the German administrations should operate independently but only to execute the jointly-issued orders of the Control Council [57], it would have been very difficult for them to outlive the Control Council. The hopes subsequently placed by German writers in these German administrations would have been justified only if a central German Government could have developed rapidly out of these agencies. This was, however, in direct opposition to the express decision of the Potsdam Conference to allow no all-German Government "for the time being".

The Soviet tactics in the German problem can be summarised by saying that their "minimum aim" [58] was that the Soviet Zone should stand on its own feet. Should it prove impossible to draw the whole of Germany within the Communist sphere via the Control Council and the German administrative offices, Communist infiltration of the Zone, which in the long run offered new opportunities, could suffice for a start. Probably the western part of Germany would be permanently handicapped in its competence to perform legal acts by the fact that a substantial part of the country had been drawn within the Soviet sphere. [59] The Soviet Zone could, in the long run, become a German "Piedmont" as a starting-point for a unification of the country under the distinctive marks of the Soviets. [60] In Iran [61] and Korea there was a subsequent attempt to realise this policy.

It is staggering how precisely the Potsdam decision which later made the cleavage of Germany manifest corresponded with the Soviet "minimum aim policy". In the decision on German reparation deliveries, the Soviet Union was allocated everything that was taken out of the Soviet Zone as well as 25 per cent. of the dismantlement in the three Western Zones. Still more staggering seems the fact that this ruling was based not on a Soviet, but on an American, proposal [62], which was snatched at solely by Stalin. [63] However, the process loses all its mystery when one sees from the memoirs of Senator Byrnes, the United States Secretary of State, that the decision on reparations was nothing more than

ecognition of a fact that had been accomplished, as in so
ıy other cases, by the Soviets prior to the taking of common
resolutions. At Yalta, the Soviet demand that Germany should
be called upon to pay reparations totalling 20,000 million dollars
and that half of this should be given to the Soviet Union was
accepted as a basis of discussion.[64] However, in spite of the set-
ting-up of a reparations commission, nothing was decided in the
following month. Nevertheless, that did not prevent the Soviets,
directly after invading Germany, from making a start on the
indiscriminate transportation of all attainable goods and valu-
ables, ranging from household effects and industrial plant to
works of art.[65] When at Potsdam it was pointed out to the Soviets
that such arbitrary withdrawals would prejudice any reasonable
solution of the reparations problem, they brusquely designated
what they had carried away up to then as "war booty". Feeling
themselves confronted by an insoluble problem, the Americans
therefore resigned themselves to the Soviets' pillaging of their
Zone.[66]

Thus was recognised for the first time that the western demarcation of the Soviet Zone of Occupation had a significance greater
than that of a mere occupational boundary. It seems that the
representatives of the Western Powers did not appreciate the
magnitude of these decisions. To all intents and purposes they
abandoned the illusion that it would be possible "to regard Germany as one economic whole", as mentioned in the "Political and
Economic Principles". They conceded the Soviets a special position in their Zone – and in all-Germany, too – which in the long
run left open only two possibilities: either the Soviets were allowed to ruin the whole of Germany economically and thereby
transform Central Europe into a poverty-stricken area or the
Western Powers refused the Soviets this right, with the result that
the Soviets recouped themselves in their Zone. When it was left
to the Soviet Zonal Commander to decide about dismantlings in
his territory, he could, and would have to, evolve his own
"economic policy".[67] It is difficult to image how German administrative departments "under the direction of the Control
Council" could have arrested this development.

Everything decided on at Potsdam was mere embroidery. It was artless to give the four Commanders-in-Chief a double function as "Heads of Government" in their respective Zones and members of the Control Council. When there were differences of opinion, which was inevitable when Western and Eastern ideas came up against each other, each naturally gave preference to his function as Zonal Governor. In view of the Soviet practice in the matter of reparations, it was equally artless to establish the principle that the yield accruing from exports out of domestic production should be used in the first place for payment in respect of necessary imports. The Soviets naturally did not for a moment think of helping the British and Americans in this manner to pay for the food they delivered but carried off to Russia without compensation everything that the ransacked economy of their Zone could still produce, although nowhere in the Potsdam Protocol was provision made for withdrawals from current production.[68] Basically, the decision on reparations was only a first, still barely conscious, adjustment to the fact that, as a result of the destructive Soviet policy, agreement on a common policy seemed scarcely conceivable.[69]

Stalin and Molotov made no difficulties about the decision on reparations, but at the same time they were concerned to achieve that their influence in the Western Zones was not eliminated as Western influence was in the Soviet Zone. During the Conference they very emphatically demanded placing the Ruhr under a special three-Power Commission. This demand was viewed favourably by Truman, since he himself had proposed placing the Rhineland, the Saar Territory and the Ruhr under four-Power control. However, here, too, the Americans and the Soviets pursued basically different aims. While the Americans regarded international control as a preliminary step to originating an independent Rhineland-Ruhr State[70], the Soviets were above all interested in preserving the particular possibility of having an influence on Western Europe's largest industrial area over and above the four-Power administration of Germany. For this reason they wished to prevent the Ruhr from being detached from German national territory and, indeed, asked for a written guarantee that the Ruhr would remain part of Germany.[71] It was no accident that they expressly wished to exclude France, which was casting avaricious eyes on the Ruhr and Rhineland, from controlling the Ruhr.[72] At any rate, they temporarily postponed their demands after they had received a promise from the Western Powers that a quarter of the dismantlings in the Western Zones would also be allocated to them.[73] Nevertheless, it must be noted in this connection that a substantial part of these dismantlings would have to take place in the Ruhr, so that indirectly the Soviets were, indeed, still able to secure an influence there.

The Potsdam discussions on reparations ended with a significant change of front. In the session on August 1, Stalin made a proposal in regard to the value of German assets abroad that at first sight seemed highly sensible and fair. He left to the Western Powers the gold they had found in Germany and proposed that there should be a demarcation line between the Soviet Zone and the Western Zones in respect of the distribution of German assets abroad. To Truman's question as to whether he was thereby to understand a line from the Baltic to the Adriatic, Stalin replied expressly in the affirmative, giving as an example that German investments in Roumania and Hungary would go to the Russians.[74] When after lengthy discussion the Western Powers agreed to this proposal, they did not apparently appreciate that they were thus recognising the partitioning of Europe into a Western half and an Eastern half. Certainly they did not suspect that the Soviets would also make use of this decision to place undetachable fetters on the countries they had occupied. Otherwise they would certainly not have let part of Austria also fall within the Soviets' reparations area.

Stalin's proposal reflected his view that the Soviet Union should be allocated the eastern half of Europe as far as the Elbe as the Soviet sphere of jurisdiction. At the same time, the incorporation of a part of Austria and the attempt to set up a three-Power control in the Ruhr indicated that the Soviets did not feel themselves satiated after their expansion of 1945 but saw in the retention of their Zones of Occupation in Germany and Austria only a "minimum aim". It depended on the success or failure of their further schemes whether Europe was to remain partitioned at the Elbe or whether the Soviet expansion got a grip on further parts of Europe.

176

The attempt to extend Soviet domination towards the west beyond the line reached in the spring of 1945 could succeed only if the Communists assumed governmental power somewhere in Western Europe or if the "transmissions", the "driving-belts", that were finally moored east of the Iron Curtain and reaching into the West were set in motion. But both cases failed to materialise. In France and Italy it was democracy which won the day; in Germany both attempts to set in motion such "transmissions" miscarried; while in Austria the direction of the driving-belt was changed, to the disconcertment of the Soviets, with the eastern part of the country being withdrawn from Soviet jurisdiction.

(a) The German Central Agencies

A few days after the Potsdam Conference, France vetoed the establishment of all-German central agencies.[75] This brought to naught the formation of these bodies which Moscow desired to utilise as its "transmissions". It is worthy of note that when de Gaulle visited President Truman in Washington in an attempt to gain American support for French policy, he gave as his reason that a unified Germany would be still more dangerous now than in the past, because it could come under the influence of the Soviets. Germany, because of its weakness, "makes that country all the more susceptible of becoming the political instrument of other Powers".[76] Accordingly, the French Head of Government seems to have recognised the danger of incorporating the whole of Germany into the Soviet sphere of control and the sabotaging of the central agencies seems to be linked with this perception. Apparently de Gaulle was anxious that a new German Government, whose origination out of the administrations the French in their too-lively mistrust feared[77], would join up with the Soviets and, continuing Poland's "shifting towards the west", would seek compensation in the west for the loss of its territory in the east.[78]

However, from the remedies which de Gaulle recommended to his Western allies, it became patent that fear of a Russo-German alliance was only an addition to the in any case present dislike, based on a centuries-old tradition, of a unified Germany, since the Head of the French Government was only following Richelieu's recipe when he proposed the annexation of the Saar and the separation of Rhineland and the Ruhr from Germany.[79] These demands had been made in France even during the war, at a time when the Soviet danger was not yet realised there.[80] While in the meantime the Western Powers had gradually come to appreciate that the Nazi menace to Europe had been replaced by the Soviet, the French Government was now repeating the mistake of the Western statesmen. Recalling 1940, it gazed unbendingly at Germany, beneath whose ruins it thought still to perceive the former might and menace, and failed to see that the sand in the hourglass of the history of the world had trickled further. What caused the French Government to register its veto was national egoism, which, in view of the new peril to Europe, was equally as blinkered as had been Hitler's alliance with Stalin. France, complexioned by the Franco-German hostility, which had been spent as early as 1939, wished to prevent the resurrection of a Germany unified, without accounting to itself what would be the effects of the resultant vacuum in the control of Central Europe.

The French opposition to treating Germany as an economic whole had a singular result. For the time being the Iron Curtain seemed less impenetrable than the imaginary curtain with which France cut off its Zone of Occupation from the rest of Germany. For months on end the Western Powers were occupied more with French objections than with the fact that in the meantime a sort of "People's Democracy" had been set up in the Soviet Zone. France, which during the London Foreign Ministers' Conference in September, 1945, and again on October 1 in the Allied Control Council, voted against the German central agencies, seemed to be the mischief-maker that was preventing the restoration of German economic unity, while at the same time a policy was being introduced in the Soviet Zone which was detaching this region much more lastingly than was French policy.[81] But at the moment the Western Powers were taking the annoying French claims more seriously than, for example, the fact that as early as August the Soviets had decreed a socialist land reform in their

178

Zone[82], although the Potsdam Agreement had expressly laid down that throughout Germany agricultural policy should follow "common principles".[83]

While the Soviets in ostensible loyalty were awaiting the ending of the quarrel among the Western Powers in order to assume the four-Power control of Germany, they were treating their Zone as part of their empire. While during the summer they had already taken the first step towards a "popular democratic" order by insisting on the foundation of the "Antifa Block" of the four political parties they had licensed, now further steps followed. At the end of October they introduced "Soviet joint-stock companies"[84], which were intended early on to control a considerable part of the economy. Despite American and British protestations, they placed the university which was situated in the Soviet Sector of Berlin not under the Allied Kommandatura but kept it under their supervision, so as to effect its transformation in the Socialist sense.[85] American trains running through the Soviet Zone to Berlin were stopped and searched by Soviet troops, forcing the Americans to threaten to have their trains accompanied by armed guards.[86] In December, the British and the Americans proposed opening all zonal boundaries to the German population. However, General of the Army Sokolovsky, the Soviet Commander-in-Chief's deputy, simultaneously announced that the practical implementation of this was "at the moment impossible".[87] Just as in Austria, the Soviets desired the seclusion of their Zone. On the other hand, they suspected the Americans of secretly supporting the French resistance to German central agencies.[88] Since, however, these first contretemps ran their course behind the closed doors of the Control Council, the public knew nothing of them, while being kept informed about the extent of all the difficulties Paris was creating for its Western allies.

As early as October 31, 1945, General Eisenhower, the American Commander-in-Chief, announced in a report to Washington that, as result of the rejection of German central agencies, there was no development of trading in Germany, whereupon President Truman sent a special confidant to Germany to examine the situation. The latter, at a Press conference after his return, and in his report published on December 28, blamed France solely for the "economic dismemberment" of Germany. He wrote: "The United States must itself decide whether the obstruction indulged in by the French Government, which has led to a complete paralysis of the four-Power Control Council in Berlin, is to be permitted." [89] As a result of this advice, on December 3 Secretary of State Byrnes once more called publicly on France to desist from this opposition, while Truman threatened to abolish the right of veto in the Control Council. [90] Thereupon the French Government gave a fresh turn to its demands by making its acquiescence in the establishment of central agencies dependent on the preceding detachment of the Rhineland and the Ruhr. But the Great Powers would have nothing to do with this. On December 5 the American Government replied with a proposal to establish central agencies for the three Zones other than the French. This came to naught because of British objection.

Because of these proceedings, which were conducted in full publicity, the impression has arisen that it was the French who actually instigated the partitioning of Germany, even before the Soviets. In reality, however, the Soviets were simultaneously pursuing, independently of France, a policy which was forced to lead either to the incorporation of the whole of Germany within the Soviet sphere of control or to the destruction of German economic unity, even if German central agencies had been set up as a temporary measure. It was only that it was not until later that the content and consequences of this Soviet policy first became known. Since the Soviet Zone was closed to the West, only after some time did the West perceive that the Soviets were continuing their policy of plunder without bothering about Potsdam agreements. [91] It is true that in the Control Council they cooperated on the agreements about reparations, whereby they sought to secure as much booty as possible at the cost of the progressive impoverishment of Germany, but at the same time in their Zone they were squeezing reparations out of current production, undisturbed by the fact that the treatment of Germany as an economic whole was thereby being frustrated. In practice, this process meant that the Western Powers were paying for reparations deliveries to the Soviet Union and that since, in contradiction to the Potsdam decisions, the Soviets were not making payments for the food

180

imported from the West take preference over withdrawals from current production, these imports remained without recompense.

The idea that German central agencies could have moved the Soviets sooner than the Western Powers in the Control Council to renounce this reparations policy it at least a daring one. Nevertheless, with the failure of the common reparations policy that showed itself in the spring of 1946, the idea of economic unity in all other fields collapsed at the same time. The Soviets now expressly proclaimed the policy which they had in reality been pursuing from the beginning. "Before the (reparations) programme will be fulfilled", they announced, "each Commander of the zone must be responsible for putting into operation all the industrial facilities of the zone."[92] This principle was in conformity with the incorporation of the Soviet Zone into the Soviet empire.

The controversy about the German central agencies had two main consequences. It created for the Soviets an alibi for their policy towards Germany, which allowed them to give themselves out then, and later, as being the protagonists of German unity although, at the same time, through their policy of plunder they placed the West before the choice of either preparing the soil for Communism in the whole of Germany through an appalling deterioration of the conditions[93] or allowing a sharp line divide the Soviet Zone from the Western Zones. In addition, however, for a time they retained the hope of being able, with the help of the "transmissions" of the central agencies, to draw the whole of Germany within the Soviet sphere of domination, and this hope, combined with an over-estimation of the Communist chances in Western and Southern Europe, seems to have evoked in the Soviet leaders that super-optimistic mood in which is probably to be sought the reason for a gigantic blunder in Soviet policy. This blunder was committed at the end of 1945 in Austria.

(b) Elections in Austria

At the time when the Potsdam Conference began, the Soviets were still holding the Austrian capital wholly in their hands. They had prevented American and British troops from occupying in Vienna the sectors destined for them and were conducting themselves, as in Berlin, as masters of the house.[94] Because the Western Powers had had no influence on the formation of the Renner Government, they refused officially to recognise him before the Allied Control Council had started on its activities.

In August, the Soviets attempted to exploit this situation by a cunning manœuvre directed towards undermining Austria's freedom. Here, too, they utilised, in a masterly fashion, the many-sided instrument of reparations. At Potsdam, Molotov had first demanded that Austria should be saddled with reparations totalling 250 million dollars. When the representatives of the Western Powers at once protested that this demand could not accord with the Moscow Declaration of 1943, Stalin gave way. On August 1, he expressly confirmed that Austria was not obliged to pay reparations.[95] On the last day of the Conference, he nevertheless succeeded in tricking the Western statesmen. He casually proposed to include the eastern part of Austria also in the area in which the Soviet Union was free to take over German foreign assets. It is clear that the Western representatives comprehended the economic significance of this proposal just as little as they previously had the political significance of the demarcation line running straight across Europe from north to south.[96] After a short discussion they intimated their agreement, thereby involuntarily confirming that "Eastern Austria" fell within the Soviet sphere of control.

The Soviets immediately made use of this circumstance. Referring to the Potsdam resolution, with the greatest speed they opened negotiations with the Austrian Government, even before the Allied Control Council was set up in Vienna, about the oilfields at Zisterdorf in Lower Austria. Before the "Anschluss" of Austria with Germany, foreign companies had opened up oil deposits in this district, secured prospecting rights, and installed industrial plant. After 1938, much of it had come into German ownership. Immediately on entering Austria, the Soviets had seized the plant, dismantled parts of it, and continued to operate other parts. After Potsdam they laid claim to the plant and the prospecting rights (which, moreover, had a time limit extending to 1947) as "German property". Thus they wished to prevent the

182

Austrians from disposing of one of the most valuable raw materials and currency producers. But their plans went still further. They proposed to the Austrian Government to form a joint Soviet-Austrian company for operating the plant. From the Soviet side, the "German property" was to be provided as "material investment", while Austria was to find 13 million dollars within five years – an enormous sum for that poor country – as well as concessions in respect of new oil regions throughout Austria. Here, too, the Soviet Union tried to advance westward beyond its Zone.[97]

Similar "mixed companies" had previously been founded under Soviet direction in Hungary and Roumania.[98] They served to strengthen the fetters by which these countries were chained to the Soviet Union. What the consequences might possibly have been if, in spite of the pressure of the Soviet Occupation, the Austrian Government had refused the proposal, Herr Schärf, the then Socialist Vice-Chancellor, has impressively described: "It can be taken as certain that acceptance of the Russian proposal ... would have tied the Provisional Government to Russia and that Eastern Austria must have been incorporated into the Russian economic sphere. It can also be taken as certain that the Western Allies would not have recognised a Government that had bound itself to Russia with non-observance of the rights of a third party. The non-recognition of the Provisional Government would doubtless have frustrated the unification of Austria. At that time the despatch of a delegation to Moscow ... which was to conclude a trade contract between Austria and Russia had already been agreed. The contract was to initiate a close economic cooperation between Austria and the Soviet Union. After the oil negotiations came to grief, Russia cancelled the journey of the trade delegation. The incorporation of Austria into the economic sphere of the Soviet Union did not take place."[99]

It can be contested whether or not all these consequences would of necessity have resulted. Assuredly, however, Schärf has correctly perceived the Soviet intention to draw Austria into Moscow's economic and governmental sphere. The rejection of the proposal to follow the Roumanian example was the first step to the freedom of Austria, which was quickly followed by another.

Pressed by the Federal *Länder* in the west, which had the support of the Western Powers, Dr. Renner broadened his Government and restricted the powers of the Communists. While up to then a Communist named Honner had been responsible, as Minister of the Interior, for police and elections, now, after violent controversy with the Communists, a five-man commission took over these tasks. In addition, a Tyrolean named Karl Gruber became Under-Secretary of State for Foreign Affairs.[100] After this government reorganisation, in October Renner was recognised by the Western Powers. The unity of the country had been preserved for the time being.

But perils continued to loom. The Allied Control Council in Austria had rights similar to those of the Control Council in Berlin. Above all, no laws could be proclaimed without its concurrence. It was now a question of whether or not the Austrian Government could secure enough authority vis-à-vis the Control Council. As long as it was only a tool of the Occupation Powers it could not expect to be fully acknowledged as a force on its own. It must therefore have been glad when the Control Council itself commissioned it with the task of holding elections before the end of the year. These elections were to become the most decisive event of post-war history in Austria, and they received a significance going beyond the borders of the country since they ended in a catastrophic defeat for the Communists.

Since Austria ranked not as a conquered, but as a liberated, country, it would have been very difficult for the Soviets to contest the holding of free elections, and an influencing of the elections in its Zone was too risky on account of the presence of Western observers. In the opinion of numerous witnesses, they had, however, a positive reason, too, for agreeing to the elections. Before the poll it had been agreed that after voting had taken place the new Government should have a "National Front" character[101], and the Soviets had believed that the Austrian Communists would secure sufficient votes to be able to maintain their positions in the Government. They relied on the impression of their military might, on extravagant propaganda, and on the social change that, as a result of the war and defeat, they anticipated in Austria, as in other countries. The Austrian Communists themselves counted on receiving as many votes as the Socialists [102] and reckoned on the two Leftist parties combining to form a majority.[103] The new Austrian Government was intended, as a "transmission", to propagate Soviet influence over the country from Vienna.

On election day, November 25, 1945, the expectations were, however, frustrated. With 1.6 million votes and 85 mandates, the bourgeois People's Party secured an absolute majority. On the Socialist side, the Socialist Party received 1.4 million votes and 76 mandates, while the Communists had to be satisfied with 174,000 votes and four seats in Parliament.[104] Thereby they incurred Moscow's lasting contempt. It was the natural consequence of this election result that Leopold Figl, the leader of the People's Party, should form the new Government and that the influence of the Communists should be sharply curtailed in conformity with their share of the votes. They had to give up the Ministry of the Interior in favour of a Socialist named Helmer and be satisfied with the insignificant Ministry for Power Industry.

For the Soviets, the outcome of this election betokened a sudden awakening from the sweet dream of the irresistible advance of Socialism. They now found themselves in an embarrassing position. If they avoided acknowledging the new Government, they lost face and cast off the "democratic" disguise they had so carefully observed in all other countries. But if they permitted the Figl Government to exercise its rights in the Soviet-occupied Zone also, the development of socialist concepts of society and economy would be prevented and, apart from military occupation, the territory would be detached from the Soviet empire. For the time being they seem to have wavered without deciding on either of the two alternatives. In their Zone they pursued a harsher system and gave the Communists still greater privileges.[105] When they decided to recognise the new Cabinet they did so in a bad-tempered fashion. They insisted that, beforehand, three Cabinet members, who with their consent had already belonged to the Provisional Government (including the later Chancellor, Dr. Raab), were changed.[106] But the next year they also drew the additional consequence in that they agreed to a new control agreement under which the Austrian Government received the right to proclaim within 31 days any law against which the Control Council had not registered a protest. With that, Austria's freedom was assured. Now the Soviets could no longer, by exercising their right of veto in the Control Council, prevent, as in Germany, every political and economic step forward. They relinquished their influence on the shaping of the internal conditions in Austria, including the Zone.

There are various opinions as to the reason that caused the Soviet leaders at the time to allow the eastern part of Austria to secede – except for military occupation – from the Soviet sphere of jurisdiction. Assuredly there was, in the first place, the effect of the surprise that the elections had turned out not in favour of Socialism but against it and that the Government's "transmission" had changed its revolutionary rhythm from the National Front type. Instead of linking up Western Austria with the Soviet sphere it linked up Eastern Austria with the West. Only a spectacular interference could have prevented this development after the elections, but the Soviet leaders shrank from this in 1945, when they were still intent on "moral gains" in Europe. In addition, however, there was a great practical obstacle in the way of another policy which is often overlooked. For the introduction into the Soviet Zone in Austria, as in the Soviet-occupied territory in Germany, of a development towards a State in its own right, the eastern part of Austria was too small, and a joining up with neighbouring Hungary would have been possible only if, during Soviet expansion at the end of the second World War, the Soviet leaders had adopted the former scheme of direct annexation of all Communist-dominated territories. There was, therefore, nothing for the Soviets to do but be satisfied with the military occupation of Eastern Austria, which could not be forbidden them prior to the conclusion of a State treaty. That being said, for nearly ten years they did everything possible to hinder the realisation of the treaty.

The Soviet leaders' political retreat was facilitated by the circumstance that, up to the autumn of 1945, they had made only modest attempts to secure that their ideas were realised in Austria. In contrast to Germany, Austria was treated as a "liberated country". The Government in Vienna had, therefore, from the

186

beginning to be conceded a certain measure of self-responsibility. In addition, here, too, the Soviets shrank from more drastic measures into which by force of circumstances the Western Powers would have gained an insight. They did not, however, fall into the temptation of making the bold assertion that the population wished for a "People's Democracy" Government. Thus they now incurred no ridicule from outside. This notwithstanding, they have never forgotten that this retreat was forced upon them because of free elections. Since November 25, 1945, they have never allowed within their sphere of jurisdiction any further elections which might prejudice their power and esteem.

(c) Social Democracy in Germany

The outcome of the elections in Hungary on November 4 and in Austria on November 25 had a direct reaction on Soviet policy in Germany.[107] Since the German central agencies had not materialised, here the Soviets had to be on the look-out for a new "transmission" from East to West Germany. Apparently they believed they had found this instrument in the two Socialist parties, one of which, the German Communist Party, the KPD, was at their disposal as a docile tool, while they tried to win for themselves the German Social Democratic Party, the SPD, by applying the carrot and stick. The election catastrophes in Hungary and Austria suddenly exposed the danger that the "driving-belt" of an independent SPD could change the turn of its direction and prevent the sovietisation of their Zone. Thereupon the belt was severed by the Soviet leaders themselves.

In 1945, the Communist Party in Germany was relatively weak. So far as numbers went the membership and affiliations remained far behind what they had been in the period prior to the end of the Weimar Republic. In view of Germany's situation between East and West, the key to further development lay, therefore, with the Social Democrats, insofar as German politicians still had any influence at all.

During the summer of 1945, the SPD had re-emerged, not only in Berlin and the Soviet Zone but in West Germany as well.

Up to the autumn of 1945 it had remained unclear where the party's leadership lay. In Berlin they had formed, under the leadership of Otto Grotewohl, Max Fechner and Gustav Dahrendorf, a "Central Committee of the Social Democratic Party in Germany", which laid claim to leadership of the whole party. The party headquarters, originally to have been situated in the American Sector, had at Soviet insistence been set up in the Soviet Sector.[108] In West Germany, the re-establishment of the SPD proceeded more slowly as a result of the restraint of the Occupation Powers, but, thanks to the energy of a far-sighted man, a second focal point had crystallised at Hanover. Dr. Kurt Schumacher, who before 1933 was one of the youngest members of his party to be a Reichstag deputy and who, in twelve years of bravely-borne internment in a concentration camp, had become a politician of outstanding intelligence and with an extraordinary power of decision, gave the newly-born SPD in West Germany its stamp. It was of great significance that even in the 1930s he had been dominated by a profound mistrust of the Communists, and, with his penetrating comprehension of the imperialistic character of Soviet policy, in 1945 he saw through this instead of allowing himself to be deceived by the democratic façade as so many others were. He realised that the Soviet Union wished to surround itself with a "system of belt-States" to which it intended to include "if in any way possible the whole of Germany"[109], and he did not doubt for one moment that in this the KPD were prepared to render willing assistance, since they were "not a German class- but a foreign State party".[110]

In contrast with this, the Social Democrats in Berlin were at first strongly inclined to create with the Communists a single party composed of all Socialists.[111] Since at this time the Communists were comporting themselves in democratic fashion, there seemed no unbridgeable differences of opinion standing in the way. But to the surprise of the Social Democrats, the Communists soon did away with these advances – on, as one knows today, the basis of a Moscow directive that did not apply to German Communists. Apparently the Communists were first to build up their own cadres so as to be able more safely to take over the leadership in the unity party.

At the beginning of October, 1945, the Berlin and the West German Social Democrats assembled for the first time at a joint conference. At Wennigsen, outside Hanover, whither Schumacher had invited them, Grotewohl, Fechner and Dahrendorf found themselves confronted with a massive mistrust comparable to the attitude of the West Austrian politicians towards the Renner Government that had been installed in Vienna by the Soviets. They were unable to secure that the Berlin Central Committee, following a broadening through the addition of representatives of the Western Zones, was acknowledged as the highest body of the party. Instead, the promise was extracted from Grotewohl that in no case would isolated action be undertaken in the Soviet Zone to effect a union with the Communists.[112] Since in Berlin and the Soviet Zone the Communists, supported by the Soviet organs, had meanwhile started to press the Social Democrats, as, too, the members of the two bourgeois parties, to the wall, at first Grotewohl held firmly to this course. On November 17, arrived back in Berlin, he declared at a gathering: "The unity of the working-class cannot possibly, even in the slightest degree, be the result of external pressure or indirect compulsion... Union on a zonal basis would presumably not advance union on a Reich basis but only make matters more difficult and perhaps destroy the Reich!"[113]

Grotewohl's speech was immediately suppressed by the censor, and he himself was ordered to report to the Soviet Military Administration at Karlshorst.[114] A few days before he spoke, the Soviet leaders had received the first warning signal – the Hungarian elections. Fourteen days later, the Austrian elections confirmed that the Communists had widely over-estimated their strength in Central Europe. From this day forward, the Soviets employed every means at their command to achieve the forced merger, under Communist leadership, of the two Socialist parties in their Zone. There began a brutal game which a Social Democrat has since designated as a "prelude to the cold war".

After a propagandistic beating of the drums, in which the danger of a new "reaction" in Germany was splashed upon the walls, Pieck and Ulbricht invited the SPD leaders to a conference on December 20 and 21. On the very eve of the conference they tried to take the Central Committee unawares by proposing to prepare, and accomplish, the fusion of the two parties in the *Länder* and the provinces from the bottom up. The following day, this unreasonable request to eliminate themselves was once again harshly opposed by the Social Democratic leaders, who once more demanded that first of all organisations on a national basis should be created and then, in separately organised country-wide party rallies, decisions on the fusion should be taken. However, in the joint resolution taken on the second day of the conference this proposal was no longer mentioned, so that the impression arose that the merger of the parties had been determined on regardless of the Social Democrats' prior conditions.[115] "The Conference", so runs the announcement, "was replete with the common will further to develop the effective operational unity of the two worker-parties with a view to organisational fusion".[116]

This resolution once again put the West German Social Democrats on the alert. In the first half of January, under the influence of Schumacher they spoke on various occasion against the merging of the two parties, because they did not see why the Social Democrats should be called upon to be blood-donors for the weak Communists.[117] The result of the joint elections, which took place in the second half of the month in the American Zone, proved them to be right. The Communists received only 3.5 per cent. of the votes. But this result merely spurred the Communists on to accelerate the campaign for merging.[118] Arrests by the Soviet secret police and the pressure of organised gatherings gradually undermined the SPD Central Committee's will to resist, although only on January 15 it had once more plucked up courage to refuse the merger in the Soviet Zone.[119] In "night-long" discussions at Karlshorst, Grotewohl was blackmailed with, probably among other things, threats that, even in the Zone, the Soviet Occupation authorities held thousands of honest SPD functionaries as hostages, of whose fate no one would learn if they were to vanish.[120] Force is a powerful argument.

As early as January, Schumacher had perceived that the forced merger was no longer to be held back, because the decisions had "already been taken by the Occupation Power".[121] On February 8 he now tried to get Grotewohl, at a meeting at Brunswick, to disband the SPD in the Soviet Zone so as at least not to place the ordinary party members under the compulsion of having to join a Communist-led party.[122] Moreover, such a step would have proclaimed before all the world where the responsibility lay. But Grotewohl declared that it was too late.[123] Three days later the Central Committee resolved by a bare majority to merge with the KPD in the Soviet Zone.[124] The SPD in the Soviet Zone of Occupation had pronounced its own death sentence.

On February 19, Schumacher flew to Berlin himself. Once more he pressed for the dissolution of the party, but this time it was also for him a matter of preventing the forced merger at least in the western part of the German capital. Even though the Central Committee refused both, Schumacher did find in West Berlin enough determined men to oppose the Communist intrigues. Led by Franz Neumann and Kurt Swolinski, they organised a referendum, in which a bare 3,000 Social Democrats from the Western Sectors voted for the United Party but nearly 20,000 against it. In the Soviet Sector the police prevented the referendum from being held.[125] This result, an impressive testimony to the dislike of the compulsory merger, encouraged Neumann and his friends to oppose Grotewohl and Fechner. When on April 20 the "Socialist Unity Party" was founded, West Berlin, just as West Germany, retained a free Social Democratic Party.[126]

The dramatic struggle ended in a draw. In March Schumacher had forecast precisely what was at stake. "In truth, controversies of significance for the whole of Europe, and, further, for the world, are now under way on German soil. What seems like a political party controversy, which now stands at the focal point of interest in Germany, is actually a part of the future of Europe. Social Democrats believe that the core of the problem is the struggle about whether Europe is to be fashioned on a democratic basis or a dictatorial basis." [127] Through the firm bearing of Schumacher and his friends, the Soviets were prevented from securing a new "transmission" from East to West Germany. But they were unable to prevent from the West the Communist subjugation of the Soviet area of Occupation.

Thus once more was there confirmation that the Iron Curtain, which in May, 1945, was drawn down across the centre of Europe, signified more than an administrative boundary. It signified the limit of Soviet expansion, which in the later autumn and winter of 1945–46 proved, for the Soviets, too, immovable. When in the Zones they dominated in Austria and Germany the Soviets failed to established functioning "transmissions" to look after the imposition of their will in the western parts of the countries, their strivings to conquer the whole of Europe had, for the time being, come to grief. After the floodtide of Revolution a new ebb had set in. It was intended, above all, to serve the consolidation of the new empire.[128] Europe remained partitioned at the Elbe.

ENVOI

Like everything else that is historical, the story of the partitioning of Europe is a story of might. When the Soviet Union succeeded in thrusting forward with its troops and its political system into the heart of Europe, the fate of the Continent was sealed for decades. Certainly it was still some considerable time before the conditions under the pressure of the new distribution of power became settled. For a time the Western Powers still tried to free various parts from the Soviet embrace, and the Soviet Union continued its efforts to draw the whole of Germany within its sphere of domination. Neither side was successful in changing the existing situation. After the Soviet leaders had proclaimed, through the coup d'état in Prague at the beginning of 1948, their determination not to relinquish the sphere of control they had succeeded in capturing in 1945, the West also began to consolidate the free part of Europe, with West Germany included. With the founding of the Federal Republic of Germany and the immediately following conversion of Soviet military dictatorship into a German "People's Democracy", replete with the attributes of counterfeit sovereignty, the circumstance that Europe was partitioned across the heart of Germany was made manifest to all the world. The development in these post-war years is to be examined and described in a further study.

NOTES

CHAPTER ONE · THE FIRST PHASE OF THE SOVIET
EXPANSION (1918—1921)

p. 10   [1] W. I. Lenin: *Einige Thesen*. Quoted by W. Grottian: *Das sowjetische Regierungssystem, Quellenbuch* (Cologne, 1956), p. 5–6.

[2] J. W. Stalin: *Fragen des Leninismus* (Moscow, 1947), p. 133.

[3] Hannah Arendt: *Elemente und Ursprünge totalitärer Herrschaft* (Frankfurt, 1955), p. 650. The English edition does not contain this quotation (*The Origins of Totalitarism*. New York, 1951).

p. 11   [4] L. Trotzki: *Mein Leben* (Berlin, 1930), p. 327.

[5] William Henry Chamberlin: *The Russian Revolution* (New York, 1954), vol. i. 363.

p. 12   [6] David Shub: *Lenin. A Biography* (Garden City, New York, 1949), pp. 298–9.

[7] R. Aron: *Der permanente Krieg* (Frankfurt, 1953), p. 151.

[8] Shub, p. 290.

[9] Ibid. p. 322.

p. 13   [10] Chamberlin: *The Russian Revolution*, ii. 122.

[11] See G. von Rauch: *Geschichte des bolschewistischen Rußland* (Wiesbaden, 1956), p. 43.

[12] Rauch, p. 144.

[13] See Shub, pp. 341–2.

p. 14   [14] See H. Neubauer: *München und Moskau 1918/19* (Munich, 1958), p. 70.

[15] Ibid. pp. 72, 74–5.

[16] Ibid. p. 72; Chamberlin, ii. 378.

p. 15   [17] Chamberlin, ii. 298.

[18] See A. Laeuen: *Polnische Tragödie*, 2nd edition (Stuttgart, 1956), pp. 289–93.

[19] For previous history see G. Rhode: *Die Entstehung der Curzon-Linie, Osteuropa*, vol. v. 2 (1955).

p. 15   [20] See Rauch, p. 163.

p. 16   [21] Hannah Arendt: *The Origins of Totalitarism* (New York, 1951), p. 396.

      [22] For quotation see J. M. Bocheński and G. Niemeyer: *Handbuch des Weltkommunismus* (Freiburg–Munich, 1958), p. 218.

      [23] See Chamberlin, ii. 308.

p. 18   [24] W.I. Lenin: *Ausgewählte Werke,* 2 vols. (Berlin 1951/52), i. 725.

      [25] Ibid. ii. 51–2.

      [26] See Rauch, pp. 117–8.

p. 19   [27] R. Pipes: *The Formation of the Soviet Union* (Cambridge, Mass., 1954), p. 109.

      [28] Ibid. pp. 172–6; P. Olberg: *Moskaus Doppelspiel gegenüber den Mohammedanern, Neue Zürcher Zeitung,* April 27, 1958, no. 114, and May 4, 1958, no. 121.

p. 20   [29] For details see Pipes, pp. 204–20; Chamberlin, ii. 406–14.

      [30] See Pipes, p. 224.

p. 21   [31] Ibid. pp. 225–7; G. Jäschke: *Transkaukasien. Ein Musterbeispiel sowjetischer Eroberungspolitik, Osteuropa* xi. (1935–36).

      [32] For text See Pipes, p. 227.

p. 22   [33] See Pipes, p. 332.

      [34] For text see Pipes, pp. 232–3.

      [35] See Pipes, p. 236.

p. 23   [36] See *Unveröffentlichte Dokumente Lenins. Einheit* xi. pp. 708 – 713 (1956).

CHAPTER TWO · EBB AND FURTHER FLOW OF THE REVOLUTION (1921—1940)

p. 24   [1] See Pipes, pp. 183–4; Chamberlin, ii. 424–6.

      [2] See Stalin, pp. 74–5.

      [3] See Pipes, p. 235.

p. 26   [4] See J. Deutscher: *Stalin. A Political Biography* (London, 1949), pp. 281–3; Rauch, pp. 229–32.

      [5] See Deutscher, p. 290.

      [6] Ibid. pp. 290–1.

p. 27   [7] See Shub, p. 343.

      [8] See J. Degras: *The Communist International 1919–1943. Documents,* vol. i. 1919–1922 (London, 1956), pp. 168–82.

p. 28   [9] See A. W. Just: *Rußland in Europa* (Stuttgart, 1949), p. 138.

      [10] See among other things the descriptions of former Communists, such as M. Buber-Neumann, R. Fischer, D. Hyde and H. Castro Delgado.

p. 28 11 See Stefan T. Possony: *A Century of Conflicts. Communist Technique of World Revolution* (Chicago, 1953), p. 177.

12 Possony, p. 184.

p. 29 13 Deutscher, p. 410.

14 See Deutscher, p. 392.

15 See Historicus: *Stalin on Revolution, Foreign Affairs* (1948/49), vol. xxvi. no. 6, p. 179.

16 Stalin, p. 446.

p. 30 17 As quoted from Lenin by Bocheński-Niemeyer, p. 174.

18 As cited by F. Löwenthal: *Das kommunistische Experiment* (Cologne, 1957), p. 145.

p. 31 19 From Stalin's works (Russian edition, 1949), quoted by Grottian: *Quellenbuch,* p. 14.

20 See Deutscher, p. 201.

21 Stalin, p. 73.

22 Quoted by Grottian: *Quellenbuch,* p. 14.

p. 33 23 See M. Buber-Neumann: *Von Potsdam nach Moskau. Stationen eines Irrweges* (Stuttgart, 1957), p. 284; H. Castro Delgado: *J'ai perdu ma foi à Moscou* (Paris, 1950), p. 208.

24 See Rauch, pp. 361–2; Possony, p. 217.

25 See Stalin, pp. 520–5.

p. 34 26 Ibid. pp. 685–90.

27 Deutscher, p. 429; see also Rauch, p. 367.

28 See *Akten zur Deutschen Auswärtigen Politik 1918–1945,* Series D, vols. vi. and vii. (Baden-Baden, 1956). Cited as: *Deutsche Akten.*

p. 35 29 Ibid. vii. 206–7.

30 Aron, p. 277.

31 See Stalin, p. 687.

32 See Aron, p. 277; Deutscher p. 464.

p. 36 33 See Deutscher, p. 439; Possony, p. 254.

34 See Deutscher, p. 438.

p. 37 35 See *Das nationalsozialistische Deutschland und die Sowjetunion 1939–1941* (Berlin, 1948), p. 113; English edition: *Nazi-Soviet Relations 1939–1941* (Washington, 1948), pp. 102–3.

36 See the speech of the British Foreign Secretary on October 26 in the House of Lords. *Parliamentary Debates, House of Lords,* vol. cxiv, col. 1563.

37 See *Das nationalsozialistische Deutschland...,* p. 118; *Nazi-Soviet Relations...,* p. 107.

38 Ibid. pp. 102–5; pp. 92–5.

p. 37   [39] David J. Dallin: *Soviet Russia's Foreign Policy* (New Haven, 1942), pp. 70–1.

p. 38   [40] See B. Kusnierz: *Stalin and the Poles* (London, 1949), pp. 51–4.

      [41] See G. von Rauch: *Die baltischen Staaten und Sowjetrussland 1919–1939, Europa-Archiv* (1954), vol. ix. 6864.

      [42] See B. Meissner: *Die Sowjetunion, die baltischen Staaten und das Völkerrecht* (Cologne, 1956), pp. 60–1.

      [43] See Meissner, pp. 63 and 66; P. Olberg: *Die Tragödie des Baltikums* (Zurich, 1941), p. 36.

      [44] See Makarov: *Der sowjetrussisch-finnische Konflikt, Zeitschrift für ausl. öffentl. Recht und Völkerrecht* (1940–41), vol. x. 296.

p. 39   [45] Ibid. pp. 302–7.

      [46] Ibid. p. 318.

p. 40   [47] Ibid. p. 317.

      [48] See Mannerheim: *Erinnerungen* (Zurich, 1952), p. 414.

p. 41   [49] For text see Makarov, pp. 331–4.

      [50] See Meissner, p. 72.

      [51] Meissner, p. 67.

      [52] See Meissner, pp. 78–80.

p. 42   [53] Ibid. pp. 82–90; Olberg, pp. 66–73.

p. 43   [54] Ibid. pp. 91–2.

p. 44   [55] Meissner, p. 67.

      [56] See Olberg, pp. 61–5.

      [57] See G. Gafencu: *Vorspiel zum Krieg im Osten* (Zurich, 1944), pp. 385–92; A. Hillgruber: *Hitler, König Carol und Marschall Antonescu* (Wiesbaden, 1954), pp. 70–4.

      [58] For text see Makarov: *Die Eingliederung Bessarabiens in die Sowjetunion. Zeitschrift für ausländisches öffentliches Recht und Völkerrecht* (1940–41), vol. x. 356.

      [59] See Hillgruber, p. 72.

p. 45   [60] See Gafencu, p. 392.

      [61] Ibid. p. 104.

      [62] See Deutscher, pp. 438–9.

p. 46   [63] *Geschichtsfälscher. Neue Welt* (1948), vol. iii. 3.

      [64] See Rauch, p. 395; Gafencu, pp. 402–3.

      [65] See Löwenthal, p. 193.

p. 47   [66] See B. Meissner: *Sowjetrussland zwischen Revolution und Restauration* (Cologne, 1956), pp. 51–3.

      [67] See M. Beloff: *The Foreign Policy of Soviet Russia 1929–1941* (London, 1952), 2nd edition, vol. ii. 78, as well as, with a different text, Meissner: *Sowjetrussland ...*, p. 51; Rauch: *Die baltischen Staaten ...*, p. 69.

S. 48   [68] See Beloff, p. 78.

       [69] See David J. Dallin: *The Real Soviet Russia*, 3rd edition (New Haven, 1950), p. 100; Possony, pp. 269–70.

       [70] See J. Degras (Ed.): *Soviet Documents on Foreign Policy* (London, 1951), vol. i. 464–5.

p. 49   [71] Bolschewik (1940), no. 4, p. 63; for quotation see K. Krupinski: *Die Komintern seit Kriegsausbruch* (Berlin), p. 47.

       [72] Internationalnyj majak (1940), no. 4, p. 2; for quotation see Krupinski, p. 32.

       [73] See Hillgruber, pp. 98–100.

p. 50   [74] See *Das nationalsozialistische Deutschland ...*, pp. 187–8; *Nazi-Soviet Relations ...*, pp. 166–8.

       [75] See Deutscher, p. 443.

       [76] Ribbentrop to Stalin, Oct. 13, 1940. *Das nationalsozialistische Deutschland ...*, p. 329; *Nazi-Soviet Relations ...*, p. 213.

       [77] See *Das nationalsozialistische Deutschland ...*, pp. 248–87; *Nazi-Soviet Relations ...*, pp. 217–54.

       [78] See *Geschichtsfälscher*, p. 39.

p. 51   [79] Gafencu, pp. 403–4.

       [80] See *Das nationalsozialistische Deutschland ...*, pp. 291–5; *Nazi-Soviet Relations ...*, pp. 260–4.

       [81] See G. L. Weinberg: *Germany and the Soviet Union 1939 till 1941* (Leiden, 1954) pp. 151–4.

       [82] See W. Cornides: *Die Weltmächte und Deutschland* (Tübingen and Stuttgart, 1957), p. 33.

p. 52   [83] See Cornides, p. 33.

CHAPTER THREE · THE UNNATURAL ALLIANCE BETWEEN EAST AND WEST (1941—1944)

p. 53   [1] See G. Hilger: *Wir und der Kreml* (Frankfurt, 1955), p. 313.

       [2] See Weinberg, p. 167.

p. 55   [3] See mainly Stalin, pp. 24–5.

       [4] See Historicus, p. 176.

       [5] For quotation see Krupinski, p. 45.

       [6] See Historicus, p. 197.

p. 56   [7] See M. Beloff, ii. 392, 394–5.

       [9] G. F. Kennan: *The Sources of Soviet Conduct, Foreign Affairs* (1946–47), vol. xxv, no. 4, p. 572.

       [9] For quotation see Dallin, *The Real Soviet Russia*, p. 91.

       [10] J. Stalin: *Über den großen Vaterländischen Krieg der Sowjetunion* (Berlin, 1951), pp. 36–7.

p. 57 [11] See E. Sarkisyanz: *Russland und der Messianismus des Orients* (Tübingen, 1955), pp. 168–85.

[12] See Dallin: *The Real Soviet Russia*, p. 49.

[13] Just, p. 146.

p. 58 [14] See Castro Delgado, pp. 219–20.

[15] See Douglas Hyde: *I believed, The Autobiography of a former British Communist* (London, 1951), pp. 170–4.

[16] See W. Leonhard: *Die Revolution entlässt ihre Kinder* (Cologne, 1955), pp. 254–60.

[17] See Castro Delgado, pp. 227–8.

p. 59 [18] See F. Borkenau: *European Communism* (New York, 1953), pp. 282–5.

[19] Stalin: *Über den grossen Vaterländischen Krieg*, p. 13; Possony, who speaks of a "hitherto unknown prediction" of Stalin (p. 273) evidently overlooked this passage.

[20] Stalin: *Über den grossen Vaterländischen Krieg*, pp. 120–2.

p. 60 [21] See David J. Dallin: *Russia and Postwar Europe, 5th edition* (New Haven, 1948), p. 162.

[22] See J. v. Puttkamer: *Von Stalingrad zur Volkspolizei* (Wiesbaden, 1951), pp. 37, 45; H. v. Einsiedel: *Tagebuch der Versuchung* (Berlin, 1950), pp. 54–63.

[23] See Puttkamer, pp. 51–4.

p. 61 [24] Ibid. p. 38; Einsiedel, p. 49.

[25] See Puttkamer, p. 73.

[26] See Leonhard, p. 293.

[27] For quotation see Dallin: *The Real Soviet Russia*, p. 48.

p. 62 [28] See P. Kleist: *Zwischen Hitler und Stalin* (Bonn, 1950), pp. 235–84; Leonhard, pp. 294–5.

[29] G. F. Kennan: *American Diplomacy 1900–1950*, 2nd edition (London, 1952), pp. 74–5, 83.

p. 63 [30] The Supreme Allied War Council's resolution of February 5, 1940, was announced in the House of Commons by Chamberlain on March 19, 1940. *Parliamentary Debates, Commons.* vol. ccclviii, col. 1838.

[31] See *Deutsches Weissbuch*, vol. vi.; *Die Geheimakten des französischen Generalstabes* (Berlin, 1941).

[32] See Hull: *The Memoirs of Cordell Hull* (New York, 1948), vol. ii. 1169.

p. 64 [33] See New York Times, June 24, 1941.

[34] See Deutscher, p. 494.

[35] *Documents on American Foreign Relations* (Boston, from 1940 on), vol. iv. 600–1.

p. 64 36 W. Churchill: *The Second World War* (London, 1950–54), vol. ii. p. 331.

37 See also Kennan: *American Diplomacy*, p. 84.

p. 65 38 See Dallin: *Soviet Russia's Foreign Policy*, pp. 388–9.

39 See Hyde, p. 91.

40 Possony, p. 291.

p. 66 41 Löwenthal, p. 199.

42 See J. Carl: *Das amerikanische Leih- und Pachtgesetz* (Berlin, 1957), p. 79: for further details see J. R. Deane: *The Strange Alliance. The Story of our Efforts at Wartime Cooperation with Russia* (New York, 1947), pp. 93–5.

43 See Carl, pp. 62–3.

44 Ibid. p. 85.

45 See Hull, ii. 1272; Also criticised by Kennan: *American Diplomacy*, p. 86.

46 See Leonhard, p. 335.

p. 67 47 See S. L. Sharp: *Poland – White Eagle on a Red Field* (Cambridge, Mass., 1953), Chapter ii.

48 See H. W. Baldwin: *Great Mistakes of the War* (London, 1950), pp. 23–42; Ch. Wilmot: *The Struggle for Europe* (London, 1952), p. 130 and elsewhere.

49 See Churchill, v. 226.

p. 68 50 See Robert E. Sherwood: *Roosevelt and Hopkins. An Intimate History* (New York, 1945), p. 748.

51 See Deutscher, pp. 509–10; W. Wagner: *Die Entstehung der Oder- Neisse-Linie*, 2nd edition (Stuttgart, 1959), pp. 528–9; English edition: *The Genesis of the Oder-Neisse Line* (Stuttgart, 1957), pp. 68–9.

p. 69 52 See St. Mikołajczyk: *The Pattern of Soviet Domination* (London, 1948), p. 17.

53 See L. W. Holborn (ed.): *War and Peace Aims of the United Nations* (Boston, 1943), vol. i. 354.

p. 70 54 Churchill, iv. 504.

55 See Wagner, German ed. pp. 37–41; English ed. pp. 38–41.

p. 71 56 See R. Umiastowski: *Poland, Russia and Great Britain 1941 till 1945* (London, 1946), p. 218.

57 J. Ciechanowski: *Defeat in Victory* (New York, 1947), p. 213.

p. 72 58 See W. H. McNeill: *America, Britain and Russia* (London, 1953), p. 270.

59 See Ph. E. Mosely: *Dismemberment of Germany, Foreign Affairs* (1949–50), vol. xxviii.

p. 73   ⁶⁰ Precise details given by H. Strauss: *The Division and Dismemberment of Germany*, Treatise, (Geneva, 1952); E. Deuerlein: *Die Einheit Deutschlands* (Frankfurt, 1957); R. Thilenius: *Die Teilung Deutschlands* (Hamburg, 1957).

  ⁶¹ See Churchill, iii. 558.

  ⁶² See Sherwood, p. 711.

  ⁶³ An excellent summary of the extensive literature on this subject is given by G. Moltmann: *Amerikas Deutschlandpolitik im zweiten Weltkrieg* (Heidelberg, 1958), pp. 121–35.

p. 75   ⁶⁴ See Churchill, v. 356.

  ⁶⁵ Ibid. vi. 210.

  ⁶⁶ See *Foreign Relations of the United States, Diplomatic Papers, The Conferences at Malta and Yalta 1945* (Washington, 1955), pp. 612, 615.

p. 76   ⁶⁷ Washington: See *The Conferences at Malta and Yalta*, p. 187; London: See Eden's proposal, only to decide on "measures for the dissolution of the German unitary state" (*The Conferences at Malta and Yalta*, p. 656).

  ⁶⁸ See *The Conferences at Malta and Yalta*, p. 978.

  ⁶⁹ Ibid. p. 809; see also the British assertions, pp. 874, 885.

  ⁷⁰ See W. Wagner: *Besatzungszonen und Spaltung Deutschlands, Aussenpolitik* (1954), vol. v. 8.

p. 77   ⁷¹ See Lord Strang: *Home and Abroad* (London, 1956), p. 200.

  ⁷² See Churchill, vi. 206; Strang, pp. 213–4.

  ⁷³ See Mosely: *The Occupation of Germany: New Light on How the Zones were Drawn, Foreign Affairs* (1949–50), xxviii. 588.

  ⁷⁴ See Th. Eschenburg: *Das Problem der deutschen Einheit nach den beiden Weltkriegen, Vierteljahrshefte für Zeitgeschichte* (1957), vol. v, no. 2, pp. 117–8.

  ⁷⁵ See Mosely: *Occupation*, p. 589.

p. 78   ⁷⁶ See McNeill, p. 481.

  ⁷⁷ See D. D. Eisenhower: *Crusade in Europe* (New York, 1952), pp. 249, 476–7.

  ⁷⁸ Strang, p. 214.

  ⁷⁹ See Mosely: *Occupation*, p. 207.

  ⁸⁰ See Strang, p. 207.

p. 79   ⁸¹ See M. Balfour and J. Mair: *Four Power Control in Germany and Austria* (London, 1956), pp. 283–4.

  ⁸² Ibid. pp. 287–8.

p. 80   ⁸³ Ibid. pp. 287–9.

  ⁸⁴ Ibid. pp. 289–90.

p. 80   [85] See also K. Gruber: *Zwischen Befreiung und Freiheit* (Vienna, 1953), p. 59.

        [86] See *The Conferences at Malta and Yalta*, pp. 616–8.

p. 81   [87] Strang, p. 215.

        [88] See Mosely: *Occupation*, p. 588.

CHAPTER FOUR · THE THIRD PHASE: EXPANSION TO THE
ELBE (1944—1945)

p. 82   [1] See F. Fejtö: *Histoires des Démocraties populaires* (Paris, 1952), p. 48, note.

        [2] See Deane, p. 295.

p. 83   [3] Ibid, p. 319.

p. 84   [4] W. Z. Foster: *History of the Three Internationals* (New York, 1955), pp. 452–3.

        [5] Aron, p. 172.

        [6] See Borkenau, p. 484.

        [7] David J. Dallin: *The New Soviet Empire* (New Haven, 1951), p. 27.

        [8] See Borkenau, pp. 484–5.

p. 85   [9] See Sharp, Chapter iv.

        [10] For text see G. Rhode and W. Wagner: *Quellen zur Entstehung der Oder-Neisse-Linie*, 2nd edition (Stuttgart, 1959), pp. 134–6; English edition: *The Genesis of the Oder-Neisse Line, Sources and Documents* (Stuttgart, 1959), pp. 119–21.

        [11] *Documents on American Foreign Relations*, vii. 854.

p. 86   [12] See Rhode-Wagner, German edition pp. 137–8; English edition pp. 121–3.

        [13] See Hull, ii. 1442.

        [14] See Mikołajczyk, p. 81.

        [15] W. Anders: *An Army in Exile* (London, 1949), p. 211.

p. 87   [16] See Mikołajczyk, pp. 104–10.

p. 88   [17] The well-known "Cadogan Letter" of November 2, 1944 (*Poland, Germany and European Peace, Official Documents 1944–1948*, published by the Polish Embassy in London, 1948, pp. 105–6).

        [18] See A. B. Lane: *I saw Poland Betrayed* (New York, 1948), pp. 73–6.

p. 89   [19] See *The Conferences at Malta and Yalta*, p. 781.

p. 90   [20] Ibid. pp. 973–4.

        [21] See New York Times, February 6, 1945.

        [22] See Churchill, vi. 370.

p. 91   23 See Z. Stypułkowski: *Invitation to Moscow* (London, 1951), Churchill, vi. 434–5.

24 See *United Nations Treaty Series* (New York), vol. xii. 391 –403 (no. 70).

25 See H. S. Truman: *Memoirs* (Garden City, New York, 1955), vol. i. 78–82.

p. 92   26 See Sherwood, pp. 899–901.

27 See Hillgruber, pp. 169–70.

p. 93   28 Ibid. pp. 173–5.

29 See Cretzianu: *The Roumanian Armistice Negotiations: Cairo, 1944, Journal of Central European Affairs* (1951–52), vol. xi, no. 3, p. 245.

30 Ibid. p. 250.

p. 94   31 See Churchill, vi. 64–7; Hull, ii. 1451–5; Hillgruber, p. 199.

32 See Hillgruber, pp. 215–29.

33 See R. R. Betts (ed.): *Central and South East Europe 1945 –1948* (London and New York, 1950), p. 4.

p. 95   34 See H. Seton-Watson: *The East European Revolution* (London, 1950), pp. 204–5.

35 For this and the following see Betts, pp. 4–8; Seton-Watson, pp. 205–6; Fejtö, pp. 103–5; Borkenau, pp. 462–3.

p. 96   36 See Churchill, vi. 368–9.

p. 97   37 See Seton-Watson, p. 96; Hillgruber, p. 213.

38 See Churchill, vi. 65–7; Hull, ii. 1454–5.

39 Possony, p. 275.

40 See J. A. Lukacs: *The Great Powers and Eastern Europe* (New York, 1953), pp. 615–6.

p. 98   41 See Seton-Watson, p. 88. The following according to Seton-Watson, pp. 90–2; Betts, pp. 30—2; A. Gyorgy: *Governments of Danubian Europe* (New York, 1949), pp. 218–20.

42 See Strang's verdict, p. 225.

p. 99   43 See V. Dedijer: *Tito* (Berlin, 1953), pp. 95–103.

44 Ibid. pp. 109–10.

p. 100   45 See Borkenau, pp. 365–8.

46 See St. Clissold: *Whirlwind* (London, 1949), p. 34.

47 See Dedijer, pp. 172–3.

48 See Borkenau, pp. 377–8.

49 See Seton-Watson, pp. 219–20.

50 See Borkenau, p. 389; Betts, p. 55.

p. 101   51 See Dedijer, pp. 216–7; Churchill, vi. 80–4.

52 See Borkenau, pp. 391–2.

p. 101 [53] See Seton-Watson, pp. 219–20.

[54] See Churchill, vi. 198.

p. 102 [55] See Fotitch: *Tito and the Western Democracies. Journal of Central European Affairs* (1951–52), xi. no. 4, p. 354.

[56] See Borkenau, pp. 396–8.

[57] Ibid. pp. 403–6.

[58] See Seton-Watson, p. 146.

p. 103 [59] See N. Kállay: *Hungarian Premier* (New York, 1954), pp. 370–90.

[60] See N. von Horthy: *Ein Leben für Ungarn* (Bonn, 1953), p. 282.

[61] See Churchill, v. 354–6.

[62] Ibid. vi. 198.

p. 104 [63] See Seton-Watson, pp. 190–1; For the following see Gyorgy, pp. 115–7; Seton-Watson, pp. 191–4; Betts, pp. 101–5; Borkenau, pp. 465–6.

p. 106 [64] See E. Táborský: *Beneš and the Soviets. Foreign Affairs* (1948–49), xxvi. 304.

[65] See E. Táborský: *Beneš and Stalin – Moscow 1943 and 1945. Journal of Central European Affairs* (1953–54), xii. no. 2, pp. 155–6.

[66] See *Memoirs of Dr. Eduard Beneš* (London, 1954), p. 253; Táborský: *Beneš and Stalin*, p. 164.

p. 107 [67] See Táborský: *Beneš and Stalin*, pp. 162, 167.

[68] See Churchill, v. 400.

[69] See Táborský: *Beneš and Stalin*, p. 171.

[70] Ibid. pp. 172–3.

[71] W. M. Molotov: *Fragen der Aussenpolitik* (Moscow, 1949), p. 24.

p. 108 [72] See Táborský: *Beneš and Stalin*, pp. 180–1.

[73] See Borkenau, p. 497.

[74] See Baldwin, p. 51.

p. 109 [75] See Deane, pp. 159–60.

[76] According to Seton-Watson, p. 181.

[77] See A. Schärf: *Österreichs Erneuerung 1945–55* (Vienna, 1955), p. 53.

p. 110 [78] See Churchill, vi. 451–3.

[79] See Gruber, p. 28.

[80] See Leonhard, p. 343.

[81] Ibid. p. 358.

p. 111 [82] See Churchill's message to Stalin, February 20, 1944. *Corre-*

spondence between the Chairman of the Council of Ministers
of the U.S.S.R. and the Presidents of U.S.A. and the Prime
Ministers of Great Britain during the Great Patriotic War of
1941–1945 (Moscow, 1957), vol. i. 203.

p. 111 [83] J. F. C. Fuller: *The Second World War 1939–45* (New York, 1949), p. 400.

p. 112 [84] See for instance Roosevelt's message to Stalin, beginning of February 1944. *Correspondence between the Chairman ...*, ii. 119.

[85] See Hull, ii. 1612; Balfour-Mair, p. 284.

[86] See the second section of the following chapter.

p. 113 [87] See St. G. Xydis: *The secret Anglo-Soviet Agreement on the Balkans of October 9, 1944. Journal of Central European Affairs* (1955–56), xv. no. 3, p. 265.

[88] See McNeill: *America, Britain and Russia*, p. 295.

[89] See M. Bundy: *The Test of Yalta. Foreign Affairs* (1948–49), xxvii. 621.

p. 114 [90] J. L. Snell (ed): *The Meaning of Yalta* (Baton Rouge, 1956), p. 206.

[91] See Snell, pp. 102–26, and the relative literature.

[92] See the telegrams of December 28, 1944 and January 16, 1955. *The Conferences at Malta and Yalta*, pp. 64–6, 450–5.

[93] See *The Conferences at Malta and Yalta*, p. 93.

[94] Ibid. p. 97.

[95] Ibid. pp. 566, 569–70.

[96] Ibid. pp. 566, 569–70.

p. 115 [97] See E. R. Stettinius: *Roosevelt and the Russians* (London, 1950), p. 42.

[98] See *The Conferences at Malta and Yalta*, p. 861.

[99] Ibid. p. 863.

[100] Ibid. pp. 848, 863.

[101] Ibid. pp. 873, 878.

[102] Ibid. pp. 873, 878.

[103] For final text see *The Conferences at Malta and Yalta*, pp. 971–3, 977–8.

p. 116 [104] See Snell, p. 122.

[105] See Truman, i. 384–5.

p. 117 [106] See W. D. Leahy: *I was there* (New York, 1950), pp. 405–6; Truman i. 384.

[107] See J. F. Byrnes: *Speaking Frankly* (New York and London, 1947), p. 73; Truman, i. 346.

p. 117 [108] See Churchill, vi. 550–1.

p. 118 [109] Fuller, p. 355.

[110] *Correspondence between the Chairman . . .*, i. 317.

p. 119 [111] Ibid. i. 318.

[112] See *The Memoirs of Field-Marshal the Viscount Montgomery of Alamein* (London, 1958), 331.

[113] See Churchill, vi. 449.

[114] See Montgomery, pp. 332–4.

p. 120 [115] See Churchill, vi. 528.

[116] Ibid. vi. 448.

[117] Ibid. vi. 448–9.

p. 121 [118] Ibid. vi. 497.

[119] Ibid. vi. 499, 522–3.

[120] See Truman, i. 287.

[121] Ibid. i. 362; Montgomery, pp. 376–7, 379.

[122] Ibid. i. 302.

p. 122 [123] See Montgomery, pp. 384–5.

[124] See Churchill, vi. 523.

p. 123 [125] Montgomery, p. 386.

CHAPTER FIVE · CAUTIOUSNESS IN VICTORY (1945)

p. 124 [1] B. Meissner: *Russland, die Westmächte und Deutschland* (Hamburg, 1953), p. 54.

p. 125 [2] At Yalta, Roosevelt had countered a question posed by Stalin by saying that the American troops could remain in Europe not much more than two years. See *The Conferences at Malta and Yalta*, pp. 617, 628; Stettinius, p. 121.

[3] See also W. Höpker: *Europäisches Niemandsland* (Düsseldorf, 1956), p. 11.

p. 126 [4] See A. and V. Toynbee (eds.): *The Realignment of Europe. Survey of International Affairs* (London, 1955), p. 265.

p. 127 [5] See Mannerheim, p. 505.

[6] See W. von Harpe: *Die Sowjetunion, Finnland und Skandinavien 1945–1955* (Tübingen, 1956), p. 16.

[7] See Mannerheim, p. 520.

p. 128 [8] Ibid. p. 525; Toynbee, p. 269.

[9] See Mannerheim, p. 543.

[10] See Borkenau, p. 487.

p. 129 [11] Ibid. p. 487.

[12] See C. M. Woodhouse: *Apple of Discord* (London, 1948), pp. 112, 180–3.

p. 130 [13] See Churchill, v. 476–86.

p. 130 [14] Ibid. vi. 63.

[15] See Woodhouse, pp. 197–9. Borkenau, who attributes the change of mind to the failure of the mutiny, overlooks the fact that in the meantime the first Balkan Agreement had been concluded (p. 403).

[16] See Xydis, p. 258.

p. 131 [17] See Churchill, vi. 252.

[18] See Toynbee, p. 396.

p. 132 [19] See *The Conferences at Malta and Yalta,* pp. 849, 857.

[20] Ibid. pp. 873, 878.

p. 133 [21] See H. Sturmhöfel: *Die Türkei und die Sowjetunion 1939 bis 1954. Osteuropa* (1955), v. 21.

[22] See *Das nationalsoz. Deutschland und die Sowjetunion 1939 bis 1941,* p. 277; Engl. ed. : *Nazi-Soviet Relations,* pp. 245–6.

[23] See Sturmhöfel, p. 24.

p. 134 [24] See Sturmhöfel, p. 27; G. Kirk: *The Middle East 1945–50* (London, 1954), p. 21.

[25] See G. Jäschke: *Die Türkei in den Jahren 1942–1951* (Wiesbaden, 1955), p. 42.

[26] See N. Sadak: *Turkey faces the Soviets. Foreign Affairs* 1948–49), xxvii. 458; Sturmhöfel, p. 27.

[27] See McGhee: *Die Türkei in der westlichen Welt. Aussenpolitik* (1955), vi. 369.

[28] See Sadak, p. 458.

[29] See Kirk, p. 21.

[30] See Byrnes, p. 77; Truman, i. 376.

p. 135 [31] Ibid. p. 78; Ibid. i. 376.

[32] Ibid. p. 76; Ibid. i. 374.

p. 136 [33] Hyde, p. 218; see also Borkenau, p. 453.

p. 137 [34] See H. Seton-Watson: *From Lenin to Malenkov. The History of World Communism* (New York, 1954), pp. 218–9, 333–4.

[35] See Toynbee, p. 491.

[36] See Borkenau, pp. 442–5.

[37] See R. J. Guiton: *Paris–Moskau* (Stuttgart, 1956), p. 54.

[38] Ibid. p. 80.

p. 138 [39] Ibid. p. 54.

[40] Ibid. p. 54.

[41] See 4th section of this chapter.

p. 139 [42] See Borkenau, pp. 444–5.

[43] See. M. Einaudi, J. M. Domenach and A. Garosci: *Communism in Western Europe* (Ithaca, N. Y., 1951), pp. 76–7.

p. 139 [44] See Seton-Watson: *From Lenin to Malenkov,* pp. 219–20; Borkenau, pp. 326–7.

[45] See Guiton, p. 54.

[46] Ibid. p. 116.

[47] See Borkenau, p. 456.

p. 140 [48] See Foster, p. 458; Toynbee, p. 513.

[49] See Borkenau, pp. 469–70.

[50] See Guiton, p. 117.

[51] See Borkenau, p. 470.

[52] See Toynbee, p. 516.

p. 141 [53] See Borkenau, p. 471.

[54] See Toynbee, pp. 539–43.

p. 142 [55] See Borkenau, p. 451.

[56] See Toynbee, pp. 535, 548.

p. 143 [57] See Borkenau, p. 461.

[58] See Einaudi-Domenach-Garosci, pp. 184–5.

p. 144 [59] See Hull, ii. 1557.

[60] See Borkenau, p. 460.

p. 145 [61] Ibid. p. 461.

[62] See Toynbee, p. 427.

[63] Ibid. p. 430.

p. 146 [64] See Einaudi-Domenach-Garosci, pp. 184–5.

[65] See Borkenau, p. 479.

[66] Foster, p. 457.

p. 147 [67] For quotation see B. D. Wolfe: *Der Tito-Stalin-Konflikt. Ostprobleme* (1953), v. 462.

p. 148 [68] See Lenin, ii. 733.

[69] See Löwenthal, p. 155.

[70] In: *The United Front* (New York, 1938).

[71] See Fejtö, p. 47 note.

p. 149 [72] See Castro Delgado, p. 216.

[73] See first section of chapter iv.

[74] See Foster, p. 453.

[75] See Possony, pp. 211–2.

p. 150 [76] See Löwenthal, p. 219.

[77] G. Dimitroff: *Rolle und Bedeutung der Volksdemokratie* (Berlin, 1953), p. 63.

[78] See Fejtö, p. 172.

[79] Borkenau, p. 494.

p. 151 [80] This is alleged by Borkenau, p. 482.

p. 152 [81] See Harpe, p. 17.

p. 153 [82] See Woodhouse, p. 213; W. H. McNeill: *The Greek Dilemma* (London, 1947), p. 121.

[83] See Borkenau, pp. 418–9.

p. 154 [84] Ibid. pp. 450–1.

p. 155 [85] Ibid. pp. 463–4.

[86] See Leonhard, p. 533.

[87] See Deutscher, pp. 339–400.

[88] See Leonhard, pp. 425–6.

p. 156 [89] See Mikołajczyk: *Challenge in Eastern Europe*, edited by C. E. Black (New Brunswick, N. J., 1954), p. 68.

[90] See Dedijer, p. 165.

[91] See 2nd section of chapter iv.

[92] See Toynbee, pp. 257–60.

p. 157 [93] See Aron, p. 172.

CHAPTER SIX · THE STRUGGLE FOR CENTRAL EUROPE
(1945—1946)

p. 158 [1] See Stettinius, p. 277.

[2] See Soviet Government Note dated November 27, 1958, to United States Government ("Berlin Note").

p. 159 [3] The concept is not a product of the 1950s, as is often assumed, but it was already making its appearance in Communist revolutionary theory in the middle of the 1920s.

[4] Lenin, ii. 355.

p. 160 [5] See Forrestal, p. 47.

[6] Ibid. p. 57.

[7] *Correspondence between the Chairman ...*, i. 343–4; Churchill, vi. 433.

p. 161 [8] See Churchill, vi. 438–9.

[9] Ibid. vi. 498–9.

[10] Aron, p. 238.

[11] Information from Prof. Fraenkel, Berlin.

[12] See Dallin: *The New Soviet Empire*, p. 8, however, the reference is to Germany only.

p. 162 [13] See Mosely: *Dismemberment*, p. 493.

[14] See Stalin: *Vaterländischer Krieg*, p. 23.

[15] See Sherwood, p. 745.

[16] B. Meissner, who was the first to recognise the problem, still alleges this circumstance as a possible motive, although more incidentally. See *Stalin und die Oder-Neisse-Linie. Osteuropa* (1951), i. 7–8. R. Thilenius puts forward this thesis categorically, pp. 52, 56.

p. 162   17   See B. Meissner: *Der Kreml und das Ruhrgebiet. Osteuropa* (1951), i. 2; Meissner: *Russland, die Westmächte und Deutschland*, p. 70; Thilenius, p. 56.

p. 163   18   See *The Conferences at Malta and Yalta*, pp. 616, 625.

      19   At the turn of the year 1945/46, Kurt Schumacher characterised the aim of Soviet policy as "to keep Central Europe in a permanent state of unrest, with Russia ... continuing to play the role of the political aggressor and strengthening its position to an extraordinary degree." See A. Scholz and W. G. Oschilewski: *Turmwächter der Demokratie* (Berlin, 1958), vol. ii. 60.

      20   See G. Castellan: *La politique allemande de l'U.R.S.S. 1941–1945. Revue d'histoire de la deuxième guerre mondiale* (1956) vol. vi. nos. 21 and 22, especially no. 22, pp. 45–6.

      21   See also Deuerlein, pp. 149–51, 175.

p. 164   22   See Meissner: *Russland, die Westmächte und Deutschland*, p. 58.

p. 165   23   See Cornides, p. 45. At Yalta there was still being discussed the possibility of a German counter-government with which, under certain circumstances, cooperation would be possible "as with Badoglio in Italy". See *The Conferences at Malta and Yalta*, p. 613.

      24   See Mosely: *Occupation*, p. 578; Strang, pp. 215–21; Strang: *Germany between East and West. Foreign Affairs* (1954–55), xxxiii, no. 3, p. 390.

      25   See Strang, p. 218; Mosely: *Occupation*, p. 583.

      26   See *The Conferences at Malta and Yalta*, pp. 113–8.

      27   See *The Axis in Defeat* (Washington), pp. 23–4.

      28   See Strang, pp. 221–5.

      29   See *Official Gazette of the Control Council for Germany*, Supplement no. 1 (Berlin, 1946), p. 11.

      30   See W. Grewe: *Punkt vier. Archiv des öffentlichen Rechts* (1952/53) vol. lxxviii. 496. The Declaration bases its legality on Art. 4 of the Instrument of Surrender, into which it is certainly difficult to read intentions of this character.

      31   See also K. Altmeyer: *Die Dokumente vom 5. Juni 1945 und die politische Einheit Deutschlands. Europa-Archiv* (1955), vol. x. 7366. There is frequently a failure to recognise this connection (which is confirmed also by Mosely: *Dismemberment*, p. 496) as with Thilenius, p. 57, and with W. Abendroth: *Die aktuelle Tragweite und die Fortgeltung des Pots-*

damer Abkommens (Untersuchungen zur Lösung der deut-schen Frage, published by the Königsteiner Kreis, Göttingen, 1952, p. 11).

p. 165   [32] See A. Kohn-Brandenburg: *Das System der Provisorien, die Zentralverwaltungen der sowjetischen Besatzungszone und die Verwaltung Berlins. Europa-Archiv* (1947), ii. 1017–22.

p. 166   [33] See Leonhard, pp. 402–3.

      [34] Ibid. pp. 389–90.

      [35] See Puttkammer, p. 46.

p. 167   [36] See Ruth Fischer: *Stalin und der deutsche Kommunismus* (Frankfurt, 1948), p. 624.

      [37] Buber-Neumann, pp. 251–65.

      [38] See Eisenhower, p. 498; L. D. Clay: *Decision in Germany* (Garden City, N. Y., 1950), pp. 46–7.

      [39] Leonhard, p. 396.

      [40] The Soviet secret police took part in all political discussions. See. J. P. Nettl: *Die deutsche Sowjetzone bis heute* (Frankfurt, 1953), p. 23.

p. 168   [41] See Wagner: *Die Entstehung der Oder-Neisse-Linie,* p. 125; English edition: *The Genesis of the Oder-Neisse-Line,* p. 127.

      [42] See Scholz, ii. 60.

      [43] See Leonhard, p. 410. According to Nettl, p. 43, Hörnle had, indeed, brought with him the text from Moscow as early as July.

p. 170   [44] See Leahy, p. 390.

      [45] See Truman, i. 300, 306.

      [46] See Leahy, p. 400.

p. 171   [47] Ibid. p. 309.

      [48] See Truman, pp. 552, 353; Leahy, p. 401.

      [49] See *Official Gazette of the Control Council for Germany,* Supplement no. 1 (Berlin, 1946), p. 11; H. Kraus and K. Heinze: *Völkerrechtliche Urkunden zur europäischen Friedensordnung seit 1945* (Bonn, 1953), vol. viii. 8.

      [50] Thus was the task even in those days. When other authors say that the central agencies could have prevented Germany's partitioning, they evoke the false impression that the division made its appearance only after Potsdam. See W. W. Schütz: *Die Stunde Deutschlands* (Stuttgart, 1954), pp. 50–2; Paul Sethe: *Zwischen Bonn und Moskau,* 3rd. edition (Frankfurt, 1957), pp. 7–11; Thilenius, pp. 113–4.

p. 171   51 But see Altmeyer, p. 7371.

        52 See Nettl, p. 17; Balfour-Mair, pp. 104, 125.

p. 172   53 See Stalin: *Fragen des Leninismus,* pp. 148–51.

        54 See Löwenthal, p. 155.

        55 See Clay, p. 131.

        56 In, for example, the communes and in press matters. But one is wide of the mark if one believes there was a sort of Communist conspiracy between Moscow and Washington, as H. zu Löwenstein believes: *Deutschlands Schicksal 1945 bis 1957* (Bonn, 1957), pp. 17–20.

p. 173   57 See Cornides, p. 74.

        58 See Aron, p. 238.

        59 Ibid. p. 238.

        60 See W. Erfurt: *Die sowjetrussische Deutschland-Politik* (Eßlingen, 1959), 4th edition, pp. 12–3.

        61 See D. Geyer: *Die Sowjetunion und Iran* (Tübingen, 1955), pp. 58–60.

        62 See Byrnes, p. 83.

        63 See Truman, i. 406–7.

p. 174   64 See *The Conferences at Malta and Yalta,* pp. 978–9.

        65 See Nettl, pp. 183–4; Harriman reported to Washington on the matter as early as the beginning of April. See Forrestal, pp. 40–1.

        66 See Byrnes, pp. 83–4.

        67 See Cornides, p. 95.

p. 175   68 See also Byrnes, p. 86.

        69 There is occasionally too little value placed on this fact, particularly if Germany's partitioning is traced to the circumstance that the Allies had failed to work out a common policy towards Germany in good time. See W. Dorn: *Die Debatte über die amerikanische Besatzungspolitik für Deutschland (1944–45). Vierteljahrshefte für Zeitgeschichte* (1958), vol. vi., no. 1, p. 76; Deuerlein, pp. 153–4, 180–1. It is scarcely possible to imagine what a common policy of partners so different in character could look like if it was not to be limited to negative things. See Cornides, p. 61.

        70 See Leahy, p. 390.

        71 See Truman, p. 406.

p. 176   72 Ibid. i. 401; Churchill, vi. 580–1.

        73 See Byrnes, p. 86.

        74 See Truman, i. 407.

p. 177 [75] See the note dated August 7, 1945, in: *Documents français relatifs à l'Allemagne (August 1945 – February 1947)*, (Paris, 1947), p. 8–9.

[76] See Byrnes, p. 170.

[77] See the statements quoted in Altmeyer, p. 7371.

[78] See Byrnes, pp. 169–70, and the interviews with the London "Times". Guiton, p. 113, and Thilenius, p. 130.

p. 178 [79] See Byrnes, p. 70; Guiton, pp. 11, 13–4.

[80] See Guiton, p. 69.

[81] In regard to the spring of 1946, Clay (p. 145) writes that the French opposition to the administration seemed of less importance "as the intransigent Soviet position made it appears unlikely that these central agencies could operate successfully". What applied for 1946 was, however, also correct for 1945, since Soviet policy had not changed in this period. See also Balfour-Mair, p. 125.

p. 179 [82] Text of the law for Saxony. B. Ruhm von Oppen: *Documents on Germany under Occupation 1945–1954* (London etc., 1955), pp. 59–64.

[83] The Western Powers' way of looking at things has often been adopted in German contemporary literature, e. g., by Schütz, Sethe and Thilenius.

[84] See H. Duhnke: *Stalinismus in Deutschland* (Cologne, 1955), p. 94.

[85] See Clay, p. 111.

[86] Ibid. p. 115.

[87] Ibid. p. 112.

[88] Ibid. pp. 39–40.

p. 180 [89] See Schütz, p. 51.

[90] See Guiton, p. 125.

[91] Clay gives "by the end of 1945" as the point of time when this was realised.

p. 181 [92] See Clay, p. 122.

[93] Ibid. p. 123.

p. 182 [94] See Balfour-Mair, pp. 304–9.

[95] See Byrnes, p. 162.

[96] See Ph. E. Mosely: *The Treaty with Austria. International Organisation* (1950), vol. iv. 229.

p. 183 [97] See Schärf, p. 64.

[98] See Balfour-Mair, p. 350.

[99] Schärf, p. 67.

213

p. 184 [100] See Gruber, pp. 35–6; Balfour-Mair, pp. 319–20.

[101] See Balfour-Mair, p. 321.

p. 185 [102] See Schärf, pp. 79–80; Leonhard, p. 425.

[103] See Gruber, p. 37.

[104] See Schärf, p. 80.

[105] See Balfour-Mair, p. 323.

[106] See Gruber, p. 39.

p. 187 [107] See Leonhard, p. 425; *Das Präludium des Kalten Krieges. Europa-Brücke* (1957), vol. ii., no. 9, p. 25.

p. 188 [108] See Scholz, i. 54.

[109] Ibid. ii. 56.

[110] Ibid. ii. 59.

[111] See *Das Präludium des Kalten Krieges* (1957), v. 21–3, pp. 18–20.

p. 189 [112] See F. Wesemann: *Kurt Schumacher (Frankfurt*, 1952), pp. 94 –95; Scholz, i. 46.

[113] See *Das Präludium des Kalten Krieges* (1957), ix. 23; G. Stern: *Porträt einer bolschewistischen Partei* (Cologne, 1957), p. 29.

[114] See Stern, p. 29.

p. 190 [115] Ibid. pp. 31–2; Leonhard, p. 426; Duhnke, p. 56.

[116] The greatest significance is accorded this resolution in *Das Präludium des Kalten Krieges* (1957), x. 22.

[117] See Stern, pp. 32–3; Wesemann, p. 96; Scholz, i. 53.

[118] See Duhnke, p. 57.

[119] See Stern, p. 34; *Das Präludium des Kalten Krieges* (1958), iv., no. 1, p. 26.

[120] See *Das Präludium des Kalten Krieges* (1958), iv., no. 2, p. 18.

[121] See Scholz, ii. 54.

p. 191 [122] See Wesemann, p. 99.

[123] See *Das Präludium des Kalten Krieges* (1958), iv., no. 3, p. 17–8; Wesemann, p. 99; Stern, p. 35.

[124] See Duhnke, p. 58.

[125] See Duhnke, p. 60; Leonhard, p. 433.

[126] See Duhnke, p. 60; Scholz, i. 59–60; Wesemann, p. 104.

[127] Neue Zeitung, March 22, 1946, as quoted by Scholz, i. 59.

p. 192 [128] See Historicus, pp. 212–3.

BIBLIOGRAPHY

From the very large amount of literature dealing with the events of the last forty years, in general only those books and essays referred to in this book are detailed below.

I. DOCUMENTS

Akten zur Deutschen Auswärtigen Politik 1918–1945. Aus dem Archiv des Deutschen Auswärtigen Amtes (Baden-Baden, 1956), Series D 1937 till 1945, vols. vi. and vii.

The Axis in Defeat. Department of State Publication 2423 (Washington).

Correspondence between the Chairman of the Council of Ministers of the U.S.S.R. and the Presidents of the U.S.A. and the Prime Ministers of Great Britain during the Great Patriotic War of 1941 to 1945. Published by the Ministry of Foreign Affairs of the U.S.S.R., 2 vols. (Moscow, 1957).

Degras, Jane (ed.): *The Communist International 1919–1943. Documents.* Vol. i, 1910–1922 (London etc., 1956).

Degras, Jane (ed.): *Soviet Documents on Foreign Policy.* 3 vols (London etc., 1951–53).

Deutsches Weissbuch, vol. vi. *Die Geheimakten des französischen Generalstabes* (Berlin, 1941).

Documents on American Foreign Relations (Boston, from 1940 on).

Documents français relatifs à l'Allemagne (August 1945–February 1947). (Imprimerie Nationale J. U. 707 018, Paris, 1947).

Foreign Relations of the United States. Diplomatic Papers. The Conferences at Malta and Yalta 1945. Department of State Publication (Washington, 1955).

Grottian, Walter: *Das sowjetische Regierungssystem. Die Grundlagen der Macht in der Sowjetunion. Leitfaden und Quellenbuch* (Cologne and Opladen, 1956).

Holborn, Louise W. (ed.): *War and Peace Aims of the United Nations.* 2 vols. (Boston, 1943 and 1948).

Kraus, Herbert, and Heinze, Kurt: *Völkerrechtliche Urkunden zur europäischen Friedensordnung seit 1945* (Bonn, 1953).

Meissner, Boris: *Das Ostpakt-System. Dokumentensammlung* (Frankfurt, 1955).

Das nationalsozialistische Deutschland und die Sowjetunion 1939–1941. Akten aus dem Archiv des Deutschen Auswärtigen Amtes. Department of State (Berlin, 1948). English edition: *Nazi–Soviet Relations 1939–1941. Documents from the Archives of the German Foreign Office.* Department of State Publication 3023 (Washington, 1948).

Official Gazette of the Control Council for Germany, Supplement No. 1 (Berlin, 1946).

Parliamentary Debates. Official Report. House of Commons. Vols. ccclxxiii to cdxiii.

Parliamentary Debates. Official Report. House of Lords. Vols. cxiv to cxxx.

Poland, Germany and European Peace. Official Documents 1944–1948. Published by the Polish Embassy in London (London, 1948).

Rhode, Gottfried, and Wagner, Wolfgang: *Quellen zur Entstehung der Oder-Neisse-Linie. Die deutschen Ostgebiete,* vol. iii, 2nd edition (Stuttgart, 1959). English edition: The Genesis of the Oder-Neisse Line. Sources and Documents (Stuttgart, 1959).

United Nations. Treaty Series. Vols. i to xii (New York).

Unveröffentlichte Dokumente Lenins. Einheit (1956), vol. xi. 8.

II. MEMOIRS AND MONOGRAPHS

Abendroth, Wolfgang: *Die aktuelle Tragweite und die Fortgeltung des Potsdamer Abkommens. Untersuchungen zur Lösung der deutschen Frage.* Published by Königsteiner Kreis (Göttingen, 1952).

Anders, Wladyslaw: *An Army in Exile* (London, 1949).

Arendt, Hannah: *Elemente und Ursprünge totaler Herrschaft* (Frankfurt, 1955). English edition: The Origins of Totalitarism (New York, 1951).

Aron, Raymond: *Der permanente Krieg* (Frankfurt, 1953).

Baldwin, Hanson W.: *Great Mistakes of the War* (London, 1950).

Balfour, Michael, and Mair, John: *Four-Power-Control in Germany and Austria 1945–1946. Survey of International Affairs 1939–1946* (London etc., 1956).

Beloff, Max: *The Foreign Policy of Soviet Russia 1920–1941.* 2nd edition, 2 vols (London etc., 1949–52).

Beneš, *Memoirs of Dr. Eduard Beneš* (London, 1954).

Betts, R. R. (ed.): *Central and South East Europe 1945–1948* (London and New York, 1950).

Black, C. E. (ed.): *Challenge in Eastern Europe. 12 Essays* (New Brunswick, N. J., 1954).

Bocheński, Joseph M., and Niemeyer, Gerhart (eds.): *Handbuch des Weltkommunismus* (Munich, 1958).

216

Borkenau, Franz: *Der europäische Kommunismus. Seine Geschichte von 1917 bis zur Gegenwart* (Berne, 1952). English edition: European Communism (New York, 1953).

Buber-Neumann, Margarete: *Von Potsdam nach Moskau. Stationen eines Irrweges* (Stuttgart, 1957).

Byrnes, James F.: *Speaking Frankly* (New York and London, 1947).

Castro Delgado, Enrique: *J'ai perdu ma foi à Moscou* (Paris, 1950).

Chamberlin, William Henry: *America's Second Crusade* (Chicago, 1950).

Chamberlin, William Henry: *The Russian Revolution 1917–1921*. 3rd edition, 2 vols (New York, 1954).

Churchill, Winston Spencer: *The Second World War*. 6 vols (London, 1948 to 1953).

Ciechanowski, Jan: *Defeat in Victory* (Garden City, New York, 1947).

Clay, Lucius D.: *Decision in Germany* (Garden City, New York, 1950).

Clissold, Stephen: *Whirlwind. An Account of Marshal Tito's Rise to Power* (London, 1949).

Cornides, Wilhelm: *Die Weltmächte und Deutschland. Geschichte der jüngsten Vergangenheit 1945–1955* (Tübingen and Stuttgart, 1957).

Dallin, David J.: *The New Soviet Empire* (New Haven, 1951).

Dallin, David J.: *The Real Soviet Russia*. 3rd edition (New Haven, 1950).

Dallin, David J.: *Russia and Postwar Europe*, 5th edition (New Haven, 1948).

Dallin, David J.: *Soviet Russia's Foreign Policy 1939–1942* (New Haven, 1942).

Deane, John: *The Strange Alliance. The Story of our Efforts at Wartime Co-operation with Russia* (London, 1947).

Dedijer, Vladimir: *Tito. Autorisierte Biographie* (Berlin, 1953).

Dennett, Raymond, and Johnson, Joseph E. (eds.): *Negotiating with the Russians* (Boston, 1951).

Deuerlein, Ernst: *Die Einheit Deutschlands. Ihre Erörterung und Behandlung auf den Kriegs- und Nachkriegskonferenzen 1941–1949* (Frankfurt and Berlin, 1957).

Deutscher, Isaac: *Stalin. A Political Biography* (London, 1949).

Dimitroff, Georgi: *Rolle und Bedeutung der Volksdemokratie* (Berlin, 1953).

Duhnke, Horst: *Stalinismus in Deutschland. Die Geschichte der sowjetischen Besatzungszone* (Cologne, 1955).

Einaudi, Mario, Jean-Marie Domenach and Aldo Garosci: *Communism in Western Europe* (Ithaka, N. Y., 1951).

Einsiedel, Heinrich von: *Tagebuch der Versuchung* (Berlin and Stuttgart, 1950).

Eisenhower, Dwight D.: *Crusade in Europe* (New York, 1952).

Erfurt, Werner: *Die sowjetische Deutschland-Politik. Eine Studie zur Zeitgeschichte*, 4th edition (Esslingen, 1959).

Erfurth, Waldemar: *Der finnische Krieg 1941–1944* (Wiesbaden, 1950).

Fejtö, François: *Histoire des démocraties populaires* (Paris, 1952).

Fischer, Ruth: *Stalin und der deutsche Kommunismus. Der Übergang zur Konterrevolution* (Frankfurt, 1948).

The Forrestal Diaries (New York, 1951).

Foster, William Z.: *History of the three Internationals. The World Socialist and Communist Movements from 1848 to the Present* (New York, 1955).

Fuller, J. F. C.:*The Second World War 1939–1945* (New York, 1949).

Gafencu, Grigoire: *Vorspiel zum Krieg im Osten. Vom Moskauer Abkommen bis zum Ausbruch der Feindseligkeiten in Russland* (Zurich), 1953).

Garthoff, Raymond L.: *Soviet Military Doctrine* (Glencoe, Ill., 1953).

Geyer, Dietrich: *Die Sowjetunion und Iran. Eine Untersuchung zur Aussenpolitik der UdSSR im Nahen Osten 1917–1954* (Tübingen, 1955).

Gruber, Karl: *Zwischen Befreiung und Freiheit. Der Sonderfall Österreich* (Vienna, 1953).

Guiton, R. J.: *Paris–Moskau. Die Sowjetunion in der auswärtigen Politik Frankreichs seit dem zweiten Weltkrieg* (Stuttgart, 1956).

Gurian, Waldemar (ed.): *Soviet Imperialism. Its Origins and Tactics* (Notre Dame, Ind., 1953).

Gyorgi, Andrew: *Governments of Danubian Europe* (New York, 1949).

Harpe, Werner von: *Die Sowjetunion, Finnland und Skandinavien, 1945–1955* (Tübingen, 1956).

Hilger, Gustav: *Wir und der Kreml. Deutsch-sowjetische Beziehungen 1918–1941* (Frankfurt, 1955).

Höpker, Wolfgang: *Europäisches Niemandsland. Moskaus Zwischeneuropa vom Nordkap bis Kreta* (Düsseldorf, 1956).

Horthy, Nikolaus von: *Ein Leben für Ungarn* (Bonn, 1953).

House of Representatives. 83rd Congress, 2nd Session. House Report No. 2684. Special Report of Select Committee on Communist Aggression (Washington. 1954–55).

Hull: *The Memoirs of Cordell Hull*. Vol. ii (New York, 1948).

Hyde, Douglas: *I Believed. The Autobiography of a former British Communist* (London, 1951).

Jäschke, Gotthard: *Die Türkei in den Jahren 1942–1951* (Wiesbaden, 1955).

Just, Arthur W.: *Russland in Europa. Gedanken zum Ostproblem der abendländischen Welt* (Stuttgart, 1949).

Kállay, Nicholas: *Hungarian Premier. Personal Account of a Nation's Struggle in the Second World War* (New York, 1954).

Kennan, George F.: *American Diplomacy 1900–1950*. 2nd edition (London, 1952).

Kirk George: *The Middle East 1945–1950. Survey of International Affairs* (London etc., 1954).

Kleist, Peter: *Zwischen Hitler und Stalin* (Bonn, 1950).

Krupinski, Kurt: *Die Komintern seit Kriegsausbruch* (Berlin).

Kusnierz, Bronislaw: *Stalin and the Poles* (London, 1949).

Laeuen, Harald: *Polnische Tragödie. 2nd edition* (Stuttgart, 1956).

Lane, Arthur Bliss: *I saw Poland Betrayed (New York, 1948).*

Leahy, William D.: *I was There* (New York etc., 1950).

Lenin, W. J.: *Ausgewählte Werke.* 2 vols. (Berlin, 1951–52).

Leonhard, Wolfgang: *Die Revolution entlässt ihre Kinder* (Cologne, 1955).

Löwenstein, Hubertus Prinz zu, und Volkmar von Zühlsdorff: *Deutschlands Schicksal 1945–1957* (Bonn, 1957).

Löwenthal, Fritz: *Das kommunistische Experiment. Theorie und Praxis des Marxismus–Leninismus* (Cologne, 1957).

Lukacs, John A.: *The Great Powers and Eastern Europe* (New York, 1953).

Mannerheim, Gustav: *Erinnerungen* (Zurich, 1952).

McNeill, William Hardy: *America, Britain and Russia. Their Co-Operation and Conflict 1941–1946. Survey of International Affairs 1939–1946* (London etc., 1953).

McNeill, William Hardy: *The Greek Dilemma* (London, 1947).

Meissner, Boris: *Russland, die Westmächte und Deutschland. Die sowjetische Deutschlandpolitik 1943–1953* (Hamburg, 1953).

Meissner, Boris: *Sowjetrussland zwischen Revolution und Restauration* (Cologne, 1956).

Meissner, Boris: *Die Sowjetunion, die baltischen Staaten und das Völkerrecht* (Cologne, 1956).

Mikołajczyk, Stanisław: *The Pattern of Soviet Domination* (London, 1948).

219

Molotov, W. M.: *Fragen der Aussenpolitik. Reden und Erklärungen. April 1945–June 1948* (Moscow, 1949).

Moltmann, Günter: *Amerikas Deutschlandpolitik im zweiten Weltkrieg. Kriegs- und Friedensziele 1941–1945* (Heidelberg, 1958).

Montgomery: *The Memoirs of Field-Marshal the Viscount Montgomery of Alamein* (London, 1958).

Nettl, J. Peter: *Die deutsche Sowjetzone bis heute. Politik, Wirtschaft, Gesellschaft* (Frankfurt, 1953).

Neubauer, Helmut: *München und Moskau 1918/1919. Zur Geschichte der Rätebewegungen in Bayern* (Munich, 1958).

Olberg, Paul: *Die Tragödie des Baltikums* (Zurich, 1941).

Pipes, Richard: *The Formation of the Soviet Union. Communism and Nationalism 1917–1923* (Cambridge, Mass., 1954).

Possony, Stefan T.: *A Century of Conflicts. Communist Technique of World Revolution* (Chicago, 1953).

Puttkammer, Jesco von: *Von Stalingrad zur Volkspolizei. Geschichte des Nationalkomitees „Freies Deutschland"* (Wiesbaden, 1951).

Rauch, Georg von: *Geschichte des bolschewistischen Russland* (Wiesbaden, 1956).

Renner, Karl: *Österreich von der ersten zur zweiten Republik* (Vienna, 1953).

Roucek, Joseph S. (ed.): *Moscow's European Satellites. The Annals of The American Academy of Political and Social Science.* Vol. 271 (Philadelphia, 1950).

Ruhm von Oppen, Beate: *Documents on Germany under Occupation. 1945–1954* (London etc., 1955).

Sarkisyanz, Emanuel: *Russland und der Messianismus des Orients. Sendungsbewusstsein und politischer Chiliasmus des Ostens* (Tübingen, 1955).

Schärf, Adolf: *Österreichs Erneuerung 1945–1955. Das erste Jahrzehnt der neuen Republik* (Vienna, 1955).

Scholz, Arno and Walther G. Oschilewski (eds.): *Turmwächter der Demokratie. Ein Lebensbild von Kurt Schumacher.* 3 vols. (Berlin, 1953–1954).

Schütz, Wilhelm Wolfgang: *Die Stunde Deutschlands. Möglichkeiten einer Politik der Wiedervereinigung* (Stuttgart, 1954).

Sethe, Paul: *Zwischen Bonn und Moskau. 3rd edition* (Frankfurt, 1957).

Seton-Watson, Hugh: *The East European Revolution* (London, 1950).

Seton-Watson, Hugh: *From Stalin to Malenkov. The History of World Communism* (New York, 1954).

Sharp, Samuel: *Poland – White Eagle on a Red Field* (Cambridge, Mass., 1953).

Sherwood, Robert E.: *Roosevelt and Hopkins. An intimate history* (New York, 1948).

Shub, David: *Lenin. A Biography* (Garden-City, New York, 1949).

Snell, John L. (ed.): *The Meaning of Yalta. Big Three Diplomacy and the New Balance of Power* (Baton Rouge, La., 1956).

Stalin, Joseph: *Fragen des Leninismus* (Moscow, 1947).

Stalin, Joseph: *Über den grossen vaterländischen Krieg der Sowjetunion* (Berlin, 1951).

Stern, Carola: *Porträt einer bolschewistischen Partei. Entwicklung, Funktion und Situation der SED* (Cologne, 1957).

Stettinius, Edward R.: *Roosevelt and the Russians. The Yalta Conference* (London, 1950).

Strang, Lord: *Home and Abroad* (London, 1956).

Strauss, Harold: *The Division and Dismemberment of Germany. Treatise* (Geneva, 1952).

Stypułkowski, Z.: *Invitation to Moscow* (London, 1951).

Thilenius, Richard: *Die Teilung Deutschlands. Eine zeitgeschichtliche Analyse* (Hamburg, 1957).

Trotzki, Leo: *Mein Leben. Versuch einer Autobiographie* (Berlin, 1930).

Truman, Harry S.: *Memoirs. Vol. i: Year of Decision* (London, 1955).

Toynbee, Arnold and Veronica M. (eds.): *The Realignment of Europe. Survey of International Affairs 1939–1946* (London etc., 1955).

Umiastowski, R.: *Poland, Russia and Great Britain 1941–1945* (London, 1946).

Wagner, Wolfgang: *Die Entstehung der Oder-Neisse-Linie in den diplomatischen Verhandlungen während des zweiten Weltkrieges. Die deutschen Ostgebiete,* vol. iii., 2nd edition (Stuttgart, 1959). English edition: *The Genesis of the Oder-Neisse Line. A Study in the Diplomatic Negotiations during World War II* (Stuttgart, 1957).

Weinberg, Gerhard L.: *Germany and the Soviet Union 1939–1941* (Leyden, 1954).

Wesemann, Fried: *Kurt Schumacher. Ein Leben für Deutschland* (Frankfurt, 1952).

Wilmot, Chester: *The Struggle for Europe* (London, 1952).

Wiskemann, Elizabeth: *Germany's Eastern Neighbours. Problems relating to the Oder-Neisse Line and the Czech Frontier Regions* (London etc., 1956).

Woodhouse, C. M.: *Apple of Discord* (London, 1948).

Altmeyer, Klaus: *Die Dokumente vom 5. Juni 1945 und die politische Einheit Deutschlands. Europa-Archiv* (1955), vol. x.

Bundy, McGeorge: *The Test of Yalta. Foreign Affairs (1948–49)*, xxvii, 4.

Čakste, Mintauts: *Latvia and the Soviet Union. Journal of Central European Affairs* (1949–1950), ix, 1 and 2.

Carl, Joachim: *Das amerikanische Leih- und Pacht-Gesetz (Lend-Lease Act). Entstehung und Bedeutung für den Ausgang des zweiten Weltkrieges. Wehrwissenschaftliche Rundschau* (1957), Supplement 6.

Castellan, G.: *La politique allemande de l'U.R.S.S. 1941–1945. Revue d'histoire de la deuxième guerre mondiale* (1956), vi. 21 and 22.

Cattell, David T.: *The Hungarian Revolution of 1919 and the Reorganisation of the Comintern in 1920. Journal of Central European Affairs* (1951–1952), xi, 1.

Cretzianu, Alexander: *The Soviet Ultimatum to Roumania* (June 26, 1944. *Journal of Central European Affairs* (1951–1952), xi. 3.

Cretzianu, Alexander: *The Soviet Ultimatum to Roumania* (June, 26, 1940). *Journal of Central European Affairs* (1949–1950), ix. 1.

Dorn, Walter L.: *Die Debatte über die amerikanische Besatzungspolitik für Deutschland (1944–1945). Vierteljahrshefte für Zeitgeschichte* (1958), vi, 1.

Eschenburg, Theodor: *Das Problem der deutschen Einheit nach den beiden Weltkriegen. Vierteljahrshefte für Zeitgeschichte* (1957), v. 2.

Fotitch, Constantin: *Tito and the Western Democracies. Journal of Central European Affairs* (1951–1952), xi. 4.

Geschichtsfälscher. Eine historische Richtigstellung. Neue Welt (1948), iii. 3.

Grewe, Wilhelm: *Punkt vier. Archiv des Öffentlichen Rechts* (1952 bis 1953), vol. lxxviii.

Grewe, Wilhelm: *Die Vereinbarungen von 1945 und die Politik der Wiedervereinigung. Aussenpolitik* (1954), v. 6.

Historicus: *Stalin on Revolution. Foreign Affairs* (1948–1949). xxvii. 2.

Hoptner, J. B.: *Soviet Policy in Eastern Europe since 1945. Journal of Central European Affairs* (1954), viii. 1.

Jäschke, Gotthard: *Transkaukasien. Ein Musterbeispiel sowjetrussischer Eroberungspolitik. Osteuropa* (1935–1936), xi. 1.

Kennan, George F.: *The Sources of Soviet Conduct. Foreign Affairs* 1946–1947), xxv. 4.

Kohn-Brandenburg, Alexander: *Das System der Provisorien. Die Zentralverwaltungen der sowjetischen Besatzungszone und die Verwaltung Berlins. Europa-Archiv* (1947), ii.

Lütkens, Gerhard: *Anstatt Potsdam etwa Jalta? Aussenpolitik* (1954), v. 4.

Makarov: *Die Eingliederung Bessarabiens und der Nordbukowina in die Sowjetunion. Zeitschrift für ausländisches öffentliches Recht und Völkerrecht* (1940–1941), x.

Makarov: *Der sowjetrussisch-finnische Konflikt. Zeitschrift für ausländisches öffentliches Recht und Völkerrecht* (1940–1941), x.

McGhee; George C.: *Die Türkei in der westlichen Welt. Aussenpolitik* (1955), vi. 6.

Meissner, Boris: *Der Kreml und das Ruhrgebiet. Osteuropa* (1951), i. 2.

Meissner, Boris: *Stalin und die Oder-Neisse-Linie. Osteuropa* (1951), i. 1.

Moltmann, Günter: *Die Genesis der Unconditional-Surrender-Forderung. Wehrwissenschaftliche Rundschau* (1956), vi. 3 and 4.

Mosely, Philip E.: *Dismemberment of Germany. The Allied Negotiations from Yalta to Potsdam. Foreign Affairs* (1949–1950), xxviii. 3.

Mosely, Philip E.: *The Occupation of Germany: New Light on How the Zones were Drawn. Foreign Affairs* (1949–1950). xxviii. 4.

Mosely, Philip E.: *The Treaty with Austria. International Organisation* (1950), iv.

Das Präludium des Kalten Krieges. Europa-Brücke (1957 and 1958). iii and iv.

Rauch, Georg von: *Die baltischen Staaten und Sowjetrussland 1919 bis 1939. Europa-Archiv* (1954), ix. 17, 20 and 22.

Rhode, Gotthold: *Die Entstehung der Curzon-Linie. Osteuropa* (1955), v. 2.

Rothholz, Walter: *Finnlands völkerrechtliches Schicksal seit 1917. Archiv des Völkerrechts* (1948–1949), vol. i.

Strang, Lord: *Germany between East and West. Foreign Affairs* (1954 to 1955). xxxiii. 3.

Sturmhöfel, Heinz: *Die Türkei und die Sowjetunion 1939–1954. Osteuropa* (1955), v. 1.

Táborský, Eduard: *Beneš and the Soviets. Foreign Affairs* (1948–1949), xxvii. 2.

Táborský, Eduard: *Beneš and Stalin – Moscow, 1943 and 1945. Journal of Central European Affairs* (1953), viii. 2.

Sadak, Necmeddin: *Turkey faces the Soviets. Foreign Affairs* (1948 to 1949), xxvii. 3.

Die Technik der Sowjetisierung am baltischen Beispiel. From the Bulletin de l'association d'études et d'informations politiques internationales (Paris, January 1 to 15, 1951).

Wagner, Wolfgang: *Besatzungszonen und Spaltung Deutschlands. Aussenpolitik* (1954), v. 8.

Wolfe, Bertram D.: *Der Tito-Stalin-Konflikt. Ostprobleme* (1953), v. 12.

Xydis, Stephen G.: *The Secret Anglo-Soviet Agreement on the Balkans of October 9, 1944. Journal of Central European Affairs* (1955 to 1956), xv. 3.

INDEX

Here, as in the text, names are spelled in the way current for the non-academic reader – for example, Trotsky, instead of Tročkij. Names such as Soviet Union, Bolshevism and Europe are not included, since they occur throughout the book.

CONTENTS

589 ⚹ 27